T.E.D. Klein
and the Rupture
of Civilization

T.E.D. Klein and the Rupture of Civilization

A Study in Critical Horror

THOMAS PHILLIPS

McFarland & Company, Inc., Publishers
Jefferson, North Carolina

This book contains square brackets in some
quoted material to maintain present-tense verb consistency.

LIBRARY OF CONGRESS CATALOGUING-IN-PUBLICATION DATA

Names: Phillips, Thomas, 1969– author.
Title: T.E.D. Klein and the rupture of civilization : a study in critical horror / Thomas Phillips.
Description: Jefferson, North Carolina : McFarland & Company, Inc., Publishers, 2017. | Includes bibliographical references and index.
Identifiers: LCCN 2017028612 | ISBN 9781476670287 (softcover : acid free paper) ∞
Subjects: LCSH: Klein, T. E. D.—Criticism and interpretation. | Horror tales, American—History and criticism.
Classification: LCC PS3561.L374 Z83 2017 | DDC 813/.54—dc23
LC record available at https://lccn.loc.gov/2017028612

BRITISH LIBRARY CATALOGUING DATA ARE AVAILABLE

ISBN (print) 978-1-4766-7028-7
ISBN (ebook) 978-1-4766-2937-7

© 2017 Thomas Phillips. All rights reserved

No part of this book may be reproduced or transmitted in any form or by any means, electronic or mechanical, including photocopying or recording, or by any information storage and retrieval system, without permission in writing from the publisher.

Front cover images © 2017 iStock

Printed in the United States of America

McFarland & Company, Inc., Publishers
 Box 611, Jefferson, North Carolina 28640
 www.mcfarlandpub.com

Table of Contents

Acknowledgments — vi
Introduction: "Sabbats likely" — 1

1. "The Weird Tradition of America" — 9
2. Events and Ceremonies — 34
3. White, Black and Other People: "Children of the Kingdom" and "Black Man with a Horn" — 65
4. Sorceries of Self-Negation: "Petey" and "Nadelman's God" — 81
5. Goosebumps and the Haunting Conscience — 97
6. "We are not saved": Critical Horror Today — 116

Appendix I—Reassuring Words: An Interview with T.E.D. Klein — 155
Appendix II—The Singular Ceremonies — 165
Chapter Notes — 175
Bibliography — 181
Index — 185

Acknowledgments

A number of people have helped make this book possible. Thank you: Dean King, for the crucial act of introducing me to Klein's work; Richard di Santo, for his always thoughtful editorial insights and *joie de vivre*; S.T. Joshi, for his generosity; Jonas Ploeger of Zagava Books, for allowing me to use "The Singular Ceremonies"; David Carter, for his wisdom, theological and otherwise; Tannon Penland, for poetry, ideas, metal, laughter, and all that is Bag; Todd Campbell, for pushing me to reach out to the inestimable Klein; J. Winston Phillips, for brotherhood, music, and productive horror; my parents, for allowing the right kind of horror into a young, impressionable life; Becca Woodward, for love in a world of non-understanding; and T.E.D. Klein, for his unique contribution to a never ending conversation between critical horror and those who read.

Introduction: "Sabbats likely"

In one of his journal entries in T.E.D. Klein's novel *The Ceremonies*, protagonist Jeremy Freirs writes, "sat up reading—or trying to—'The Jolly Corner.' James seems so goddamned labored. M.R. James of Cambridge, now *he* had the touch. Why so little fuss about him?" (357). On a number of levels, this passage captures the literary orientation and imagination (along with a dose of *jeu d'esprit*) of Klein's slender horror oeuvre consisting of the novel, the related story that preceded it ("The Events at Poroth Farm"), four novellas compiled in the *Dark Gods* collection, some essays, and a few scattered, minor texts, some of which appear in the limited edition *Reassuring Tales*. Klein also co-wrote the screenplay of Dario Argento's *Trauma* with the director. The passage is indicative of Klein's literary reach. He values Henry James; his protagonist makes the effort because, as many traditional literary aficionados would agree, it is an effort worth making despite the labored style. And yet, it is the other James—not William, but Montague Rhodes, a *true* Brit, incidentally—who elicits praise from Jeremy for exercising exceptional skill with his many early 20th-century ghost stories. But what does "the touch" mean, exactly? This study endeavors to answer that question by examining Klein's major texts and offering a parallel—and paraphrased—assertion, followed by the inevitable question: T.E.D. Klein of New York, now *he* has the touch. Why so little fuss about him?

Widely lauded but largely undervalued horror or "weird fiction" author, initial editor of *Twilight Zone* magazine, and aspiring optimist, Klein, relative to the genre's key figures, is probably not as popular due to the scarcity of his output. That the current batch of talentless "YouTube stars" can garner ample "fuss" simply by maintaining a constant presence in the spotlight of the already omnipresent screen would seem to testify to this claim in a depressingly timeless manner. But many, including noted authors and blogging connoisseurs of the genre, speak

Introduction

of him as one of the great horror writers of M.R. James' own century. Klein is highly literate, a quality that shines in his prose as tremendous enthusiasm for his chosen field despite his much-lamented writer's block. He brings an urban savvy to his narratives but one born of Columbia University or The New School of Social Research milieu as much as of gritty New York City streets. S.T. Joshi asserts that "perhaps his greatest feat is a seamless blending of the mundane realism so prevalent in weird writing today ... with the cosmic horror of Machen, Blackwood, and Lovecraft" (*Modern* 96), an observation that finds solidarity with the James of *The Turn of the Screw* fame when he comments on "the strange and sinister embroidered on the very type of the normal and easy" (xxiv) with regards to his own efforts at the ghost story. It is here, in this appealingly organic synthesis of the quotidian and the supernatural, communicated with the sophistication of an erudite belletrist and a staunch admirer of the genre, where one might find a functional sense of that particular quality identified as "the touch." Klein knows precisely how to lay hands, so to speak, on the delicate nexus between the sacred and the profane and to conjure spirits with accessible but charged discourse where there are often only formulas of evocation in the genre.

To push this characterization further is to situate Klein in the domain of what I call critical horror, a form of horror fiction (and film) that is aligned, overtly or, more commonly, peripherally, with critical theory as a philosophical and exploratory approach to culture, as well as with the notion of "imperative" inherent in one meaning of "critical." Critical horror is concerned with the mechanisms of injustice and ideological oblivion. It frames them in conjunction with evil; or, it actualizes the profound otherness of malevolent forces as a sinister but creative counter to material, lived evil unfolding between individuals and communities, on city streets, in forests, and in otherwise quiet neighborhoods. And it manifests its seemingly malign, critical vision as an urgent response to aspects of the human experience in desperate need of the kind of interrogation that can meet its subject matter with comparable or exceeding phantasmagoria, with spectral absurdity even, that horror alone can provide.

Moreover, critical horror is ultimately productive, comparable to the compensatory and therapeutic becomings heralded by Gilles Deleuze and Felix Guattari, as opposed to the prevailing 21st-century chic of pessimism or nihilism; which does not mean that it relents in the face of

"Sabbats likely"

what Arthur Machen observes as genuine evil in his influential "The White People." Sometimes horror just wants to be scary, but even here, it is inclined to present a distinctive—but Machenian—vision of life that runs howlingly against the grain of bourgeois, populist cosmology, the kind that delivers comfort and answers in consumerism and infantile brands of theology. "Sabbats likely," Jeremy learns of "Lammas Eve, the last day of July" (Klein, *Ceremonies* 384–85). Witchery, Satanism, the myriad forms of occultism that might offend religious orthodoxy or middle-class rationalism are all likely where critical horror buries its acuminous fangs, as the antidote to toxicity is often contained in the poison itself. Critical horror is "homeopathic," to use one of Klein's own references, which means that sabbats are likely as long as people and politics, the material of any civilization, are essentially, venomously unconscious and self-absorbed, and thus in dire need of a healing agent.

The aim here is not to pin Klein down as a rabid leftist, or a sugary romantic, for that matter. He would doubtless have written these texts for the sake of producing quality horror alone, though it will become apparent in the course of the following chapters that he reveals an eminently intelligent and perceptive social conscience (on subjects ranging from race, to patriarchy, and class) that positions his work in the province of a critical mode of horror. Chapter 1 lays the theoretical foundation for Klein's unique and, I argue, ethical variety of horror fiction by examining the nature and discontents of civilization. I am aware that some readers may find the theory a bit plodding, or completely superfluous in relation to the great and generally immediate pleasures of Klein's work. To this I can only say, with W. Somerset Maugham concerning a chapter-length philosophical conversation in his mighty *The Razor's Edge*, "I feel it right to warn the reader that he [sic] can very well skip this chapter without losing the thread of such story as I have to tell." But he goes on: "I should add, however, that except for this conversation I should perhaps not have thought it worthwhile to write this book" (243). What unfolds in chapter one is in fact a conversation, between Klein and the general operations of critical horror and certain theoretical imperatives around the productive development of communities, individuals, and, indeed, a species that is edging ever closer to insidious dehumanization. As the study proceeds beyond this initial foray into theory, it will occasionally bring other texts, other voices outside the canon of horror, into the conversation in hopes of further

Introduction

expanding its depth and significance with regards to the machinations (or *Machenations*) of American civilization in particular, how the latter informs the human and inadvertently demands consideration of supernatural intervention in the form of horror.

Another caveat: the central methodology here exercises what the current ambitions of Digital Humanities tend to eschew for the sake of relevancy, power, and money—close-readings of literary fiction that endeavor to engage precisely, meaningfully, and personally with the language of a text, here applied equally to theory. This practice, a *process* that rewards not with immediate compilations of data but with substance born of effort, can sometimes feel tedious to non-scholars, though I have made every effort to brighten the path with cultural and other contexts in ways that foreground the distinct enjoyment of Klein's style and thematic concerns. Nor is this to say that my approach is bound to the New Criticism school of literary exploration; its theoretical scope is far more diverse than that and is ultimately aligned with the kind of poststructuralism that cuts through a text from any number of vantage points, class and gender being central given where Klein and his cultural environments lead us. Chapters 2 through 4 thus exemplify this nexus of methodologies regarding Klein's major texts, while chapters 5 and 6 return to the meeting point of theory and cultural critique, with specific emphasis on texts that address the nature of horror, from its fantasy to its actuality, its aesthetic difference to its hauntology. Chapter 5 considers the necessary but highly problematic tendency toward negation in the common recipe of horror, the latter becoming decreasingly critical as it dovetails with ideologically based skepticism. Chapter 6 locates the logical extension of non-critical, cultural horror in the form of religious fundamentalism and literalism as forces against which critical horror exacts its own powerful, often ferocious dynamism.

My own fiction work is noted for its minimalism and its brevity, a direction to which this study adheres in the context of conventional, scholarly monographs. Unlike Klein, most fortunately, I have yet to encounter the demon of writer's block, though I am a firm believer in the value of efficiency and concision. The common injunction against brevity in particular, from the pulpits of fiction and non-fiction publishers alike (and thus their readers) in North America, as opposed to some European publishers, is a regrettable expression of bloated capitalism that critical horror is prone to attack. The physical object of the

"Sabbats likely"

text, that dying animal, tucked into a purse or a hipster cycling bag, must weigh heavy on the shoulder, give the reader his or her money's worth. I hope that, as with the most compelling and economical fiction (Jean-Philippe Toussaint, Christian Gailly, or the shorter novels by Don DeLillo come to mind), the immediacy of the language has done justice to the subject matter here. Interestingly, the general consensus seems to be that Klein's far more compact "The Events at Poroth Farm" is superior to the expanded novel. I would agree, though there are times when even the most devoted minimalist must concede to—and revel in—the splendid and transformative accomplishment of a five hundred page testament to literary (or theoretical) vitality in the contemporary world. It should also be clear that the current book is hardly the final word on Klein. Perhaps it will motivate others to continue Kleinian scholarship from alternative angles. Perhaps—and this is truly wishful thinking—it will inspire the writer himself to complete that long-awaited second novel, however succinct or expansive.

Nevertheless, the two appendices serve to both flesh out the text and provide a kind of update around Klein's work and the subgenre of critical horror. The first is an exclusive interview with Klein that addresses some of the central concerns of this study. Though distant from the writer whose creative drive brought us such eerie, consequential narratives, in terms of age and sensibility, it will be apparent that Klein continues to be fascinated by the aesthetic concerns and impetus around the horror genre. It should also be a delight to those admirers of his work to recognize a familiar character, an older Jeremy, perhaps, who, having survived the hazards of horror, has put the genre's books and films down without having lost his curiosity and sense of humor. The second appendix, completed long before beginning work on this book, is a hybrid of sorts, a version of which initially appeared in an anthology (Zagava Books' wonderful *Booklore*) on the subject of cherished, rare, or out of print books. It investigates *The Ceremonies* via relatively traditional literary criticism but merges the critical process with fiction whereby the novel becomes-actual, as Deleuze might put it, becomes a kind of grimoire in the immediate space and time of the critic. "The Singular Ceremonies" is hardly comparable to Klein's exceptional abilities, though it is a relevant expression of critical horror's potentiality in the 21st century.

One last point, on Klein's optimism. Ursula Le Guin, in her oft-

Introduction

anthologized "The Ones Who Walk Away from Omelas," identifies "the trouble" of modernity as our "bad habit, encouraged by pedants and sophisticates, of considering happiness as something rather stupid. Only pain is intellectual, only evil interesting. This is the treason of the artist: a refusal to admit the banality of evil and the terrible boredom of pain" (532). Much will be said about Klein's appreciation of "happy endings" and its ostensible discontinuity with the fact that most of his narratives end in palpable doom, but for now, and by way of clarifying the introduction, I would like to consider Le Guin's observation from a more general standpoint. There is undoubtedly "trouble" afoot. It springs from everyday occurrences as much as from—and realistically, more than—what H.P. Lovecraft and his many literary descendants would call the "unutterable" or the "unnamable." And yet, to presume that said trouble necessitates a brooding pessimism as the foremost technique of confronting the many predicaments of a lived life is, at best, short-sighted, and at worst, reactionary. It is tantamount to the middle-aged queuing up for the Bauhaus reunion show, donned in black, gloomily committed to sharing a sullen disposition with the choir (if for no other reason than the sake of nostalgia), when really this experience of willfully forlorn interiority (as opposed to what was, in fact, a fantastic performance...) would have been more appropriate twenty years prior, when such self-involved angst and the wonderful music it can create is genuinely fortuitous relative to the youthful energy that spawns it. "The treason of the artist" has nothing to do with losing that energy; rather, it means reducing one's vision to a limited conception of evil, one that dedicates the force of creative energy to mere personal tumult (as morose interiority or mere exterior performativity), to ego, or worse, intolerance. Such "treason" is thus bereft of humor and the profound pleasure of modesty. It cannot state, with Woody Allen, that "more than any other time in history, mankind faces a crossroads. One path leads to despair and utter hopelessness. The other, to total extinction. Let us pray we have the wisdom to choose correctly" (*Side* 81). It lacks the self-awareness required, paradoxically, to step back from oneself and laugh or to recognize the absurdity of solipsistic designs, however bereft of ontological certainty they may be, upon the twin projects of life and death.[1]

As Joshi implies, Klein is deeply interested in the evil that permeates banality, in addition to otherworldly malevolence. This prerogative is different from evil for evil's sake. Pain is not boring to the individual experiencing it but when cultivated, as an identity, a way of relating to and framing the world, it soon becomes tiresome; even fairy tales bear this out. We were supposed to get it as children, that the drama of crying wolf to fill one's time is a kind of unconsciousness that can deaden one, and one's community, to the actual wolf lurking in the shadows, waiting to strike. The unjust law in the making. The pervasive discourse of narcissism and prefabricated culture. Evil for the sake of evil is ultimately an orientation of self-aggrandizement, that in which "pedants and sophisticates," as well as some children, tend to excel. Why are otherwise functional adults so averse to happiness? Probably because they are alone in the agriculture of their intellectual and aesthetic trajectories, isolated journeyers amidst countless others invested in mediocre formulas of existence, who do not seem to understand the poetry of that existence. Klein brings this poetry alive in his prose, in the critical nature of his horror. He courts the Lovecraftian "unknowable," the bleakness of a potentially gutting, or merely indifferent universe; despair, hopelessness, and extinction are real and present dangers in what may, for many, be the familiar scenarios he orchestrates in the context of everyday atmospheres and contrivances. On the other hand, he articulates both the momentousness and the great pleasure found in the subversive, abjection, strategic marginalization, modes of radical becoming that draw inspiration from the criticalness of critical horror to propel an energized, perhaps a revolutionary life, rather than an inconsequential or shoegazing death. He foregrounds belonging and humanity, that category that demands attention even as it is being deconstructed or blacked-out by philosophical catatonia. Klein reassures that sabbats are restoratively, productively imminent.

CHAPTER 1

"The Weird Tradition of America"

In setting the cultural and historical context for the advent of American horror fiction, H. P. Lovecraft observes, in an extended passage,

> the free rein given under the influence of Puritan theocracy to all manner of notions respecting man's relation to the stern and vengeful God of the Calvinists, and to the sulphureous Adversary of that God, about whom so much was thundered in the pulpits each Sunday; and the morbid introspection developed by an isolated backwoods life devoid of normal amusements and of the recreational mood, harassed by commands for theological self-examination, keyed to unnatural emotional repression, and forming above all a mere grim struggle for survival ... [*Supernatural* 60–61].

Published in 1945, Lovecraft's seminal *Supernatural Horror in Literature* provides a vision of America that is as compelling (offering, in these few observations alone, some of the material of which critical horror texts are made) as it is subjective and thus representative of a particularly pessimistic sensibility, one that held to the inevitability of cosmic foreboding filling every crevice of cultural and psychological space. Part of what makes this passage so convincing is the degree to which it remains applicable to 21st-century North American culture, even as it speaks to cultural underdevelopment that has become monstrously overdeveloped seventy years after the fact. Fundamentalist Christianity continues to seek, if not enact, "free rein" in its "vengeful" wielding of a sword against the "Adversary" in his many contemporary guises, as the tradition understands him. The Evangelical pulpit remains a powerful voice in a culture given to phantasy and contrived hysteria.[1] "Backwoods life," though still prevalent in a country the size of the United States, has become the metropolis, the medium-size city, the town, the suburb, the rural community, all interpenetrated by technology, all online and consequently, as is often the case with virtual life, "isolated," locked into the addictive glare of screens, as opposed to the

T.E.D. Klein and the Rupture of Civilization

density of forests or the open sky. Now the morbidity of introspection lies in the very lack of "self-examination," fixated on rather than "devoid" of what have become the "normal amusements" that generate a privileging of recreation over self-reflection as our collective reveries have become. Examination remains theological but its gaze is exterior; it assumes the form of a theistic super-ego, or simply the more or less anonymous recriminations of countless "friends" and strangers in the universe of virtual networking. "Emotional repression" is always "unnatural" and always already integral to a culture founded on the interrelated principles of technological and Puritan progress, and thus a "grim" domination, for its struggle to survive.

Subjective perspectives indeed, and yet immediately preceding the above quote, Lovecraft displays his notorious racism by including a characteristic dig at the "coppery Indians ... of infernal origin" (60) as a component of America's fertile ground for horror narrative. While the historical tension and violence perpetuated against and by Native Americans is undeniable, "infernal" is hardly an accurate claim here; or at least no more than it might be regarding the followers of John Calvin. Demonizing an ethnicity is of course tantamount to sanctioning its slaughter. Much has been said about the violence of Lovecraft's racist propensity, though I mention it here merely for the sake of adumbrating certain aspects of civilization in which critical horror is produced, reflected, and, crucially, that it in turn mirrors. Whether it results in genocide or not, racism, for example, reflects unconsciousness and ignorance, the critique of which may rely on subjective standpoints, personal histories, while its lived realities are scarred on real bodies and psychologies. Racism stands as one more link in the chain of real, historical events among many—class structure operating as another significant series of such moments—all of which lead to a dialectic of empowerment and disempowerment.[2] As Fredric Jameson puts it with regards to the postmodern milieu of which early 21st-century culture is arguably a hyper-extension, "this whole global, yet American, postmodern culture is the internal and superstructural expression of a whole new wave of American military and economic domination throughout the world: in this sense, as throughout class history, the underside of culture is blood, torture, death and *horror*" (my italics, *Jameson* 192). This cultural base that Lovecraft and Jameson attempt to communicate ultimately eludes

1. "The Weird Tradition of America"

discourse; it is *too real* for words and thus exists outside our capacity to delineate it. And yet, the critical horror narrative endeavors to make the leap, to pierce the skin and reach into the blood-written self that becomes-subject via foundational structures and superstructures of civilization.

In its contemporary incarnations, the "grim struggle for survival" produces monsters, people for whom happiness and wellbeing reside precisely in languid, amorphous discourse (in what Jacques Lacan famously calls the "symbolic") while "real" life happens beneath the glossy surfaces of our words, the signifiers that determine, as if by magic, our likes and dislikes, dramas, preoccupations, quotidian circumstances—in short, our identities. Freud goes so far as to claim that "we are so made that we can derive intense enjoyment only from a contrast and very little from a state of things. Thus our possibilities of happiness are already restricted by our constitution. Unhappiness is much less difficult to experience" (*Civilization* 23–24). Whether humanity is doomed to such a constitution *ab aeterno* is perhaps a matter of debate, though there can be no doubt that culture contributes to its promulgation. It is as though schooled in the perverse pleasures of "contrast" (the anomaly of the car accident on the highway, the melodrama of office or familial politics, the latest sensational because moronic statement tweeted by a power-hungry politician), we are uncertain as to what to do with a mere "state of things," a space and time of relative stillness and silence in which the "recreational" subject might actually step up to the demands of productive self-examination, the kind that must finally deem racist and other infantile tendencies to be unworthy of human dignity. In lieu of this "state," we often long for narrative, the re-presentation of unsavory circumstances that approximates or becomes horror. Such is the condition, as Freud instructs, of civilization, a predicament that requires rupture (which for some literalists goes by the name of rapture) to meet the disjunction, the quiet or boisterous shattering of everyday experience, as much as its super-egoic and monstrously willful constraints require rupture of a different sort, also willful but productively antagonistic to said strictures. Hence Freud's *Civilization and Its Discontents*, and perhaps the entirety of his oeuvre, as testament to the many pitfalls and, in their exposure to the light of something more than everyday unconsciousness, the possible liberation of human experience from its destructive leanings.[3]

T.E.D. Klein and the Rupture of Civilization

Despite his numerous psychological and anatomical miscalculations, Freud makes a strong case for "our constitution" and the degree to which it allows for an effortless unfurling of general unhappiness. Civilization rests upon our solipsism, our self-enclosure and the invariable attack-thoughts that seek, unconsciously, to secure the fortress of what we take to be a static—and vulnerable—"I" whose penchant for repression, as Lovecraft alerts us, is unnatural. Perhaps, then, this constitution has its origin elsewhere than the fetal, ontological self? Cultural theory has much to say about this question, but for now it is useful to elaborate on Freudian insights into the phenomenon of civilization and its potent impact on the psychology, or mass psychology, of its inhabitants, the North American variety of which stands as a truly weird tradition indeed and will ultimately be the focus of this study, as it arguably is in the work of T.E.D. Klein.

Prosthetic Pleasures

The ground of civilization in Freud's view can be encapsulated by what he calls the "prevailing cultural super-ego" (89), that collection of social mandates that at once informs and is informed by individuals and their respective communal affiliations. This baseline indoctrination "is largely responsible for our misery," he tells us, leading to the conclusion that "we should be much happier if we gave it [civilization] up and returned to primitive conditions" (33). Simply put, we are miserable because our instincts (for self-preservation, sexual satisfaction, and possessiveness or territoriality, among others) are always already under fire, compromised, diminished, or precluded altogether by cultural sanctions. However, to "primitive conditions" the general "we" shall never return given the immense power of influence that civilization exercises and, consequently, the equally intoxicating force of unconscious mechanisms, both individual and collective, employed to sublimate or merely soften the brunt of said instincts. Of that instinctual armory known as the pleasure principle, for example, Freud suggests that it perpetrates "unrestricted domination" in its "tendency … to separate from the ego everything that can become a source of unpleasure, to throw it outside and to create a pure pleasure-ego which is confronted by a strange and threat-

1. "The Weird Tradition of America"

ening 'outside'" (14). Such domination might assume the form of what Freud considers "cheap enjoyment" (35), relative to the happiness of genuinely uninhibited instinctual practice. The "pure pleasure-ego," then, indulges in deceptive fulfillment, that which can assuage a temporary (and as cultural theory asserts, contrived) desire, but eventually gives way to the vacuum that is its original and ultimately enduring state. Nevertheless, if the populist sensibility that governs contemporary Western culture is any indication, the dominating quality of our shoddy pleasures is enough to stave off the void, at least in pockets of the everyday, and to foster the delusion that our "misery" can be bribed, that a menacing exteriority can be contained, understood, and assimilated by the frame of a computer screen. Freud famously refers to such bravado as humanity having "become a kind of prosthetic God" (38–39), the implication being that our countless appendages, or more generally, the increasingly magnificent *objets fétiches* that we create and literally incorporate into our lives, our bodies, provoke an illusion of godliness. We might consider the ubiquity of the mobile phone in this regard, an obvious example but one that, exigently, at once provides a sense of jurisdiction over the self and its environment and infiltrates the human by becoming an extension of the body and annexing consciousness. When pleasure is merely adjunct to immediate experience, unhappiness—the malfunction of the mechanical limb, the crashing of the computer—is there, lurking in the otherwise luminous interior, poised to subsume the "God" and affirm the First Noble Truth of Buddhism that "all life is suffering."

In the Freudian scheme, of course, the fallibility of human, all too human happiness may be most apparent in the ascendency and inevitable regulation of its investment in sexual congress. Sexual imagery and innuendo abound on the multitude of screens, in the discourse between friends and strangers, entertainers of the world, in labia-mimicking lipstick, yoga tights, sports magazines, machismo gestures and chest-beating; though the sexual impulse itself has a way of bending tropistically toward the mandate of weird, "unnatural" taboo when asserted as the constitutional (in every sense of the word), even the prosaic quality, or inalienable right, that it is. While culturally (over)determined, sexual impulses are obviously integral to human experience. And yet Freud claims "a large amount of the psychical energy which [civilization] uses for its own purposes has to be withdrawn from sexuality" (51). Such "purposes" require interrogation, particularly when they foster unnecessary and potentially destructive prohibitions on individuals and communities. Who are they intended to benefit and how? What ideological structures undergird their processes? Who and what do they keep in power? To what degree do they sacrifice the fundamental multiplicity and heterogeneity of life for the sake of moralistic certitude? "The requirement ... that there shall be a single kind of sexual life for everyone," Freud tells us, "disregards the dissimilarities, whether innate or acquired, in the sexual constitution of human beings; it cuts off a fair number of them from sexual enjoyment and so becomes the source of serious injustice" (*ibid.*). One need not look too hard to locate examples of castigation in this regard—from real-life Hester Prynnes to modern day victims of homophobia, such injustice is more or less overt in a "Puritan theocracy." Naturally, Freud is interested in the rich psychology of sexual social dynamics from a developmental perspective. What emerges from such repression, he observes, is guilt, which operates "as the most important problem in the development of civilization," and further, "that the price we pay for our advance in civilization is a loss of happiness through the heightening of the sense of guilt" (81). Critical horror, and Klein's single novel to date in particular, has a great deal to say about this condition, the inherited sense that abjection is forever haunting our dreams and our bodies, like unhappiness in the shadows; the tendency of critical horror, its *raison d'être*, in fact, is to pull no punches in presenting scenarios in which the abject may be perceived as natural and as *pleasurable* as it is horrifying.

And a very peculiar pleasure it is, one that shares its instinctual basis with another common product of guilt that is most likely in league with a certain perverse form of gratification. There is much more to say about the nature of horror's general appeal, the particular nuances of this pleasure, though it is the less congenial quality of aggression that may superintend the former as it orients the everyday by virtue of both its inauspicious birth from the non-gendered womb of civilization and as "the greatest impediment to civilization" (69). For Freud, human psychology cannot be reduced to an imperative of belonging, a cry for love. Human beings are, rather,

> creatures among whose instinctual endowments is to be reckoned a powerful share of aggressiveness. As a result, their neighbor is for them not only a

1. "The Weird Tradition of America"

> potential helper or sexual object, but also someone who tempts them to satisfy their aggressiveness on him, to exploit his capacity for work without compensation, to use him sexually without his consent, to seize his possessions, to humiliate him, to cause him pain, to torture and to kill him [58].

Somewhere in this quagmire of impulses is, at the very least, a desire for intimacy, be it sexual or otherwise, a recognition not only of the inevitability but the convenience and even the preferability of having neighbors. Nevertheless, as an "instinctual endowment," and a powerful one at that, aggression pervades the human experience, an observation that does not necessarily need to be pointed out to anyone who views news, dramas, comedies, and most of what emerges from Hollywood. But the psychoanalyst, not unlike the astute writer of critical horror, works his or her way into the mire of this teeming "share" of the human condition for the sake of amplifying what may skirt the immediate—or extended—attention of the cultural consumer. Without drifting too far into the platitude of modern desensitization, it is (un)safe to say that the sublimation of aggression (through relatively safe media) invariably fails to address aggression's "temptation" that lies at the core of civilization's development, a "struggle between Eros and Death, between the instinct of life and the instinct of destruction" (69). Freud refers to this dialectic as the "battle of the giants that our nursemaids try to appease with their lullaby about Heaven" (*ibid.*). Though the "our" in this claim is presumptuous, speaking as it does to a privileged class, the nursemaid of the 21st-century American bourgeoisie may assume numerous forms that appease with comparable "lullabies," the problem of which resides in the notion that "every piece of aggression whose satisfaction the subject gives up is taken over by the super-ego and increases the latter's aggressiveness (against the ego)" (76). So the instinctual self, predisposed to aggression, must generally repress or sublimate this "satisfaction" and thus add fuel to the prohibitive, super-egoic tendencies of civilization; hence the deep-seated guilt that, according to Freud, diminishes the capacity for happiness, replacing it with the more or less overt violence of aggression, even in the face of middle-brow Christianity's emphasis on the hopes and aspirations of the prime cosmic real estate known as heaven.

It is easy to dismiss what is both obvious and below the surface of civility in Freud's proclamations. We are all familiar with the technologies that graft a sense of distracted divinity upon the human experience, or the nethermost internal and external aggression, especially in the confines of the domestic sphere, among friends, family, lovers, the degree to which self-possession can rapidly become possession of a very different variety with the spark of a word, a glance, an insinuation on the part of a sometimes painfully familiar other. On the other hand, when our collective capacity to become unraveled, or simply vacant, assumes the form of social, political, and/or economic malignity, the aggressive, guilt-ridden microcosm of the home or the office may be identified as inexplicably mapped onto, or into, the fabric of civilization at large. Or not. It goes unrecognized; the subtleties of its proliferation escape attention for, among other reasons, their sobering inconvenience. Freud holds that "a real change in the relations of human beings to possessions would be of more help ... than any ethical commands; but the recognition of this fact among socialists has been obscured and made useless for practical purposes by a fresh idealistic misconception of human nature" (90). Psychoanalytic theory and practice is largely oriented toward exposing "misconceptions of human nature," a program that takes on considerable importance where relationality is concerned. Who determines these (mis)conceptions of human nature and according to what criteria, under what auspices? What power structures are at stake and to what degree are they dependent upon objects and ownership? Baudelaire's scathing observation, *"Aux objets répugnants nous trouvons des appas; / Chaque jour vers l'Enfer nous descendons d'un pas"* ("We find charm in repugnant objects; / Each day we descend one step closer to Hell") (my translation, "To the Reader" 16), is perhaps indicative of an inevitable consumerist trajectory. That identification with "possessions"—be they quotidian or fetish objects, other people, or even ideas—can so diminish the quality of life, necessitating, in Freud's view, "real change," suggests that the pragmatism that is so fundamental to the general American sensibility is best served, for a start, by shattering, or to be more academic, problematizing, said identification.

"Uncritical consensus"

In keeping with the general aims of cultural criticism, Jameson is concerned with what he calls "the omnipresence of culture," without an

1. "The Weird Tradition of America"

understanding of which "realistic conceptions of the nature and function of political praxis today can scarcely be framed" (*Jameson* 136). Horror need not be concerned, overtly or otherwise, with politics. However, insofar as its relatively critical expression seeks to interrogate civilization and the many tendrils of the latter's reach into our psychologies, our behaviors and presumptions around social mores, ontology, cosmology, and otherness, it is necessarily invested, consciously or not, in particular modes of framing or reframing collective and individual relationships to culture as a tapestry of ubiquitous, dominant forces. One of the effects of such force is to generate rifts between people(s) that invariably lead to political or ideological alienation and hegemony, and thus social instability. Capitalism, for example, "systematically dissolves the fabric of all cohesive social groups" (*ibid.*), as Jameson explains, and does so in a manner that reifies the pervasive presence and "naturalness" of consumer culture. While the Bible admonishes us to "die daily," contemporary American "death" appears more akin to shopping daily, a mild witticism that speaks nonetheless to isolated, compulsive subjectivities in the face of a relatively profound and spiritually productive self-effacement (against which the seductions of popular culture militate with increasing coercion). Theodore Adorno is thus led to characterize the consumer "masses" as "secondary" relative to the larger mechanisms of capitalism; "they are," he asserts, "an object of calculation" and "an appendage of the machinery" (*Culture* 85). They are both the dupes and the media of "a general uncritical consensus" (86) around the reified "scaffolding of rigidly conservative basic categories" (87) that informs culture. There are, of course, any number of qualifications to be made concerning such critique, not least of which is that much of what operates as "culture" is in fact quite revolutionary.[4] Nevertheless, Adorno will claim that "what parades as progress in the culture industry [his well-known term for culture as the widespread manufacturing of consent and consumption], as the incessantly new which it offers up, remains the disguise for an eternal sameness; everywhere the changes mask a skeleton which has changed just as little as the profit motive itself since the time it first gained its predominance over culture" (*ibid.*). Here the horror is the cadaverous substructure of a homogenized consumerism, the function of which is to conceal its bromidic sameness and conformity, to maintain the consensus that the new (the incessant digital update culture, to put it in contemporary terms, for example) is both genuinely fresh and worthy of indulgence.

Adorno's screed against the "culture industry" has received a great deal of critical attention, mostly concerning his tendency to dismiss such potentially rich phenomena as jazz, cinema, and television. Modern horror, on or off screen, would doubtless figure into his critique and would, in large part, occupy a justified position there given what Adorno identifies as the formulaic propensity of popular genres. And yet, in spite of the "omnipresence" of culture, its enterprises consist of individuals with rich material and psychological histories, subjects of an industry to be sure, but not, one might think optimistically, entirely bereft of agency. As this study argues, certain texts have the capacity to jar our complacency, to push against the ceiling of the dubious cultural and personal boundaries to which we are heir. We are amenable, in exceptional moments, to what Kaja Silverman refers to as "textual intervention" that "would 'light up' dark corners of the cultural screen" (*Threshold* 81). Though perhaps where horror is concerned, the inverse is true—the darkness of horror blackens the superficiality and sentimentality of light; and such illumination is indeed excessively bright, more often than not casting a polished, depthless, neon sheen rather than a contemplative shadow on the individual who absorbs more than he or she sieves.

When Adorno refers to intellectuals who embrace more than they repudiate popular culture, they do so, he suggests, with "a tone of ironic toleration" (*Culture* 89), a characterization that captures much of what passes for contemporary hipster culture. The latter reemerged as a media-inscribed category in the 1990s, an extension of pre–Internet bohemia that quickly became commodified (if it wasn't always, already) and consequently subject to mass appeal. It warrants attention here insofar as its indiscriminate irony and cultural permissiveness is highly indicative of the "screen" or "image-repertoire" (Silverman, *Threshold* 10) that harbors normative, and thus dominant, capitalist reflections of all that is acceptable and, in the case of hipster culture, fashionable. Its raiment, its weird confluence of permeability, exhibitionism, and indifference, its appropriation of everything from artistic to, in the case of males, facial hair styles that probably deserved their former burials, together constitute what Jameson, among countless others, regards as the superficiality of postmodernism. Like radio-friendly pop music, hipster cul-

1. "The Weird Tradition of America"

ture "insensibly becomes part of the existential fabric of our own lives, so that what we listen to [or view, or read, or don] is ourselves, our own previous auditions" (*Jameson* 133). It is culture that unconsciously engages in "the imitation of dead styles, speech through all the masks and voices stored up in the imaginary museum of a now global culture … the random cannibalization of all styles of the past" (202). How could such culture be anything but ironic and therefore incompatible with the relatively sincere, contemplative knowledge of self and other, with what I will identify below as the real? Ever poised to subsume the potentially insurgent "intervention" of texts, hipster culture is in some respects the epitome of what critical horror ultimately seeks to undermine and wither.

A Warning from the Imperious: Horror and the Curious Fear of Trampling

Culture, as the linchpin of civilization, may be omnipresent, though it certainly plays favorites. The hipster sensibility, which is essentially a relatively progressive materialization of the 1980s prep and every other historical manifestation of privilege, tends to look more subversive than it is. In their 21st-century incarnations, identity-hipsters absorb the formulas of fashion, music, art school, or cheap American beer with a knowing wink. If the prevailing characteristic of hipster culture is irony that thrives on surface appropriation of former styles and thus worships at the altar of postmodern-era global capitalism, the far right of the cultural and political spectrum, with its increasing bevy of populist voters, builds its own shrine on the base instincts of paranoia and aggression. Hipster culture, at its most educated, engages the sinews of civilization with response rather than reaction; it responds to the "total," Internet-obtained knowledge of everything that can be usurped and incorporated into its self-construction, and on rare occasions does so with considerable cleverness that transcends its banality. A response is always more elevated than a reaction. The reactionary right wing of American culture, on the other hand, with its tendencies toward the very fundamentalist thinking that provides the engine of terrorism, at once inimical to and endowing of far right American vulgarity and boorishness, constructs

T.E.D. Klein and the Rupture of Civilization

a self without a sense of possibilities—without, to put it in more theoretical terms, a sense of multiplicity. Its brand of culture fortifies itself against what Freud calls "a strange and threatening 'outside'" to such a degree that interiority, with its vast promises of intellectual and emotional becoming, becomes calcified. And yet, if we are to agree with the father of psychoanalysis in his claims about the proclivities of ego, extreme conservatism is merely brandishing the reactionary impulses that make garden-variety civilization the neurotic quagmire that it often is.

Critical horror has a unique way of sobering up the sensibility that is intoxicated by its own sequestration, the impulse to quarantine the self against all that would complicate and thus crack the stone of its essentialism. Of course, horror in general understands the beleaguered self, the desire for seclusion that every writer or contemplative requires in a world of insensitivity and crudeness, and, on a different level, that every extreme social conservative venerates for the purposes of rallying one's immediate, ideologically-based community around the benefits of segregation. Horror understands, aesthetically and philosophically, the "outside(r)," a discernment that can appeal on any number of levels: to one for whom its liminal qualities produce elation, as well as to the embittered fortress of a self that perceives progressive others and their ideologies as malignant, as the giants of cultural progress that are eager to stamp out more or less culturally sanctioned forms of bigotry and mediocre thinking. What follows here is a reading of the current day mantra of the far right—"Don't Tread on Me"—through the revealing horror of a story by M.R. James, with a little added sobriety from Jacques Lacan.

I've written elsewhere about James's compelling tale, "A Warning to the Curious," the story of a man, Paxton, who digs up a legendary crown meant to protect the inhabitants of an English seaside town from foreign invasion and soon faces the haunting, and fatal, consequences.[5] For the purposes of this study, it is worth noting certain aspects of the text that align with the peculiar admonishment to avoid treading upon what Lacan calls the *"moi"* (the ego that commonly objectifies or misrecognizes itself), as opposed to the *"je"* (the subjective ego), distinctive terms to which I'll soon return. The Gadsden flag that bears the warning dates back to the 18th century and has since been employed by various communities and organizations. There is a certain logic to its longevity, of

1. "The Weird Tradition of America"

course; if we consider human nature, and thus civilization, according to Freud's scheme, any expression of defiance against others who might spoil our visions of selfhood, and around which collectives can rally, is destined for bumper sticker status, or comparable historical venues. Lacan's work on human aggression and diversionary self-conception foregrounds both the vitriol and the mistaken identity inherent in the exhortation that, for the average Tea Party enthusiast, essentially means "don't take my money and give it to lazy people, or to those less fortunate, Heaven help them." Nonetheless, Don't Tread on Me, like any slogan, parades a message via specific discourse that warrants analysis, as a thoughtful horror story demands to be read at once closely and in a larger cultural context.

Paxton's central problem is that he has acquired the crown and is now unable "to put it back" (James, "A Warning" 571), initially a mystery to the narrator with whom the protagonist is sharing his plight until the latter explains "I've never been alone since I touched it" (574). The malevolent presence that follows Paxton is for the most part obscured but palpable as "a restrained hostility ... like a dog on a leash that might be let go at any moment" (579). It also "has some power over your eyes" so that "sometimes ... you see him, and sometimes you don't, just as he pleases" (575). Even after the haunted man returns the crown to its strategic position in the earth, Paxton is aware of the fact that he is "not forgiven," and further, that though he may seek refuge in religion, "it is the body that has to suffer" (581). And suffer it does—Paxton is eventually found dead on the beach, "his mouth ... full of sand and stones, and his teeth and jaws ... broken to bits" (585). Both prior to and in death, he is said to be "so totally without connections that all inquiries that [are] subsequently made [end] in a No Thoroughfare" (587).

On the surface, we might take this story as a warning to anyone who would tamper with security against potential "invaders," a reading that would likely find support with the NRA. On the other hand, the monster, apparently a male figure though animalistic in its viciousness and cadaverous in what is at one point observed as a skeletal quality, constantly obfuscates his pursuers/victims. He is an amorphous figure, a fluid weapon, a super-ego that embodies, however ephemerally, the desire to protect *identity* from foreign incursion, from "a strange and threatening 'outside'"; which is not to say that assaults do not occur in

T.E.D. Klein and the Rupture of Civilization

civilization, that seemingly innocent bodies do not suffer. How could they not, given the degree to which we ourselves are fluid, vulnerable to any number of unpleasant "instinctual endowments?" But such an investment in the superstition surrounding a buried crown suggests that fear of "the Danes or the French or the Germans" (567) is equally fanciful, as much about exercising the identity-politics of nationalism as it is full-scale battle. Thus the imperious warn against the dangers of crossing boundaries. The "curious," however, must transgress borders, be they cultural lines, psychological or corporeal frontiers, or interred mysteries. Paxton is obsessed, an understandable propensity in light of his archaeological work but one that is ultimately damning. What the story intimates, then, is the notion that such curiosity can lead not simply to the undoing of national security but to collapsed borders of body and selfhood, particularly where the latter is most dogged in its assertion or expression.

Another way of framing this intimation is to observe the inherent discrepancy in what Lacan calls "*meconnaissance*" or misrecognition. His well-known "mirror-stage" of human development posits a period of the infant's life between the ages of six to eighteen months when he or she "misrecognizes" a sense of corporeal and thus psychic integrity in the mirror image (be it literal or in the form of a caregiver) of an ideal self, one, in other words, that appears more cohesive than how the infant actually feels. Lacan elaborates on what this experience can produce as

> a drama whose internal thrust is precipitated from insufficiency to anticipation—and which manufactures for the subject, caught up in the lure of spatial identification, the succession of phantasies that extends from a fragmented body-image to a form of its totality that I shall call orthopaedic—and, lastly, to the assumption of the armor of an alienating identity, which will mark with its rigid structure the subject's entire mental development [*Écrits* 4].

The developmental process that follows is essentially defined by the ongoing search for this ideal self or "Ideal-I" on the part of the "*je*" or subjective ego, a hopeless enterprise in so far as the ideal constitutes "a fictional direction" that is incongruent with the reality of subjective and therefore cultural fragmentation (2). The distance between the identificatory ideal and the real is tremendous; it marks the gaping hole separating discontinuity of self and a fraudulent "totality." Paxton, an adult, a professional man, is unforgiven and thus suffers the consequence of

1. "The Weird Tradition of America"

death and the final realization of his own fragmentation, his own "bits," smashed and exposed. No friendship, no "orthopaedic" illusion, no "prosthesis," can help when psychological identification with the object of his obsession is so pronounced.[6]

Thus both the imperious, the far right Gladsden waver, and the curious are susceptible to plummeting into this hole unawares, though it is the former who are particularly vulnerable to its depths. The curious seek possessions, answers, political influence, personal stability, as participants in the human experience, but they do so at the risk, more or less conscious, of compromising identification with the subjective self, and they know such a compromise is in fact essential to common maturation and intellectual, emotional, and spiritual development. They seek, intentionally or not, multiplicity. The imperious, equally implicated in the innumerable conditions of being human, never quite graduate from the safety of mirror-stage delusion and its haunting ideality.[7] They don't step outside of themselves, of their comfortable, psychic homes; or, to put it another way, they refuse the opportunity to scrutinize interiority, the potential result of which is a recalculating, or a diminishing, of the "*moi*." They might pontificate amongst familiars, or on talk shows, or on the windows of their vehicles with the warning not to inhibit what they have worked so hard (or paradoxically, not at all) to create—a static, monolithic sense of self. Built into this "*moi*" may be a bank account, a particular line of employment, certain anti-socialist views that repudiate any and all efforts to address disparities and discrimination beyond self-serving charity, even well-intentioned if not uncritical attempts to savor something called liberty, though what is finally at stake in the Gladsden flag is a "me" brazenly announcing to the world that it must back off or else an ego will strike with the venom of a coiled snake. "Don't Tread on Me," it trumpets in a middle-America culture that, despite ever-present injustices, is as far as one can get from the infernal havoc that besieges less privileged nations in the everyday. And for all intents and purposes, from certain vantage points, this brand of misrecognition has been remarkably successful.

But only on the exterior. From a psychoanalytic perspective, "Don't Tread on Me" is a defining characteristic of civilization at its psychological base, irrespective of political affiliation or income bracket. Thesis V of Lacan's seminal "Aggressivity in Psychoanalysis" asserts that "a

T.E.D. Klein and the Rupture of Civilization

notion of aggressivity as one of the intentional co-ordinates of the human ego, especially relative to the category of space, allows us to conceive of its role in modern neurosis and in the 'discontents' of civilization" (*Écrits* 25). And yet, he continues, "the pre-eminence of aggressivity in our civilization ... is usually confused in 'normal' morality with strength" (*ibid.*). Here we see both the ethos and the pathos of the Gadsden flag unpacked; at its center lies aggression in relation to "space," with this term's connotations of room (or property) and freedom, a nexus that produces what Lacan calls the "vertigo of the domination of space" (28), a "*moi*" dizzied and unhinged by the impossible dream of dominion. Moreover, despite the confusion of potentially violent reactivity—signified by the snake—with economic or cultural potency, the former inevitably results in the "neurosis" and the "discontent" of which Freud warned us as early as 1930 with the original publication of *Civilization and Its Discontents*, a lesson in the danger of pathetic, if not forceful egocentricity from which Hitler's Germany, and indeed, civilization in its great diversity, could have benefitted nine years later. The "*moi*" of war, however, or of any life circumstance involving impending conflict, is less concerned with an existential apprehension around death, as Lacan explains, and more with "the narcissistic fear of damage to one's own body" (*ibid.*), of being "tread" upon. Narcissism strikes hardest when its surface identity is challenged, as it must eventually be in the precarious, even ludic, vicissitudes of life. James's Paxton, on the other hand, is clear that "it is the body that has to suffer," a moment defined not by confusion or vertigo but by clarity, a profound and arresting sense of the real.

Prior to Paxton's physical undoing is the primary concern of having entered a liminal (as opposed to a reified) space, a threshold that, once crossed, transforms the self for better or, in this case, most certainly for worse. The ominous repetition of "I don't know how to put it back" signifies the new porosity of his being and mortality, the extent to which he has become the subject of a specter, entered in turn by another, an apparition, an ideology. Paxton has been driven to paranoia—but, crucially, by curiosity rather than unrefined arrogance. The latter coincides with what Lacan calls the aggression-laden "paranoic knowledge" that corresponds to "certain critical moments that mark the history of man's mental genesis, each representing a stage in objectifying identification"

1. "The Weird Tradition of America"

(17). The uncanny entity that haunts the story's protagonist is aggression given form, however opaque, a quintessential "*moi*" whose objectification can only subsume or demolish. Paxton is seduced and victimized by the form's own guardianship of paranoia and thus provides the reader with a warning. Of course, James is right to admonish because by its very nature, horror antagonizes the subject that would mistake himself or herself for anything other than one who is vulnerable to the multiplicity inherent in nature, through the webs of other people, known or unknown forces. Some horror, however, reminds us that the thing we cannot put back is far more prosaic than a mythical crown and, consequently, is indubitably inscribed into the fabric of quotidian desires, dreams, and nightmares.

David Robert Mitchell's 2014 film *It Follows*, a "period" piece that has no definitive period (70s? 80s? 2014?), underscores the "it" as a commonplace product of the desiring, coming-of-age self at the same time that, as in the James text, "it" is dramatized as correlative to monstrosity. The protagonist, a female high school student, has sex with her boyfriend in the back seat of his car, only to find herself drugged and bound soon thereafter. But the boyfriend's action is deceptive; he is not a sadist, but a young man for whom previous sex has led to being followed by a murderous force visible only to its prey. Though slow-moving, it assumes the form of random or familiar bodies and pursues the young lover to the death, only to travel down the line of his or her sexual lineage to further the killing spree. Apparently, the only way to rid oneself of what follows is to sleep with someone else, and even then, "it" may reappear, though without the intention to destroy; "it" merely haunts, disavowing the possibility of a return to separation, lovelorn or otherwise.

Like Stanley Kubrick's *The Shining* and any number of horror films involving young people, *It Follows* is clearly invested in studying the inevitable processes of maturation, if not adulteration. Children may be closer to their innate powers of intuition than their jaded elders and thus confront the wrath of jealousy. Having crossed the border into sexuality beyond adolescent masturbation, into that space in which adults tend to be both absent and obsolete, teenagers must face the consequences of mixing fluids and inexperienced sensibilities. Horror is a fitting genre for these scenarios because they necessarily entail fear, vulnerability, and sometimes crisis born of inquisitiveness. Both Paxton

T.E.D. Klein and the Rupture of Civilization

and coming-of-age lovers are curious. Once this impulse is satisfied by stepping into foreign terrain, however ordinary, there is no returning to one's former self. "It" cannot be put back, "it" will always follow and the child always becomes an adult, if only in age. Nonetheless, advancing into maturity, whatever that might mean for a given individual, is obviously essential to participating in civilization, regardless of neurosis-producing social structures. Neurosis, for Freud, is integral to civilization, both a key component of the machinery that drives it (the "it" here can also include capitalism to the degree that mass consumerism may be framed as a form of neurosis) and an entanglement that is tremendously difficult to overcome. On the other hand, unlike James's story, *It Follows* concludes with two young friends having revived their pre-teen amorousness and consummated their (particularly the male's) longstanding desire for the sake of facing "it" together in the wake of numerous deaths; such fellowship that transcends the specificity of a particular era and particular teenagers so as to highlight common bonds of alliance against the adversity of growing up. After they have sex, the film's final scene depicts them walking toward the camera, tenderly holding hands, though clearly apprehensive, and the ominous presence of a blurred figure following behind in the distance, a figure who may or may not be a manifestation of the "it."

Nobody wants to be followed with malicious intent, limited, or in some way aggressed. What *It Follows* presents is a phantasmagoric and horrifying but realistic response to the desire for self-reliance taken to extremes. The fact is that it is impossible not to be "tread upon" in life. People need one another emotionally, sexually, intellectually, economically, logistically, to different degrees at different stages of a life, or a day. Moreover, there is potential pleasure in entering these stages that demand the selflessness of intimacy, compassion, and an awareness of multiplicity that transcends the true horror of laissez-faire or ideological isolationism. That the monster in the film and in the story exercises "some power over your eyes" suggests that we "see" only what we have invited into our lives via impulses, reactions, behaviors, and ideological assumptions that can serve either to push us toward productive, liminal spaces or into the "vertigo" of self-containment and poignantly turgid misrecognition. To wave the Gadsden flag is to see the "threat" of an amorphous, "strange outside" as an ever-present enemy rather than the

1. "The Weird Tradition of America"

valuable challenge to egocentricity and narcissism that it is, that other people, irrespective of their stations in life, are.

Coming Attractions

In assigning and observing the creative projects of students in a horror seminar, it is impossible to avoid the fact that those of a conservative, and certainly an evangelical bent, often create the most riveting literary and filmic texts. Why is this? Perhaps it has something to do with said students being immersed in opposition, the penchant for antagonism mentioned above, or, in the case of conservative religious individuals, the taste of blood on their lips, so to speak, that coincides with the foregrounding of hellfire and indictments of damnation. Sartre's well-known contention that "hell is other people" says infinitely more about the self than it does the other, especially in the case of one who employs some variation of this notion to berate and condemn as a central practice in the munitions factory of his or her ideological operations. There is a perverse pleasure in adversarial thinking that resonates with the violence of horror, but such pleasure is as cheap and ephemeral as the egocentrism it is propping up. It ultimately negates itself rather than the abhorred other, the abject situation, and is too blinding to reveal the self-defeating mechanisms that give rise to what is ultimately the baring of crippled fangs. To put it in Lacanian terms, conservative pleasure in horror may be rooted in the deluded "*moi*" as opposed to the "*je*."[8]

Stephen King's popular claim that the most compelling horror is at once "reactionary, anarchistic, and revolutionary" is convincing if for no other reason than its grounding in the conditions of civilization. Horror reflects the promises and perils of being human among other humans, or the sense of being alone in a potentially malevolent or indifferent universe. But King's assessment could be more specific; the smartest, most effective horror—critical horror—averts reactivity and is too savvy, too aesthetically and intellectually advanced to be merely anarchic (which is not to dismiss the unique albeit throwaway pleasures of B-movie or pulp schlock). The genre is at its best when its horror is organic, seemingly effortless, original, and provocatively critical. It is most vital when it transcends its own formulas, and thus the formulaic expectations of popular culture. It burns brightest when its filmic adaptation upsets the writer of the original text, as Kubrick's version of *The Shining* affected King, who, apparently, has since come around to appreciating the film's genuinely revolutionary quality. In distinguishing popular culture from modernism, Jameson asserts that both

> entertain relations of repression with the fundamental social anxieties and concerns, hopes and blind spots, ideological antinomies and fantasies of disaster, which are their raw material; only where modernism tends to handle this material by producing compensatory structures of various kinds, mass culture represses them by the narrative construction of imaginary resolutions and by the projection of an optical illusion of social harmony [*Jameson* 138].

Critical horror is kindred to modernism in this regard without necessarily being as "anarchistic" or self-consciously iconoclastic. It motions toward but ultimately displaces formulas. It resists, with ferocity, what Jean Baudrillard refers to as "the unclean promiscuity of everything [inherent in mass culture] which touches, invests, and penetrates without resistance" (quoted, Modleski 163). It replaces the façade of social or subjective harmony with turbulence but it also subverts the reactionary appropriation of anarchic violence by unleashing "an unprecedented assault on all that bourgeois culture is supposed to cherish" (158), including delusions of pitiable self-reliance and the demonization of abjection.

But what of the "compensatory structures" of horror? In what way can it be said to ameliorate the challenges of confronting civilization in the everyday of its persistent, galvanic wash over our lives? What compensation does critical horror offer in the wake, or *in flagrante delicto*, of our seemingly endless reactions, the minutiae of our identifications, misrecognitions, ignorant prejudices—in short, our egos both in the service of and at odds with civilization? As an extension of Lovecraft's canonical *Supernatural Horror in Literature*, Thomas Ligotti's "Professor Nobody's Little Lectures on Supernatural Horror" suggests an answer in proclaiming "we have been force-fed for so long the shudders of a thousand graveyards that at last, seeking a macabre redemption, a salvation of horror, we willingly consume the terrors of the tomb ... and find them to our liking" (188). Horror as "salvation," "redemption," the Lovecraftian uncanny, the marginal ontology that should not be appealing to one's sense of proper alignment; perhaps we are saved from our-

1. "The Weird Tradition of America"

selves, from those features of the self that have been styled and manicured by the indoctrination of civilized culture, by all that dehumanizes in the age of digital consumerism, facile relations, and vacuous sloganeering. And curiously, ideally, rather than devolving into the dysfunctional, neurotic playthings of a domineering nihilism, a juvenile investiture in despondency, we "like" "the terrors"; we find satisfaction in this alternative mode of consumption, one whose marginalization subverts the cronyism of mass subjectivities. The latter have a tendency to "like" according to popular taste, by virtue of knowing all the right people and their minute-to-minute preoccupations, Facebook façades. Perhaps there is something redemptive in closing off the entrance of one's mouth, rejecting toxic food, and, without necessarily repudiating those who would gorge (thus creating yet another lurking, barricaded monster of a "*moi*"), stepping into the tomb to confront the gravity and the profundity of death, its boundaries that can inspire as much as they threaten, its harrowingly mortal atmospheres.

Stephen King's essay "Why We Crave Horror Movies" offers another perspective. Somehow we recognize the importance of confronting the egoic murk beneath the digital networking profile picture in its formulaic sheen, its ongoing glee and gripes, what King refers to as "the hungry alligators swimming around in that subterranean river beneath" (3–4). Critical horror aids us in the confrontation by forcing the issue in a semi-popular medium, one that, perhaps ironically, is far more palatable for most than rigorous philosophical or spiritual practice. Obviously the beasts must be kept in check for the efficient running of civilized life, and to maintain the scaffolding of collective ethics that in turn keeps more people out of a deeply problematic, racially skewed prison system. And somehow we "like" the tension inherent in the interior skirmish, facing off with ethical boundaries that horror delights in pushing, especially when one's political and philosophical ethos is amenable to the responsibilities of personal and cultural multiplicity. We, some of us, crave horror. We desire the suspension of the intumescent self, however temporary, that is akin to de Chardin's omega point, the evolution of consciousness to a point of extinguishing the profile, or what G.I. Gurdjieff calls "personality" that struts, emotes, and intellectualizes itself into delusional being. Don DeLillo's haunting novel *Point Omega* characterizes de Chardin's belief as a transpersonal "introversion" that is

T.E.D. Klein and the Rupture of Civilization

"what we want" (52–53). Isaac Asimov's science fiction story "The Last Question" posits a scenario in which humans and god-like computer technologies merge in an endless round of rebirth, "each physical body losing its mental identity in a manner that [is] somehow not a loss but a gain" (*Nine* 89). We crave horror because we want to loosen the human grip on all that we hold dear given our intuitive knowledge that this grip is phantasy, that it is always already vulnerable to disengagement, to rupture. What we have to gain in the process of dissolution is, in yet another irony, a profound sense of pleasure.

Roland Barthes's distinction between the "text of pleasure" and the "text of bliss" is significant here. The former, he explains, is one that "contents, fills, grants euphoria; the text that comes from culture and does not break with it, is linked to a *comfortable* practice of reading," while the latter "imposes a state of loss, the text that discomforts … unsettles the reader's historical, cultural, psychological assumptions, the consistencies of his tastes, values, memories, brings to a crisis his relation with language" (*Pleasure* 14). Of course, if we follow the Lacanian observation that "the unconscious is structured like a language" (Lacan, *Four* 203), this "crisis" applies to the very mechanism at the core of civilization's discontents. And yet, the afflictive dilemma with language and subjectivity is provoked by textual *bliss*, the French term for which is *jouissance*, with its larger, postmodern implications of both sexual orgasm and a de-centering capacity that operates on the seemingly static, cohesive self. Bliss signifies pleasure that transcends corporeal euphoria, the kind that emerges from the comfort of prescribed gratifications; it arouses the "gain" of lost platitudes and furtive, unconscious psychopathologies of everyday life. Bliss results in a form of self-effacement (or rather, *l'effacement de moi*), a kind of extinguishing of the distended self. At its best, horror gives us the gift of bliss.

On the other hand, this "crisis" has a tendency to provoke (particularly in 21st-century considerations of horror's import) a trendy, prevailing pessimism. There is something noble in embracing pessimism as a response to the quintessentially American (and as Lovecraft observes, the "smirking" [*Supernatural* 12]) optimism that garners much of its resilience from capitalist power structures. Kafka's heroic hunger artist, for example, can find nothing to eat, so to speak, in a world dazzled by (or "force-fed") trivial pleasures for which it is always willing to pay.

1. "The Weird Tradition of America"

Melville's famed Bartleby expresses his unsettlingly powerful preference for anything but what a hypocritical, mediocre Wall St. lawyer has to offer. Where pessimism becomes self-defeating, however, is where it (mis)identifies and generates the deluded, isolated self against which Freud, and revolutionary horror, warns us; it postulates cosmic indifference to a point of rather un-postmodern essentialism that denotes the philosophizing subject as much as the philosophy. Hell is other people. But even the dour critique of Adorno allows for a condition beyond such self-absorption. He speaks of it in different ways, as "immediacy and life" that operates in contradistinction to "the completely reified and mediated" that is the culture industry (*Culture* 87). The latter requires time, the cultural nurturing of false consciousness, and ultimately resembles death, or utter mechanicalness, while the former he later relates to "the development of autonomous, independent individuals who judge and decide consciously for themselves" (92). He even goes so far as to equate "immediacy and life" not only with "emancipation" from the circumscribed "order" of the culture industry, but with "happiness" (*ibid.*). Though an extensive examination of happiness is beyond the scope of this study, the term is by no means irrelevant. There is something more authentic about the "happiness" of *jouissance* as opposed to mere pleasure; the manner in which it accounts for a sense of horror or sublimity (or rupture) in conjunction with well-being. At the very minimum, we can safely say that Adorno's use of "happiness" necessarily entails the confident struggle of enacting subversive ways of being and thinking. It eschews the pop Zeitgeist and the reactionary subjectivities it generates. It entails productive solitude at the same time that it does not acquiesce to the aggressive, isolationist impulses that are quick to produce (and project) egoic misanthropy. It is orgasmic without being masturbatory, independent and conscious with no intransigent recourse to *Schadenfreude* (literally, "harm-joy," that unique pleasure in the misfortune of others).

Regarding the contrary valorization of pessimism, we might consider S.T. Joshi's reaction to T.E.D. Klein as a nascent "optimist who yearns for happy endings both in life and literature" (*Modern* 96). Though Klein himself has maintained that horror is "in effect, defanged, to be enjoyed in a spirit of play" (quoted 98), Joshi counters with a plea for horror's ability to destabilize the reader: "would any serious writer

T.E.D. Klein and the Rupture of Civilization

wish his work to be so 'defanged' that it would have no effect upon us after we put the book aside? Do we not retain in our minds the notion of mankind's insignificance after we finish reading a tale by Lovecraft (or Klein)?" (*ibid.*). Important questions, both, in that they speak to horror's potential role in unraveling the dichotomies that fuel civilization's base instincts, those which operate hierarchically, according to the demands of a particular order, within the subject to effect a self at the expense of other selves. What is lost in this critique of "play," however, is the distinct difference between the fangs of horror and those that would strike out of reactionary fear ("Don't Tread on Me"), of losing the precious identity, with all of its manufactured desires, opinions, and prejudices. Critical horror's rupture may very well invite the reader to weigh his or her "insignificance," but this preoccupation does not necessarily hinder agency, or happiness for that matter. Rather, as Deleuze and Guattari might put it, at its "minoritarian" best, horror "[stretches] tensors through" (*Thousand* 105) the reading self and thus removes one from the center of the universe. It proposes a form of healthy self-effacement, the confrontation with the mirror image in which one beholds a paradoxically agentic selflessness that is alert in "immediacy and life," as opposed to the conventional mirror-stage moment of merely "[reaping] the ego" (quoted, *Jameson* 96). Of course we ultimately seek happiness "in life and literature." To do otherwise is to pit one's fragile interiority against all that is other and simply reinforce the tired exhortation of far right obtuseness; and more importantly, it is to ignorantly disregard literature as "an enterprise of health," as Deleuze frames it, the aim of which "is to set free, in [its] delirium, this creation of a health or this invention of a people, that is, a possibility of life" (*Essays* 3-4). The counter-formulaic, counter-culture, ego-smashing "delirium" of critical horror generates possibilities, life, *jouissance*, with the elixir of its own singular poisons. In this respect, horror as the literature of "happiness" *par excellence*, limited though it may be to those "people" brave enough to withstand its encroachment upon cherished borders, is quite possibly the most sensible, radical approach to the genre and its deployment of all.

Nevertheless, Freud's anticipation of "someone [who] will [one day] venture to embark upon a pathology of cultural communities" (*Civilization* 91) has since been met by many critical, occasionally caustic thinkers

1. "The Weird Tradition of America"

and writers, from the "hypermodernism" of a Paul Virilio to the potent insights into Middle America of a Raymond Carver. Somewhere amidst such figures stands T.E.D. Klein, whose six major works of what Joshi astutely calls "quiet horror" (*Modern* 103) will occupy the rest of this analysis.

Chapter 2

Events and Ceremonies

The first page of Klein's monumental *The Ceremonies* informs us that "the events recorded here began as one day they would end—In mystery" (3). This admission may come as a disappointment to those readers for whom ambiguity is narrative sin, a cop out that forgoes the safety and satisfaction of Aristotelean symmetry. On the other hand, most horror enthusiasts are both savvy and brave enough to embrace uncertainty insofar as the latter is so profoundly indicative of the collective human experience, from the wily ways of the unconscious that is closer than breathing to the Hell that that can often assume the form of other people, and well beyond into the largely unknowable cosmos with its ephemeral meanings and black holes. Like any thoughtful horror writer, Klein knows that a degree of ambiguity is integral to both the condition of being human and elevated narrative satisfaction. And yet, his protagonist, Jeremy Freirs, a thirty-year-old scholar and teacher of Gothic/horror fiction who is spending a summer researching in Gilhead, home to an isolated, rural religious community, is eventually led to ask the question "what if some stories in horror books aren't fiction? What if there are White People out there, malevolent little faces grinning in the moonlight? Whispers in the grass? Poisonous things in the woods? Unsuspected evil in the world?" (439). The reference here is to Arthur Machen's seminal story "The White People," a text that produces a variety of answers to Jeremy's question, the most direct of which claims that its own events are "all true and wonderful and splendid" (142). So the "mystery," however obfuscating or deleterious, is at once grounded in reality and, to use a term commonly ascribed to the effects of horror, sublime. As such—and it is in this framework that Klein excels—critical horror is also firmly based in the mundane, the quotidian "landscapes of estrangement" that reveal "a spiritual knife-edge in the poetry of alien places, where extreme situations become inevitable and characters

2. Events and Ceremonies

are forced toward life-defining moments," as Don DeLillo puts it in his considerably shorter but equally monumental *The Body Artist* (31). The stories of horror fiction invariably speak to situations that may be removed from but are strangely akin to everyday life, to the (knife) point that the "mystery" is nearly as close, or dangerously closer than the breathing that animates a body; or it lurks in the home, in the charged dynamic of relationality, on the farm, or in the forest.

The Ceremonies, published two years after metal band Venom released its own seminal album, *Black Metal*, in 1982, opens with the following line: "The forest was ablaze" (Klein 3). The band's genre defining title would eventually and infamously inspire a group of Norwegian teens to push the satanic aggression inherent in its ethos to extremes, one of their aesthetic contributions (in addition to church burnings, corpse-like face painting, and creative post-mortem jewelry designs) being Darkthrone's *A Blaze in the Northern Sky*.[1] Though hardly related, the novel's opening suggests a comparable emphasis on nature as origin or begetter of evil—a natural element whose potentially widespread incineration of skies, forests, religious ideologies, people, ultimately transcends the natural world and operates, destroys, on a cosmic scale. Both *The Ceremonies*, along with "The Events at Poroth Farm," and the general aesthetic/behaviors/events of the Black Metal scene in Norway (circa early 80s and 90s) foreground a sense of supernatural mystery, be it in the form of a Lovecraftian Old One long embedded in the earth and flesh of life or a vision of Satan's collusion with adolescent egoism running rampant and playing with fire.[2] At the other end of the spectrum from "mystery," however, is the mundane that can be no less aggressive and malevolent. Klein's texts exert considerable force in critiquing common egotism, patriarchy, religious bigotry, consumerism, the ignorant repudiation of human desire, and the baseline of fear that fuels such tendencies. Black Metal culture often exemplifies said tendencies in the guise of the occult. "What if some stories in horror books aren't fiction?" Jeremy asks himself. Klein's answer is that some of them are in fact quite real. I would like to begin here by exploring the realities of civilization as they manifest in these central Kleinian texts before moving on to a discussion of infernal mysteries beyond the veil of culture and human presumption, or as some might have it, pedestrian arrogance in the face of the unknowable.

T.E.D. Klein and the Rupture of Civilization

Both the Prologue and the Epilogue of *The Ceremonies* follow events taking place during two consecutive Christmas seasons, a fitting timeframe given that the holiday (outside, perhaps, of pleasant choral music and familial good cheer) is often representative of five central aspects of debased civilization at the core of the novel. Aggression, puritanical sexual prohibition, patriarchy, labor/property, and cultural (i.e., religious and populist) ignorance all overlap in Klein's narrative as they do in life on the margins of fiction, as they have long done and will likely continue to do. Civilization wrestles the individual over a lifetime, they entwine and dance, with the former typically leading, and it obviously does the same with cultures over the course of millennia. The forest is invariably ablaze even while progress appears to refine. The Prologue sees "a year [pass]. And another. And then five thousand more." And eventually, "the Indians were dead, and the forest land had dwindled to a third its size. Settlers had dotted it with homesteads; engineers had crisscrossed it with roads; farmers had cleared off a patchwork of fields for pasturing and corn. Villages had sprouted, townships spread; somewhere a city was being laid out that would spell destruction for another million trees" (4). Such destruction, of course, is not limited to land and Indians; in paying only enough attention to the trees to eliminate them, the forest goes unseen. The civilized development of privileged peoples bulldozes conscience, ethical considerations, those that tend to preclude destructiveness, and thus obscures its own implication in the darkest forces propelled by "mystery." As Absolom Troet, aka Rosie, aka The Old One, aka the embodiment of evil in *The Ceremonies* observes, "No one else is watching; no one would understand. No one sees the patterns in the water, or smells the corruption beneath the flower scent, or hears the secret sound the grass makes when the wind dies" (24). This singular character's advanced senses notwithstanding, what is finally at stake in his allegation is the "corruption" that operates beneath the civilized veneer, not unlike the viciously battling ants just under the surface of an idyllic suburban backyard in David Lynch's *Blue Velvet*. The man who has the heart attack while watering his lawn at the beginning of this film will survive, though the ants remain.

And yet, unlike the happily recovering homeowner, the viewer is given access to the violence beneath the surface. We are led to understand, to distinguish the patterns, and to recognize scents other than

2. Events and Ceremonies

those of a sweet flower. Through horror and related narratives, we are given to comprehend the notion that, as Machen suggests to Jeremy and other readers, "the whole world is but a great ceremony" (quoted 230). Regardless of a ritual's point of origin, metaphysical or otherwise, it necessarily assumes discursive or physical form in the "world" and is consequently informed by civilizing processes, human impulse and inconsistency, forces of self-preservation, not the least of which is the aggressive drive. In particularly violent instances, this quality of the "ceremony" appears widespread indeed; in Klein's novel, it is firmly established on nearly every page as only a text attempting to press in on cultural and cosmic ruin would have it.

Flashes of Aggression

Perhaps the most arresting display of aggression in the novel, all the more effective than the dramatic conclusion with its disfiguration, blood, rape, and fire for its relative subtlety, occurs during a dinner scene. Rosie has invited Jeremy and his love interest, Carol (a virgin, and thus crucial to Rosie's plan to annihilate the human race), to dine at a posh restaurant. With the demeanor of a kindly, jolly grandfather, and the appearance of a diminutive, harmless, aged man, he has befriended Carol, requested her employment to help with esoteric research, and gained her trust to the degree that she has been willing to engage in his eccentric games involving dance and song—ceremony—which makes the scene all the more menacing. There is a thunderstorm. The electricity flickers out, leaving the diners in momentary candlelight, whereupon, "in that frozen moment of shadows and silence, with only the candle on the table for illumination, she [sees] Rosie regarding her—it [is] like seeing him for the first time. In the altered light, that instant, everything [looks] different: the old man's face [is] hard, icy, cruel. He [has] held the [steak] knife poised in her direction, and his tiny eyes [have] glittered like razors in the candlelight" (257). The scene is especially striking in terms of what it reveals about most any human being: the reactionary cruelty underlying even the most innocuous presence in an "instant" of regression, the manic ants in the soil.

Of course, what is on display here is a rather exceptional misan-

T.E.D. Klein and the Rupture of Civilization

thropy on the part of a transformed man, over a hundred years old, made alien and evil as a child ("Absolom Troet, the boy with the devil in him" [226], or as Jeremy later jokes upon seeing a photo of the young Absolom, "Portrait of the Devil as a Young Man" [309]) in all but his appearance, at least when the lights are on, one who "feels no trace of kinship for these odious doomed beings, only a cold and unremitting hatred" (40). Throughout most of the novel, Rosie's perspective is aligned with the reader's in all but the details of how the numerous ceremonies will play out, while other central characters, including Jeremy, Carol, and the farm owners, Deborah and Sarr Poroth, essentially and unconsciously bend to the will of the Old One.[3] While the reader might root for Jeremy in his navigation of the slowly unfolding evil on Poroth farm, or even for his conquest of Carol, whose own wholesome example warrants sympathy, it is Rosie's project that maintains the most compelling tension and therefore the fascination of the novel. One need not identify with Rosie per se to experience the appeal of his single-pointed ambition, to feel the immensity of his power (in the lifespan of his current inhabitation) over thousands of years. Klein ensures that this embodiment of hatred is both likable and still very much human in his aging, and periodically endearing, relatability, even as it charts the "doomed" course of a humanity consumed by survival and mere ego-fulfillment.[4] The reader's god-like perspective is at once gratifying and anything but benevolent, in keeping, it is fair to say, with both the attraction to narrative suspense and the malice (or simply the self-involvement) of a species that can set the forest ablaze, so to speak, with a word, a gesture, or a vote.

On the other hand, when Rosie observes a young couple in the grip of affection, his reaction extends beyond common misanthropy; it challenges, in fact, what most every human craves, namely, a sense of belonging and intimacy that will exert both its force and its appeal to the reader in the examples of the two aforementioned couples. Upon seeing the lovers in one another's arms on a beach,

> rage sweeps over him like a wave. Jerkily he begins moving toward them, lips tightening, color surging to his face. He can feel, in his fists, the pumping of their loathsome hearts; the air before him rings with ancient voices screaming for a kill. Oh, to perform the Voola'teine [a murderous ritual]! To drown the pair, to burn them where they lie, to climb the boardwalk and drop knives

2. Events and Ceremonies

upon their flesh through the cracks between the planks. In a vision he sees the thrashing young bodies buried beneath waves of smothering sand ... [150].

Two people who aren't necessarily "odious"; they are merely experiencing something approximating love. One need not worship beach culture to feel the vicarious pleasure of this exchange, the lovers in one another's arms, careless of sand and heat; one would, in fact, have to be psychotic to apply such rage and violence to their condemnation as Rosie's, even in the throes of envy. Alternatively, one could be possessed by a demon, the Demon, hungry for the world. So Absolom's aggression surpasses the human enough to situate him in a distanced horror scenario, one that transcends quotidian concerns, preoccupations, behaviors, or reductive psychoanalytic scenarios (he was not loved enough as a child, etc.). To be specific, he has transcended the category of the human by virtue of a vicious becoming-other, as Deleuze and Guattari might put it, scaling the heights of otherness as a "Thing, which arrives and passes at the edge, which is linear yet multiple" (*Thousand* 245).

But "the whole world is but a great ceremony" and the novel utilizes this Machenian trope to foreground the centrality of transformation in the human experience and beyond. The Deleuze and Guattari reference is relevant here in so far as their notion of becoming, if not ceremonial or ritualistically liminal in nature, nevertheless implies a process of "deterritorialization" (291) whereby the initial territory of the self (territorialized by cultural sanctions, the State, etc.) is liberated from said constraints to the degree that it is transformed into something new, an innovative being that is paradoxically untethered, for better and possibly for worse, to a singularity of being. Becoming has the capacity to be radically productive, though in the hands of horror narrative, it often resembles possession in one form or another; from a twelve-year-old girl in *The Exorcist* to a "dull boy" in *The Shining*, or particularly relevant to *The Ceremonies*, a cat. The "other" of becoming-other may not be authoritarian in any traditional sense but the face of its transformative operation may exert highly destructive force. Its anomalous quality "arrives and passes at the edge [of a territory], 'teeming, seething, swelling, foaming, spreading like an infectious disease, this nameless horror'" (245). Deleuze and Guattari are quoting Lovecraft here with the intent of extolling a monstrous becoming, monstrous in that it unfolds over and against hegemony and is, this study is arguing, an intrinsic quality of the "macabre redemption" of "quiet horror." And yet, no matter its literary value, no one wants the reality of an "infectious disease." To put it simplistically, not all transformations are healthy for self and other.

Deborah and Sarr Poroth, "two gravely devout children aged in the wilderness," as Jeremy observes in "The Events…" (Klein 313), are anomalous in their religious community. Deborah is an outsider though she has been raised in a comparable tradition, one that is Bible-focused and generally eschews the ways, values, and possessions of the secular world. They are 30-ish, both handsome in spite of puritan garb, and both have been educated outside their communities. In the short story, they have a television (about which Klein via Jeremy has much to say), quite scandalous in the sect, and in both texts they maintain an active, robust sex life. Sarr has even ventured to New York City as a younger man (where, incidentally, he encounters a diminutive, pink-skinned gentleman who sets him up to adopt a cat whom he will eventually call Bwada). The couple's humanity shines throughout the text, especially the case with the playful, exuberant Deborah, and lends itself to the reader's affinity considerably more than that of any of their fellow believers. Though they are certainly not beyond reproach from the perspective of a less fundamentalist or generally irreligious discernment, such qualities make their grisly demise all the more poignant. By the end of the novel, Sarr determines (finally) that it is time to request the services of his mother, who knows precisely what is happening on this last night of her son's life, because of Deborah's bizarre transformation following an attack by the possessed, undead Bwada. He leaves the house in the night, while Deborah is supposedly sleeping but fails to "see the thing that [sits] upright in the bed and [creeps] down that stairs after him" (Klein, *Ceremonies* 473). He also fails to notice "the figure wielding the axe [who is] too swift. Its blade [catches] him square in the back of the skull and [buries] itself in his brain" (474). The "thing that was the farmwife" collapses and "the thing that was the farmer shoves aside her stiffening body and gets to its feet…. It looks at the Old One and smiles" (*ibid.*).

Here the aggression is amplified by literal possession, the chaos of which provokes the couple's non-comprehending "brethren" to react in a manner that parallels the threatening, supernatural events engulfing them. Confronted with death, anomalous weather patterns, violent live-

2. Events and Ceremonies

stock, not to mention a field of snakes, they agree that the genuine outsider, Jeremy, has provoked the wrath of God and is thus responsible for havoc in their otherwise peaceful community, the plan being merely to address the interloper. "'We're not going to do him any harm now, that wouldn't be right,'" suggests one of the men, to which another replies, "'Course not, Matt. We're just gonna *call* on him, that's all. We're just gonna see that he leaves...'" (485). The italics are weighty here, signifying the convergence of both obliviousness to the reality of the situation and the inherent impulse to react with force. Though Jeremy has been drugged and is himself oblivious to what is happening—a fast-approaching apocalypse—the potential "lynching" is indicative of Jeremy's general predicament at Poroth farm, as the subject of an ongoing, if not malicious gaze. His residence on the farm, a converted chicken coop, has windows that open to both the farm and the adjacent forest area. At one point, he writes in his journal, "When you're inside here it's like being in a display case: every eye can watch you, from the woods and field and lawn. But all you see is darkness" (147). It is a moment that might call to mind the doomed Eleanor from Shirley Jackson's *The Haunting of Hill House* who receives the combination of a look and the assertion "everything is worse ... if you think something is looking at you" (120). In both cases, whether it is a cat, a raucous, chanting forest, a house, or, most commonly, another human being, the gaze is ominous in its aggressive intentionality. It seeks, at the very minimum, to lynch the wellbeing of the observed, to foster paranoia and a sense of the viewer's power under the cover of "darkness," for which there is an early precedent in *The Ceremonies*, when Jeremy first meets Sarr. In the instant of the former's awakening from a nap (in a cemetery, no less), he becomes aware that "the world [has] darkened" (Klein, *Ceremonies* 26), at which point another, a hulking man, a son and husband, a believer, Sarr Poroth, introduces himself.

Evil, too, is on display, as when Rosie becomes-evil and brandishes the knife over dinner, but it exercises methodical control over its presentation, appearing at the strategic moment in order to manipulate and eventually destroy. When Rosie rightly perceives Carol's promiscuous female roommate, Rochelle, as a threat to Carol's virginity, a bad influence that would wreck any and all ceremonies, he manifests as a still, "shapeless bundle of rags" (206) outside the elevator that the roommate is taking to their apartment. "As she [pulls] open the elevator's scarred black metal door, the bundle [rises] and [follows] her inside" (*ibid.*) and appears as a "filthy-looking" old woman with plump hands that soon elicit a "desperate scream" from Rochelle and "[close] over her throat" (207). The rising bundle is certainly striking, as is Rosie's masquerade as a harmless and decrepit woman, though the strangling that concludes this section of the chapter is perhaps a bit hackneyed in its succinct drama, the display being too obvious. Klein, like most horror writers, is prone to such affected phrasing. Where evil's exhibition is more ominous, I would argue, is where it flourishes in the guise of mundane humanity; where, for example, the two couples dine together at Poroth farm (Carol having made the trip from New York in anticipation of fostering her blossoming relationship with Jeremy). A common dynamic emerges, a collusion between opposite partners, whereupon Sarr realizes that "the lines ... [are] shifting, setting him and the new woman against his wife and guest" (183). Intimate or romantic relationships often give to the peculiar relief of such a dynamic, the minor and largely innocent empowerment of the self that finds a temporary ally in the playful safety of an other for whom there may or may not be a level of attraction. In this case, there are definitely attractions being exchanged on both sides, giving the "lines" a particular (and particularly tense) charge despite the fact that everyone at the table except Jeremy is devoted to a religious (and more or less moralistic) calling. This charge, of course, is the spark of aggression that erects borders between individuals, couples, cultures, and nations.

Of course, the shifting of borders is inevitable. Only a reactionary way of being seeks to strengthen the formerly static territory, as opposed to processing and seeking to understand its implications with intelligence and conscientiousness. To his credit, Sarr contemplates these lines and arrives at the conclusion that they are "natural," leaving him finally to "[understand] and [forgive]" (*ibid.*). Even Jeremy, with his pronounced penchant for cynicism, will later occupy a "hot, smelly New York night" while visiting Carol in the city, (only to be interrupted by Rosie, whose presence will maintain Carol's virginity), and "see why, if [he] were a bit younger and poorer, stuck in the city with nothing to lose, [he'd] be tempted to bash somebody's brains out with a tire iron"; but ultimately, "[his] impulses [are] somewhat more humane: [he feels] like pulling Carol out of the glare of the streetlamps and making love to her all night" (249). Understanding, forgiveness, loving congress: such acts that counter aggressive tendencies and reveal the potential benevolence in the face of the multiplicity and porosity of the human experience. That the qualifier "somewhat" diminishes the efficacy of these noble impulses is suggestive of the immense complexity of lines intersecting where desire, sexual or otherwise, holds sway, which brings us to the second topic of what I am identifying as Klein's central critiques of civilization.

Even Priests Do It

Klein is kind to Carol's virginity. He does not demean his character for being puritanical; on the contrary, she is complicated and well intentioned. The fact that she leaves her small town and strikes out for NYC (much as Sarr has done as a younger man) already qualifies her as a strong, inquisitive woman who is prepared to broaden her horizons. Desire is complicated and Carol is steadying herself to enter its web, its many folds and strata that are born out in the mundane impulses of a lived life. Nonetheless, it is her virginity that makes her vulnerable to both personal violence and playing a significant role in the annihilation of the human race. The reader is generally guided to favor Jeremy's relatively street-savvy agnosticism over Carol's religious convictions, equally implicated though the two are in the Old One's scheme. As Jeremy accompanies Sarr to the farm for an initial visit, the latter warns his guest of his wife's dangerously good cooking (one of many allusions to Jeremy's inevitable weight gain): "I hope you're one who struggles against the temptations of the flesh," to which Jeremy responds, "No better than the next man, I guess! You know what they say about the best way to get rid of temptation" (29). This comment may be amusing but it extinguishes any levity between host and visitor, foreshadowing as it does the sexual tension between Jeremy and Deborah, a re-mapping of social and sexual lines, Sarr's "understanding" of which is limited by virtue of desire's intricacies, especially in the context of fundamentalist Christian doctrine. Carol's observation that she has noticed even priests succumbing to what "[seems] almost a formality" (89), that of the male gaze upon her breasts, speaks to the inescapability of sexual desire, vilified, or trumpeted, though it may be.

Formality: something done in accordance with the demands of a procedure, a ritual, or a ceremony. In keeping with the term, the formality of desire makes it obligatory, a set of conventions that can be (re)negotiated and expanded but the elasticity of which has only so much flexibility before it tears. Desire is not always convenient. It is an ongoing "ceremony" that one undertakes with pleasure and/or remonstration based on the degree to which it is or is not rupturing the safety of one's self-containment. The physiological and psychological immediacy of its pleasures is obvious; if the rupture is too extensive, pushing one across the thin divide between fulfillment and self-fissure, or taboo, what follows may be the lost innocence of the bolstered ego, the psychic field where desire and aggression rally and seek to destroy. On the other hand, denial of sexual impulses and energy removes us from our bodies and may territorialize us, our embattled psychologies and corporeality, with the sanctimonious recriminations of a super-ego. It is precisely this tension between the formality (or formula) and the rich pleasures of desire that Klein explores as a potentially doomed situation, as, at the very minimum, a profound discontent at the core of (American) civilization. However, given his proclivity for happy endings, at least in the realm of everyday life outside of fictional narrative, there may be hope yet, even amidst sinister ceremonies.

Of course, hope, if it is at all warranted, must wait until the novel's conclusion (which marks a significant difference from that of the short story, a matter for later discussion). In the meantime, Jeremy ascribes to the adage about how best to quell flesh-driven temptations in terms of both food and sexual desire. Early in his stay at the farm, he is unable to hear Deborah's explanation of the various cat personalities in their household because he is too busy contemplating how "it would be heavenly ... to pile into that big soft feather bed they must have up there and lie beside her on a long winter night, slipping the flannel nightgown above her waist and breasts, feeling her warmth against the cold and darkness outside" (49). There are, in fact, numerous instances of Jeremy fantasizing about Deborah and imagining that she is wearing nothing under her long skirt. For his part in the formality of gazing and dreaming, Sarr looks upon Carol, with whom he feels a religious as well as a

2. Events and Ceremonies

sexual connection, in a similar manner. On her initial visit to the farm to meet Jeremy, over dinner, Sarr "[can't] help picturing her climbing into his bed, so thin and pale and trembling; and he [knows] that tonight, as he [makes] love to his wife, his thoughts [will] stray unbidden to this new woman, at least until he [forces] himself to think of holier things" (182). Adhering to the formality is not simply a matter of will; its cognitive action appears "unbidden," of its own accord, and thus requires great effort to shift the direction of thought. The husband can't help it. The priest glances at the breasts despite the clerical attire and the admonition to serve as an example of neutered appetite. In the privacy of her own thoughts, Carol exhibits multiple desires on the eve of her first night at the farm, alone in her guest bed while Jeremy lies frustrated by the empty bedside in his cottage and the Poroths chant various hymns. She drifts "to sleep, with Sarr's hand, Jeremy's hand, the hand of God on hers" (209) as though confused by whom she would become chaste via ravishment.[5] Deborah, about whom there will be more to say, becomes increasingly, and dangerously, eroticized after she is attacked by Bwada, an agent of the Old One.

The formatory, ceremonial movement through a given life, through the liminal moments as well as quotidian routines in the everyday, it could be argued, are replete with any number, a limitless fleet, of possessions—of material, identificatory objects and people, to be sure, but more importantly for the immediate sense of self or lack thereof, possessions as hauntings, inhabitations, co-optations of the self that desires and consumes, fantasizes and enacts its drives. Klein positions sexual desire as possession in exactly this regard, a condition that achieves remarkable, if not soap operatic alignment between the four characters once the hymns have ceased and all lights are out for the evening, Carol's first but certainly not last night at Poroth farm. Jeremy is the first to succumb, quite dramatically, by venturing outside, nude and unconscious, "hands raised as if in supplication…, [he feels] himself make overtures to the moon, gestures and faces that no one [can] see, no one [can] see, no one [has] ever seen before. Perhaps some ancient force [is] in control, but there [is] no thought of explaining what he [does], or why" (214). It is an astonishing development in light of Jeremy's general skepticism, one that might be attributed to the gothic subject matter of his research, though the others join this singular event in their own distinct ways:

T.E.D. Klein and the Rupture of Civilization

> The moment [comes]. He [wriggles] his head, [arches] his neck, [throws] his chest out in the night air. Sarr [kisses] the breasts before his face and [arches] his body into Deborah, who [leans] forward to widen herself just as Freirs [throws] his arms wide and Sarr [pushes] himself all the way in so that Deborah [gasps] and they [tremble], all three, and Deborah [makes] a moaning sound just as Carol [engulfed in a provocative dream] [cries] out in her sleep and Freirs [hears] the whispering and chanting louder now inside his head and [realizes] that the sounds he's heard [are] coming from himself [*ibid.*].

"The moment" is a nexus of occult and erotic enchantments, possessions, traced discursively through the repetition of words and motions, cries and whispers, and inaugurated by a unique bottle of wine, complements of Rosie. Does this configuration of events signal the complicity of sexual desire with malevolent intentions? Is sex an instrument of evil? It becomes a thorny question by the time such incidents converge in Deborah's shocking conversion, when Jeremy's fantasizing finally comes to fruition, near the novel's dramatic climax, and she slips into his bed while Sarr is asleep. She maneuvers him inside her, whereupon Jeremy "[feels] himself gripped as by a fist; there [is] a roughness in her, something that [abrades]. *God*, he [thinks], *she's so dry*" (464). The moment ends abruptly when he discovers something foreign in her mouth (also dry), what the reader has already identified as a sign of possession known as the "Dohl." In addition to betrayal, on the part of wife and friend, their coitus further conflates sexual desire with abjection and monstrosity. Prior to her transformation, Deborah is the least neurotic with regards to desire, her attitude one of both lighthearted acknowledgment and depth, which makes it all the more unsettling when she becomes-evil, "something that [abrades]" rather than loves. The infidelity also colors how Sarr might be perceived once his own transformation (at the violent hands of "the thing" that has been his wife) is achieved, as an all too human corollary to his jealousy.

Deborah becomes an entity for whom sexual intimacy is a mere tool in the service of destruction. The jealous partner is possessed by compulsive thoughts and paranoia as the addict is by grasping, physical and psychological ravenousness, for alcohol, drugs, clothes, cars, other people, etc. Possession, as fostered by the machinations of Western civilization, is legion. Nevertheless, at the center of the novel's earthly and supernatural havoc, Klein asserts a side of desire that, without being sanitized or saccharine, stands as a productive counter to such posses-

2. Events and Ceremonies

sion. When Jeremy decides to return home with Carol just before the final, near-catastrophic ceremony begins, "they [kiss], and she [lets] him kiss her breasts, and she [knows] that the summer [is] saved" (471). Premature though this thought may be, the exchange compels Jeremy to write, "Have been talking about her to myself. 'I'm in love with her.' 'Yeah? And what's that supposed to mean?' 'You know—the works. The whole hog. I like spending time with her, want to fuck her, marry her, give her presents. Want to have kids with her, share my old age with her, have her around when I die. All that stuff'" (472). "All that stuff" may not win the affections of the sentimental reader, though the phrase allows Klein to address the power of genuine intimacy with a realist slant, one that is legitimized by the fact that Jeremy and Carol are married by the following Christmas, once the Old One has been (seemingly) contained. Desire can unite self and other and advance the Freudian "constitution" ahead of its perilous limitations as much as it can obliterate happiness, or the prospect of happiness, over the span of an isolated predicament, a lifetime, or centuries.

Instruments, Babies, Serpents

One key difference between "The Events at Poroth Farm" and *The Ceremonies* lies in the narration. They are both epistolary, though the novel adds several hundred pages worth of third person omniscient commentary on the "events" as they unfurl between urban and rural environments. Consequently, Jeremy as first person is more relatable, confined as he is to the farm with no Carol, no Rosie, only the Poroths, some neighbors, a variety of felines (most notably Bwada, whose inherent evil is consistent in both texts), his books, and his journal. His loneliness generates sympathy, which makes his critiques of the Poroth's provincialism all the more effective. He still desires Deborah though their relationship never becomes physical; it is merely relegated to casual desires and drifting fantasies. In the novel, Jeremy can be relatively lecherous, more self-absorbed, and thus unlikable, apparent even in his journal: "Deborah seems to work as hard as Sarr does. She was cleaning up in here when he arrived, on her knees scrubbing the floor. Something enormously erotic about a woman in that position, exerting herself while you're at your ease" (143). The dual roles of labor and ownership in the novel will inform the following section, though here it is worth noting what Deborah herself identifies as "woman's work" (199), i.e., doing the dishes, general housecleaning, etc. She has interiorized the gendered dimensions of her labor, no doubt in accordance with religious strictures (and scriptures, from a perspective of biblical inerrancy). To his credit, Jeremy offers to do the dishes, and yet he remains a representative of the male "you" to whom his journal entry would seem to be addressed, the one who gets off on observing a woman working in a submissive position while "you" cast a leisurely but pointed gaze.[6] Nevertheless, he remains the protagonist, the male hero who in fact becomes heroic by the novel's spectacular conclusion and maintains a generally, albeit self-interested, social liberalism that stands against the patriarchy of the religious community, a position the reader is clearly invited to share.

It is perhaps less clear how the reader is to relate to the novel's strongest female, the shrewd but troubled Mrs. Poroth. The exceptional nature of her familial line has been that of "a female's strength ... in a kind of alliance with [nature's] laws ... with aspects of some fundamental process" (35). She engages in "other ways of knowing" (*ibid.*), other than being in opposition to nature. In a scene that mimics Rosie's own evil-promulgating trance, she "[lets] herself fall into darkness, deeper now, where other presences, indistinct but real, [hover] expectantly around her as if summoned" (351) by way of preparation for holy war. On the other hand, the exercising of her power triggers "the fear that she [is] alien in this world" (*ibid.*), in contrast to her adversary who embraces his profound otherness. It is a fear that weakens both Mrs. Poroth's force and the reader's ability to fully support her candidacy for victor in so far as it splits her psychology between cosmic justice and rigid, earthly indifference. In the tightness and severity of her person, in her divinely inspired intentions as qualified by the self-righteousness of the religious bigot, she appears to the narrator as seeming "the only truly dark thing in the landscape" (34) and thus resembles Hawthorne's Young Good Brown, a well-meaning zealot whose forest dalliance with the devil positions him as "the chief horror of the scene," for "in truth, all through the haunted forest, there could be nothing more frightful than the figure of Goodman Brown" ("Young" 354). Both characters will face a "dying hour" that is "gloom," and like Goodman Brown, Mrs. Poroth is char-

2. Events and Ceremonies

acterized as a "thing in the landscape" (357). Or she is indicative of Jeremy's frustration with Shirley Jackson, whose power as a writer towers above most (mostly male) in the horror/suspense genre (and is rumored to have exercised her own clairvoyance) but whose characters are typically "callous and vicious," leading Jeremy to prefer the "sunny disposition" and "jovial Satanism" of an Aleister Crowley (Klein, *Ceremonies* 354), a description that could apply equally to Rosie when he is at his most charming.[7]

The Old One is too ensconced in general misanthropy to be misogynistic. By contrast, the people of Gilhead, people of God and the Good Book, segregate along gender lines and relegate women to specific tasks, unambiguous subject-positions marked by an imbalanced power dynamic in keeping with extreme fundamentalism. Mrs. Poroth's unique discernment and Deborah's own jovial spirit aside, patriarchy reigns among the believers and Klein is ultimately critical of its damning but commonplace monstrosity. The notion, for example, that "a woman's body [is] His Sacred instrument" may speak to men and women being "battered," "imprisoned," "enthralled," and "ravished" by the will of God, as Donne's "Holy Sonnet 14" would have it, but the framework of imprisonment, psychological and otherwise, is historically cleft between the genders. There is a hierarchy in prison as in the world beyond the prison walls. So when Deborah's ebullience becomes exceptionally feisty, as it often does before she too becomes a "thing," she is treated to Sarr's and the others' criticism, others who "[think] her frivolous, high-spirited—dangerous even" (113). Joram, one of the more unyielding Gilhead men, complains of Deborah's robust humor and follows up with the Bible: "They that sow in tears shall reap in joy," to which Sarr responds, "Don't worry Brother Joram. I'll teach her to weep" (123–24). It is an ominous declaration, however inspired by scripture it may be, that aligns with Rosie's malevolence and makes Jeremy's less agreeable tendencies appear utterly benign—so much so that the protagonist can share a kind, intimate moment with Joram's own (very) pregnant wife, whose husband merely "glowers" at her and the life that is growing within her, and thus win the affection of the reader who may have otherwise been dubious.

In spite of exploring the self-reflections of Sylvia Plath and the inspiring philosophy of Teilhard de Chardin in her solitude, Carol comes to be "owned" by Rosie (154). He walks her, the unknowing initiate,

T.E.D. Klein and the Rupture of Civilization

through the various ceremonies in all their colors, leading to the final ritual atop a mound deep in the forest of Gilhead where others, other women, have been found murdered in the distant past. He teaches her to sing the right words, the right language, and to do the dances, her interiorization divergent from that of the Gilhead women by a mere few degrees of will. And it is this slight distinction that confers upon Carol an innocence that in turn leaves her vulnerable to a non-supernatural form of possession, Rosie's skills notwithstanding. Again, one might think of Jackson's Eleanor, who is prone to fantasy and awkward wish fulfillment, when Carol first visits the farm, walks alone by a stream, and imagines "[leaving] her clothing there on the rock and [stepping] gingerly into the water. It [will] be chilly, of course, as it [climbs] her legs. And perhaps while she [is] naked and so occupied, Jeremy [will] awaken and, walking silently down behind her, [will] surprise her, there in the warm sunlight. He [will] reach for her hand—" (220).[8] Eleanor, too, is innocent, yearning for a man to flesh out her existence, but exceptionally neurotic and selfish relative to Carol. Klein's heroine succumbs to the "ownership" of a powerful male (and desires two other men in the manner of a semi-masochistic virgin) and yet is far more independent and savvy than Jackson's child-like, suicide-driven Eleanor.[9] Her innocence may effectuate susceptibility to a monstrous patriarchy but her worldliness relative to the women of Gilhead at least ensures that she has a fighting chance to avoid the dehumanizing status of "thing."

And yet even a modern woman faces the loss of her humanity when confronting *cosmic* patriarchy. Rosemary Woodhouse in Roman Polanski's *Rosemary's Baby* (1968) is a modern woman with her short hairstyle, her hip 60s attire, and aspiring actor husband. By the end of that film, a male-dominant group of Satanists has conspired to draw Rosemary into their plot of birthing the child of their deity. She is raped by Satan and thus reduced to a breeder by the coalescence of earthly and preternatural, patriarchal designs. As Rosie returns to Gilhead and to childhood memories of becoming possessed in the woods, he recalls a discussion with the "Master": "'What do you want of me?' *Much.* 'What must I do?' *You shall perform ceremonies in my honor.* 'Ceremonies for what?' *To bring me back as my son.* 'Where is he now?' ... *He isn't born yet*" (486). Carol is to be the mother, which makes the final ceremony, in which the "thing" formerly known as Sarr becomes host to what

2. Events and Ceremonies

remains of the Master in the wake of an 18th-century fire, a rape. While Rosemary is drugged and taken on her bed, Carol, in keeping with her vision, is tied atop the forest mound by "Sarr" and submitted to what is essentially the Master's penis, "the part he'd left unburned; the organ with no clear human analogue, but corresponding roughly to a phallus, instrument of regeneration; the black thing, undying and unkillable; the Dohl" (474). Everyone in *The Ceremonies*, it would seem, is an instrument of something or someone. For Carol, however, her function as ceremonial apparatus means becoming physically conjoined with the Master via "the white rod of the man's sex" and "a long pale twisted horn [between her legs…], there upon the altar, body linked to body, end to end, a double serpent swallowing its tail" (500–501). Unlike the Gadsden snake, this serpent conjoins rather than coils, though the assertion of dominance and ultimate repudiation ("only a cold and unremitting hatred") informs each act or stance. It is finally not just the modern woman whom the Master seeks to violate and destroy but modernity itself, replete as it is with desiring, educated women and men who value a progressive life of the mind.

Nonetheless, in a rather traditional turn of events, the male protagonist will emerge as a hero and save the day. Jeremy, himself recovering from being drugged, jumps through a wall of fire surrounding the mound, scales its heights, and manages to castrate the Dohl: "With the next blow Freirs [strikes] home, the sharpened blade sweeping cleanly through the appendage that [snakes] from the farmer's mouth" (500). On one hand, horror, or at least its representative in the form of a scholar, has triumphed in castrating the radical otherness of patriarchy. On the other hand, Jeremy frees Carol from her restraints, brings her down from the mound, covers her naked body, and wonders, "reluctantly, how much pain there'd really been in those sounds she'd made, and how much pleasure" (502). But maybe the two hands meet and entwine where the defeat of patriarchy and the reality of desire that necessarily entails an element of submission overlap, where hegemonic force is dethroned in parallel with the empowerment of polymorphous pleasures. Maybe a woman intuits the fine lines between various expressions of ravishment; and maybe a scholar of critical horror fiction is capable of distinguishing between his indigenous desires and the true horror of institutionalized repression.

T.E.D. Klein and the Rupture of Civilization

Wages of Sin

What is certain is that many "events," particularly in the novel, are motivated by money or the lack thereof. While the Old One plays a significant role in orchestrating lives, he is nonetheless working with the material of the human condition that necessitates survival according to social formulas. Once settled in the city, Carol, who occupies a low-paying library position, struggles to construct a quality of life that, far from luxurious, would offer some access to the cultural offerings of NYC and an apartment that is not infested with insects. Rosie is able to capitalize on this condition and draw her into his paid "research" project. Jeremy lives in a small apartment with "a claustrophobic little bedroom" and a "secondhand air conditioner churning endlessly in the window, blocking the view of the street" (10), where he works into the night reading for his thesis, provoking images of Melville's pale, quiescent Bartleby in the depressing quarters of a small time Wall Street law office. Only, Jeremy is not in the business of copying documents; he is engaged in genuine research, on Gothic literature and, specifically, among other things, "Setting *as* Character" (*ibid.*), his ultimate aim being to maintain the teaching position he has at The New School. Sarr and Deborah require a tenant to help offset the cost of restoring their recently purchased farm to working order. Despite their hard work, like Carol and Jeremy, they struggle. Four people, averaging thirty years old, working to survive in both urban and rural America. So the two central "settings" of *The Ceremonies* are indeed characters that certainly contribute to the novel's atmosphere but do so as cultural conditions that determine the choices and outcomes of lived lives, to the degree that the gigantic, cosmic snake that engulfs the planet on the cover of my own 1984 copy of the novel may be considered, from one angle, the serpentine machine of capitalism.

A significant event occurs late in the novel as Sarr's aunt, after being kicked by a cow, lies unconscious and likely to die. Family gathers by her bed to pray and Sarr suddenly becomes aware of a shocking truth: "*she'll die if they don't get her to a hospital*"; and yet, this he quickly deems as "the devil's solution" (391). Thus he continues to pray until facing another, even more unsettling thought, "the most terrible secret of all: for while the others [have] been praying, [he's] been wrestling

2. Events and Ceremonies

with visions of losing the farm; and that mocking little voice that [has] kept whispering *Money ... ruined ... damned!*" whereupon "he [has] discovered sin, not under his roof but in his own heart" (*ibid.*). Obviously from Sarr's point of view his "sin" lies in the betrayal of a religious practice that is expected to be all-encompassing, though from the relatively secular perspective with which Klein aligns the reader, his visions constitute "sin" in so far as they are the product of what Jameson, in reference to the Frankfurt School theorists (who were, of course, associated with The New School for Social Research), calls "instrumentality" (*Jameson* 124), a corollary, I would argue, to the notion that "a woman's body [is] His sacred instrument." In the reorganization (or "reification") of labor, "the quality of various forms of human activity, their unique and distinct 'ends' or values, has effectively been bracketed or suspended by the market system, leaving all these activities free to be ruthlessly organized in efficiency terms, as sheer means or instrumentality" (*ibid.*). The human being becomes an instrument of commodification, or the reordering of object values, and thus of capitalism, what some might claim as the one true deity of the West. Sarr cannot help his aunt because he is colonized by both a religious doctrine that repudiates science and a thought process governed by the bracketing of his labor, even in the context of his community's "socialist" system (the general store where farmers acquire most of their supplies is a co-op—"Karl Marx would have been pleased," Jeremy observes [Klein, *Ceremonies* 221]). He is of two minds, as is Carol in terms of her religious convictions and her desire for sexual fulfillment: their fundamentalist values locate them psychologically and, for Sarr, geographically, on the margins of contemporary, secular society, but their bodies and the general quality of their lives suffer at the hands of a "mocking little voice" that reifies the "instruments" of both labor and sex. In other words, *The Ceremonies* is concerned with very earthly rituals indeed, ones that bifurcate the human being by reducing him or her to an apparatus of religious and/or economic systems based on power even as the need for somatic and psychological well-being invariably, and problematically in such a cultural milieu, asserts itself.

Jeremy is certainly not without his own needs. Beyond his appetite for intimacy, he finds satisfaction and comfort in food, Deborah's home cooking, to be precise, second helpings of which he disavows only to

T.E.D. Klein and the Rupture of Civilization

suffer "a crazy dream in which [he is] eating everything and everyone in sight: Carol, the Poroths, the cats, the cornfield, whole continents.... As [he recalls], it [ends] with [him] swallowing [his] own foot. Jeremy Friers, the human Uroboros" (353). The latter is a serpent that eats its tail, symbolizing cyclical time or interiority, introspection, depending on the cultural context. Yet another snake slithers its way into the pages of *The Ceremonies*, though in this case the creature's function would operate against the static, monolithic identity of the isolated Gadsden serpent in that cyclicality does not preclude becoming; rather, it reinforces the human imperative of critical introspection and self-knowledge. Of course, Jeremy is simply hungry. Moreover, his hunger drives him to acknowledge his base instinct for consumption, a proclivity that corresponds to the Old One's nefarious aims of literally consuming the world, or at least its human inhabitants. Nevertheless, Jeremy has taken steps to control his consumption, to be healthy, and unlike Carol and his landlords, he is not especially susceptible to ideological colonization. His New School education is surely enough to make him a critical thinker, enough, as it happens, to recognize the limitations of his occupation. In characterizing Henry James' "The Turn of the Screw" as "pretentious and overrated," for example, he includes its adoring audience in his critique: "perfect for the MLA crowd" (299). Jeremy is aware that the academy is as much a medium of "instrumentality" as any capitalist venture and that consumerism is not without its vainglory and hypocrisy.[10]

Consumerism naturally fosters a clinging relationship to property, be it food, books (about which Jeremy claims to be "neurotic," those gothic/horror texts that "look damned nice, lined up on the shelves" [146]), occupational positions, other people, other objects, self-identity, or land, and *The Ceremonies* is keenly aware of how compromised nature (and by extension, humanity) is by such a relation. Surely consumerism triggers an inherent capacity for addiction or grasping, though its manner of cultivating these tendencies territorializes or deforms nature, both as object and as adhesive between self and said object, a phenomenon that Sarr recognizes when he ponders their relationship to the property of Poroth farm:

> It somehow [seems] to him that the land [isn't] really his at all and that, with no human figure to mar the landscape, the farm [reverts] to what it [has] always been: a living thing, belonging only to itself[....] How foolish [he's] been

2. Events and Ceremonies

> to think that he [can] actually own this land, land which [has] been here so long before him and [will] be here so long after his body [has] crumpled beneath it [181].

From this indefensible perspective, identification with the things of the world, including the world itself, is a form of psychosis; it is, in its addictive quality, a denial of death, the inevitable and ultimate remover of the adhesive's residue. That said, it would be inaccurate to apply the stamp of Marxist to Klein's text(s). As a character in ethnologist-turned-novelist Marc Augé's *Someone's Trying to Find You* asserts, "we're not going to fight capitalism by ignoring what it does well" (98). The character is attempting to defend his automobile (a high end Mercedes) to a fellow leftist, and while no one in *The Ceremonies* is struggling with that particular dilemma, their efforts to manifest a quality of life that is largely dependent on personal property (farm equipment, seed, books, degrees, homes) suggests that economic independence is an acceptable part of Western life.

What is not acceptable to the novel's ethos is the way religion and capitalism unite through a conservative lens against what they deem the idleness of intellectualism. When Jeremy joins Sarr and Deborah for some home maintenance and "hardly [feels] useful," he questions the validity of his guilt, and thus the privileging of physical labor over intellectual pursuits, by asking "but what the hell?" (Klein, *Ceremonies* 305). "Hell" speaks both to the intensity of the interrogative and to the space to which his (pre)occupation might be condemned. This is not to say that Klein disparages physicality or a solid work ethic; rather, his texts insist on the legitimacy of Jeremy's project, especially since he is paying (rent) for his work time. Convincing the general population of Gilhead of this position, however, is finally an impossible challenge. One member of the community claims that "that sort [Jeremy] [expects] others to work for them but [won't] do a lick themselves" (376), obviously implying that Jeremy's research does not constitute work. At another point, Sarr comments to one of the brethren that his tenant "just reads books all day," the response to which, as observed by the third-person omniscient narrator, is that "idleness [is] sinful when there [is] land to be worked" (327).

The irony here is that land cannot be owned, as Sarr knows, while knowledge obtained from books, though dying with the "crumbled" body under ground, is precisely what opens vistas of self/other-awareness in life and, from a religious perspective, may reduce the amount of "sin" (as, essentially, raw egotism) one perpetrates upon oneself and others.

At the very minimum, the rigor with which Jeremy approaches his scholarly topic should be enough to silence ignorant voices. Of course, Klein's critique of anti-intellectualism is one in a relatively small chorus of voices in late 20th and early 21st century America, where "the ... commodification of labor power ... as the fundamental precondition of capitalism" (*Jameson* 124) allows little to no room for the notion of knowledge for knowledge's sake, or for its relatively abstract principles undergirding everyday realities (labor, consumption, power, desire, and aggression), realities that are at the very center of the Humanities, currently and historically under fire by right wing populism. The alternative to such knowledge, Klein implies, particularly in the short story, is current and historical ignorance.

Citadels and Idiot Boxes

Civilization arguably relies on a level of individual and collective ignorance to remain in operation. A prescribed, populist politics, left and right, along with popular culture in its infinite manifestations that drives the consumerist economy and keeps people mesmerized by a multitude of serial dramas, or a fundamentalist vision that repudiates scientific, philosophical, and historical knowledge: these powerful elements of civilization may all serve to distract people not only from large-scale corruption but from the dehumanizing conditions of the unexamined life. Without losing sight of their humanity, of all that is likable about them, Klein ridicules the Poroths for engaging in both popular culture and, of course, the stringency (and ultimately, the mythology) of their religious convictions. He does this primarily through Jeremy's criticism of television, although the one reference in *The Ceremonies* appears as another anecdote from one of the community members about a fellow "brother":

> Well, he had that thing put in, right in his living room where he could watch it all the time, and at first he thought it was something really special. But then his

> little ones took to it, and I hear it turned their heads right around. They got to scanting their dinner and their chores so they could sneak in and watch, they'd be asking for every frippery they saw, and his oldest boy near got himself thrown out of school for the way he was acting 'round the girls [Klein 285].

The father soon buries the television and does penance for the "sin" of instilling a desire for "frippery" in his children. For anyone with a critical capacity who has spent any time in front of such a box, even in the early 1980s, it might be difficult to deny this particular "sin," generative as it can be of incessant frivolity and mediocrity. Some things (the dead, ideologically deceptive and aesthetically malnourished screens) should probably be and remain buried. Klein's protagonist is more caustic in his assessment of television and the particular viewership it has found in his proprietors. He refers to "their godawful TV programs" ("Events" 320) and, joining them, is "ashamed of [himself] for sitting there like a cretin in front of that box" (335–36) watching the "offensively ignorant programs" (349). These moments are a noteworthy contrast to the journal entries in which Jeremy offers clever and occasionally insightful literary criticism, when both texts and self are under examination, as opposed to the cretinism of absorbing television schlock.

As in life outside of fiction, the nature of such benightedness extends well beyond screens, wired as they are into everyday, 21st-century phenomenological experience. Early in "The Events at Poroth Farm," Jeremy remarks on rural culture on the margins of the city as containing "pockets of ignorance, some of them, citadels of ancient superstition…, religious communities where customs haven't changed appreciably since the days of their settlement a century or more ago" (310). Television is still a prominent pastime in current American culture, and religious customs, replete, in conservative traditions, with infantile dogma and bigoted ideology, are still very much intact, allowing Klein's cultural observations around ignorance to resonate with the contemporary reader. An example of the author's cynicism concerning an uncritical approach to one's faith is found in Bwada's death (in which something has germinated and dug itself out of the feline's body) that is seemingly negated when she reanimates and reappears. Sarr claims that "her recovery demonstrates how the Lord watches over animals—affirms his faith" (329). The irony here, of course, is that Bwada is an agent of the Old One; her incessant staring (without blinking) at Jeremy mimics a young boy who stands outside Jeremy's hotel room in the wake of the tragedy, staring up at the window behind red spectacles. The urban intellectual is unsure of his future outside of feeling damned, though he is not ignorant (unlike the believers) regarding the compromised condition of such faith. Whether one pities or condemns Sarr for his ignorance in this instance, one that will lead to his and his family's brutal undoing, is obviously a matter of individual response, though it is clear that the "puritan" has been reactionary toward the scientific/veterinarian treatment that could have shifted "events" in a productive manner.

A critical part of Sarr's fundamentalist faith lies not only in the extolling of divine providence and omnipotence, but in the literalism of evil. When Jeremy accidentally lets Bwada out of the bathroom in which she has been locked for killing one of the other cats, he apologizes to Sarr, who "[says] he [isn't] mad at [his guest], that the Devil [has] gotten into his cat. It is obvious he [means] that quite literally," Jeremy comments (335). The Devil has a rich, mythological history of perpetrating evil, the supernatural nature of which I will examine in more detail below with specific reference to the views of Machen's Ambrose in "The White People." For now it is important to consider that even a cursory exploration of the contemporary Devil yields a revolving door of a character, one whose being is legend, a multiplicity that can assume any number of guises, as he does in Klein's texts. On one hand, this literalism is indicative of ignorance to the degree that its fairytale cosmology precludes critical thought around larger contexts that might involve social, psychological, historical, and philosophical nuance. The more harrowing problem of the Devil, however, is his obvious interchangeability with any demonized other.[11]

Despite his atheism, Lovecraft's racism is, of course, notorious; he found a way to sanction (if not worship) the Devil by repudiating non-Caucasians. His influence on Klein, which transcends direct references and is apparent in the latter's literary content, likely has a bearing on the role of race in *The Ceremonies*/"Events…" and other texts that will be considered in this study.[12] Though far sexier as a horned beast, the image of which may be touted in Black Metal as a tremendously successful marketing tool, the quotidian Devil appears in Klein's novel as potentially violent "blacks" and "Puerto Ricans" who make excessive

2. Events and Ceremonies

noise and lurk the night streets of New York City and its various boroughs. At one point in *The Ceremonies*, Carol refers to "those awful Puerto Ricans with their campfires" (341) after beholding a "burnt and blackened" circle of land in Central Park where Rosie has recently had her undergo (unbeknownst to her) one of the ceremonies. Ironically, however, when she questions the ethnic populations of another area where Rosie is keen to take her, *he* is the conscience when he explains that "there's nothing to worry about. There are lots of people there, people of all types, but they're all just interested in having a good time, you'll see" (276). Though his ultimate intention is to weave her into his nefarious plans, his logic is sensible and progressive; the Devil, as the saying goes, likes to mix truth with lies. Moreover, what Carol, like anyone who encounters otherness, must eventually "see" is the reality of her own projections as they co-mingle with genuine culture differences.

Jeremy is glad that the brethren do not know that he is a Jew, as this would likely add to the projections of his own otherness in Gilhead. He even speculates that Mrs. Poroth, "a nasty old hag," is also "Anti-Semitic, too" (307). Given Jeremy's ethnicity, his own wariness of others (as, perhaps, an extension of Klein's New York upbringing) reflects both an awareness of racial issues as they manifest in the life and work of the influential Lovecraft and a commonplace process of coming to terms with otherness, be it racial or otherwise. Jeremy even balks at what he perceives as Rosie's effeminate nature ("I could do without the lisp and the mincing little walk" [248]), evincing a mild homophobia. Woody Allen's 1979 film *Manhattan*, featuring, naturally, a generally progressive, intellectual, Jewish protagonist, provides a comparable process, evident in Isaac's mystification around his ex-wife's turn to lesbianism and a truly anomalous scene wherein he and his girlfriend look askance at a group of black men in traditional African garb. The protagonist holds his partner close and draws her attention to their otherness. Without excusing these behaviors as merely a product of the times *à la* Lovecraft's defenders, it is arguable that they serve as an aspect of civilization with which everyone must contend. As such, the Devil is doubtless in the detail of the civilized (American) world, from its subtle innuendos to its seething, rampaging paroxysms of intolerance. Of course, Klein and Allen, as thoughtful horror aficionado and brilliantly funny, step-daughter-marrying comedian, respectively, flawed though they may be in their humanity, as most are in their humanity, are not vile racists in the vein of a Lovecraft; they are too smart for that, at least in their art. They understand that the Devil is a collective—and thus easily absorbed into the individual psyche—mode of reactivity. In Klein's case, thankfully, the mythology is rich in both socially-resonate detail and the immense pleasure of horror that is taken seriously.

White People

Rosie gives Carol a copy of "The White People" to give to Jeremy when she first visits the farm. It comes with instructions: "Save it for Saturday night. It's the sort of tale you've got to read at bedtime; otherwise it simply doesn't *work!*"—in response to which Carol thinks "one thing about Rosie, he sure [takes] his literature seriously" (160). Klein's work, like all of the most compelling horror, invites the reader, too, to take it seriously, its captivating narrative turns and critical insights. That said, the nature of the Old One and the supernatural mystery he represents is "huge and hateful and alive" (246), nurtured by violence and aggression that must be taken seriously if their source(s) is to be understood. It may be impossible to conceive of the ontological status of uncanny and "unsuspected evil in the world," though it can nevertheless be broached by making oneself amenable to its mysteries. For Klein, this means allowing oneself to be "read" by critical horror; Jeremy, settling into "The White People" by moonlight, feels "as if he [is] no longer reading the words but [is] instead being read by them" (211). In other words, he is diminishing his wants and needs, his sense of identity, however briefly, and opening himself to incomprehensible levels of experience as well as to the gritty realities of civilization. In so doing, he "[finds] himself whispering the lines as he [reads] them, the words coming faster and faster—*I knew there was nobody here at all besides myself, and that no one could see me.... So I said the other words, and made the signs*" (*ibid.*). The "other words" recalls a statement from Nikolai Gogol's commentary on realism in literature:

> Supernatural powers have ordained that I should walk hand in hand with my odd heroes, observing the life that flows majestically past me, conveying it through laughter, which the world can hear, while seeing it myself through

2. Events and Ceremonies

> tears it never suspects. And the time is still distant when the awesome storm of inspiration will sound forth on another note, from a head immersed in holy terror and dazzling light, when the majestic thunder of other words will be heard in fear and trembling ["On Realism" 332].

Such words are immersive, liminal, aberrant, outside the formulas of conventional literature; they are as "supernatural" as they are linked to quotidian life that they invest with majesty, "holy terror," "fear and trembling." As noted above, a nighttime stroll finds Jeremy "whispering and chanting" the "other words" and making the "signs."[13] That his behavior is "ordained" by a malignant force denotes the razor's edge of horror, of walking, stripped of metaphorical clothing, on the fine line between the productively abject and the dangerously corrupt. Horror is clearly "other words" designed to expose the life that may otherwise float past us and, at its most sophisticated, to forge a space in which "holy terror and dazzling light" may coexist in the actuality of that life.

And yet, Machen's Ambrose suggests that "sorcery and sanctity [...] are the only realities. Each is an ecstasy, a withdrawal from the common life" ("White" 111). The latter refers to myriad formalities, ways of being (and seeing) that remove one from subversive pleasure, from the majesty and power of "other words" and "sign"-making. In fact, he devotes numerous passages to characterizing "the common life," antithetical as it is to the magical thrust of his narrative with its "secrets" and "ceremonies" (119). He explains that "most of us are just indifferent, mixed-up creatures; we muddle through the world without realizing the meaning and the inner sense of things, and, consequently, our wickedness and our goodness are alike second-rate, unimportant" (111). The real "sin" here, of course, is indifference to interiority and the knowledge of the latter's link to exteriority it might afford. "Our higher senses are so blunted," he goes on, "we are so drenched in materialism, that we should probably fail to recognize real wickedness if we encountered it" (115). And to continue with this thread, he further condemns "the materialism of the age, which has done a good deal to suppress sanctity ... [and] perhaps more to suppress evil. We find the earth so very comfortable that we have no inclination either for ascents or descents" (117). So Ambrose is ultimately interested in the value, substance, and interplay of "sanctity" and "wickedness." He privileges the former and recognizes the incommensurability with civilized life of the latter, though neither is generally manifested in "the common life." Moreover, in light of his interest in what he calls the "processes" (145) of occult "secrets," the potential wickedness of "sorcery" remains connected to "wonder" (*ibid.*) and is finally, and equally, legitimized.

Initiation into horror's "processes" brings us closer, then, to authenticity, the evil manifestation of which can propel us, like Jeremy making the gestures and intoning the words, into unsettling states by virtue of our curiosity. For M.R. James's Paxton, this curiosity proves fatal; for Klein's protagonist, it will ultimately confirm the reality of what he has dedicated his scholarship to interrogating. His critical distance may be highly compromised, but he is all the wiser for it. Jeremy's own curiosity has lead him to face certain realities and in so doing, at the risk of his life and that of the human species, he has accomplished what Ambrose calls the "taking of heaven by storm" (114) whereby occult inquisitiveness is exercised to such a degree that barriers of knowledge and wisdom begin to collapse. The apple is consumed, core and all, and, rather than devolve into "civilized" sexual guilt, one may discover that life is enriched in an instant charged with the force of both "ascent" and "descent." "Sabbats likely." In the example of the young girl in Machen's story, whose narrative often illustrates these "processes" with chilling nuance, the siege on heaven is deemed "true and wonderful and splendid" (142) to the extent that "[she is] changed and wonderful" (140). She is, in other words, empowered, and up to the point of her untimely death, strangely fulfilled, if not happy.

But in addition to the rich if not hackneyed debate around good and evil, acceptable and forbidden knowledge, the "taking of heaven by storm" is also productive because it demonstrates how the complexity of horror can "work," as Rosie puts it, as deterritorialization. One can read this siege as a Mephistophelian triumph, of which horror can be tremendously effective in providing vicarious experience, especially when a protagonist's death in involved, yet its deterritorializing function lies in the far more compelling reconfiguration of the psychological and cultural boundaries of a life over and against the materialistic constraints, seductions, and indifference of civilization. In the case of *The Ceremonies* and "The Events at Poroth Farm," sanctity itself is a territory in need of liberation, that of an immersion into the exposure and wisdom of horror. For example, once "events" have escalated, the brethren deter-

2. Events and Ceremonies

mine that the "fundamental disturbance" signifies "portents, signals from above, warnings of divine displeasure" (Klein, *Ceremonies* 458). In fact, it is the ignorant, infantile notion of the divine as an "angry God," as Jonathan Edwards characterizes it, that negates the pleasure and the sanctity of life. The people of Gilhead may eschew materialism and bourgeois indifference, but they are nevertheless seduced by the myth of a benevolent Father and a Devil, anthropomorphic figures who battle for the souls of those for whom "ascent" and "descent" are diametrically opposed rather than coterminous in the joint venture of a progressively refined journey through enlightening "processes."

"We are not saved"

To extend the definition of the genre further, we might say that when not capitulating to formulas and "formalities," horror is aesthetic deterritorialization. Both of Klein's "events" texts fulfill this critical function by paralleling the supernatural and the ostensibly "natural," the ideologically constructed social and psychological conditions of civilization. However, their conclusions, much to the dismay of the short story's diehard fans, are quite different and consequently divergent in terms of the extent of their cosmological and existential deterritorializations. The story concludes with Jeremy's prediction of additional deaths and "his last jeremiad: 'The harvest is past, the summer is ended, and we are not saved'" ("Events" 357). "We are not saved," it seems, from the encroaching evil, that which assumes the form of a boy outside his window and the "thing" that is Sarr still on the loose. From a social perspective, we are not saved from human fallibility that fosters and wields the gospel of "divine displeasure," which intimates, of course, the displeasure, and thus the aggression, of egos attempting to fortify their borders/identities. "We are not saved" from civilization as long as it is dominated by reactivity. The novel, on the other hand, concludes with a marriage (Jeremy and Carol) and Jeremy's ominous sense that "the roar of the dragon" (*Ceremonies* 505), omnipresent, still shrieks. Stylistically, the latter is less memorable, more banal. Thematically, its vagueness (particularly in the wake of Jeremy's rather uncharacteristic heroism when he saves Carol) weakens the story's sense of doom and thus leaves one without

T.E.D. Klein and the Rupture of Civilization

leading questions concerning one's existence, or the lack of meaning, in light of imminent destruction. And yet, the reader has no reason to disbelieve Jeremy at this point. Evil thrives and dark clouds still gather at heaven's gate.

What is easily read as schmaltzy—the male hero saving the day and possessing the heroine—is, in this reader's estimation, less compelling than the unsettling lack of hope that closes the short story. An alternative perspective, however, speaks to a central concern of this study, namely, the productive becoming of critical horror, its capacity for relying less on nihilism or pessimism while punctuating both the immense challenges and the benefits of cultivating transgression, healthy aberrance, and sublimity in the everyday. It is possible, and indeed, likely, that Jeremy has evolved over the course of *The Ceremonies*, perhaps to the point of rising to the occasion of bravery in a manner that is authentic and believable. Moreover, he is in love. He has entered a zone of relationality that requires a powerful degree of selflessness, and ideally, of relocating oneself in that sacrifice to the betterment of both self and other (however exceptional this form of ego-diminishment may be). "It was all wonderful and true and splendid" is a remarkable feature of a horror narrative, one that goes a great distance in informing the climate of Klein's novel. In context, the passage proposes a continuity between "sorcery," "sanctity," and "ecstasy," the primary ingredients, I would argue, of horror as a deterritorializing force, and also, as it happens, of love.

CHAPTER 3

White, Black and Other People: "Children of the Kingdom" and "Black Man with a Horn"

"Truth, she is far more strange"

Critical theory might challenge the validity of Truth, as it should, for ethical and countless other reasons, though one thing most (especially horror writers and fans) can agree on is the fact that the events "Truth" endeavors to represent are often quite strange. Klein's ability to marry everyday (domestic, political, cultural) events and the uncanny allows him to explore this strangeness in highly relatable contexts, so much so that it feels as though he is approaching Truth even as the supernatural, the unknown, unleashes its confounding vitality. Without necessarily being gendered, Truth's peculiarity, or aberrancy, may be indicative of what Deleuze and Guattari refer to as a process of "becoming-woman," the most fundamental of all becomings in so far as it functions in opposition to capital-M Man, to patriarchy or any form of hegemony.[1] It ultimately resists gendered conceptualization in that concepts (social, scientific, philosophical) are forever in flux. Nor is it raced, the property of a single ethnicity, though its fluidity and delusional substantiality alike have an enormous impact on the color of skin, or as Lovecraft might put it, colors out of space. It is possible that a key element of horror's appeal is exactly its simultaneous demolition and activation of something called Truth that concerns, in every sense of the word, all people.

"Children of the Kingdom," the first story in Klein's *Dark Gods* collection, foregrounds the variable "Truth" of race, or races, human and otherwise, in a manner that shares certain narrative features with the

T.E.D. Klein and the Rupture of Civilization

"events" texts. Like Jeremy, the narrator is a researcher (of "The Puritan Heritage" [Klein, *Dark* 5]) and teacher in New York City (whose wife, in an amusing turn, is identified as Karen Klein). His rascally grandfather has been placed in a retirement home and befriended by a former priest for whom Truth is strange. The story opens with his returning from Boston by train and witnessing his part of the city as though for the first time. Upon arrival, he is shocked to discover that the impoverishment of "this benighted place" (4) that he has been observing from a literal and figurative distance in the train car, where "except for [his] reflection, [he sees] not one white face," is "[his] own neighborhood" (*ibid*.). Though they live on a relatively safe, clean block, the neighborhood has of late been infiltrated by ethnically-oriented, "primitive" (28) music and "gangs of black and Puerto Rican youth" (6) in the context of what is a familiar, Kleinian, late 70s NYC, ostensibly attributing to one of the story's three epigraphic quotations—"They are everywhere, those creatures" (from August Derleth)—more than one meaning. At one point, when an elderly woman in the home is attacked by several individuals, the assistant manager claims "it must have been the blacks" (50) and later, as Karen finds herself amidst inner city turmoil during a blackout, she asserts "I swear to God, if we see another black I hope we hit him" (64).

Such moments, offensive as they are, are slowly subverted, however, by two ironies, the first being the grandfather's surprising sense of diversity. He is able to "move in either world," between middle and lower classes, and is ultimately "more at home among the poor" (5). This quality is not lost on his grandson, who is able to acknowledge that it is "just another culture or two, that's all it [is]" (15), when referring to the ethnic mix of their respective neighborhoods. The second irony lies in the strange truth surrounding the perpetrators of various assaults and, as in the case of the elderly woman, rapes. Parallel with the legends of NYC sewer dwellers, the priest, Father Pistachio (so christened by Herman, the grandfather), has written a book that he is seeking to publish in English (he is from Costa Rica), its central premise concerning the original location of the human species (Costa Rica) and the "people" who sought to seize that territory. And it is a parallel that is difficult to deny, as the narrator and his wife eventually discover. Early in the story, a child awakens to "a boy standin' right by her bed, just a lookin' down on her and doin' somethin' evil to hisself…, a white boy" (25), according

3. White, Black and Other People

to Coralette, a black woman who sits regularly with Father Pistachio and Herman to pass the time. Later, another black woman is found dead after having encountered her "first white boyfrien'" (44). The Machen reference here is obvious, but Klein invents his own "white people" mythology via the priest and, in keeping with a focus on the mundane *and* the supernatural, links them not necessarily to Caucasians but to a promising yet flawed human race.

Father Pistachio theorizes around the strange truth of these figures as "another people. One cannot be sure. No one knows where they are from. No one knows their name. Maybe they are things God make before He make a man" (38). He suggests that they may be "devils" or "children of God, but children He make wrong" (39). What seems clear is that they are capable of exceptional violence. "They love to fight," the padre continues, and to bolster this tendency, "they have something on the face. Flat places, ridges, things like little hooks. Back of head, she is like the front; all look much the same. Me, I think this mean they wear a special thing to cover the head in war" (*ibid.*). This observation is in keeping with the descriptions of numerous survivors of the creatures' attacks; and they are creaturely, anomalies with hominal characteristics. That said, they are also profoundly human. "Now, suddenly," the narrator says amidst their unusual but calm discussion, "[comes] the sounds of a scuffle, a taunt, a scream, sporadic bursts of laughter from the crowd. Pistachio [shakes] his head. Is a shame. Men. They just want to fight" (38). Minutes later, "the battle [is] still very much in progress" and the narrator hears "the echoes of a faraway war cry" (39). Without the label of "men," these lines could easily be attributed to the "roaming whites" (65) haunting the urban jungle in search of women to impregnate, an aspect of the story that will be addressed in more detail below. The "whites" are scavenging for bodies, female bodies, with the aim of increasing their numbers while, during the blackout, humans create their own chaos and begin looting: "hordes of figures … rushing from the houses, cheering, clapping, arms waving, as if [they've] been waiting all their lives for this moment" (62), a scene the narrator equates to "a travesty of Christmas shopping" (63). Although the narrator stands apart, economically and culturally, from both the violence and the rapacious roaming, his own whiteness does not necessarily leave him impervious to the multiplicities of aggression and consumption.

T.E.D. Klein and the Rupture of Civilization

A telling parallel emerges between two statements regarding "people": the first being Pistachio's claim that the "war" helmets of the white people "all look much the same" and the second, from the narrator, noting "it's said that, to whites, all blacks look alike, and years of teaching in various city classrooms have convinced me that the reverse is true as well" (9). In this correlation lies a homogenizing effect, a leveling of races and (inter)species. Two additional assertions from Pistachio take the correspondence even further, towards a universal existentialism: "All men are homeless ... we have journeyed for so many year..." (21) and "is no one safe today" (24), the latter taking the form of a declaration rather than a question. From one angle, these statements address the fundamental condition of aging and death. Most of the story's drama unfolds in the retirement home where Herman lives out his remaining years. In spite of his vivacity, he must come to terms with the reality of slowing down, with his own personal—but ubiquitous—predicament of mortality. He laments that "even [his] hair's slowing down.... Damned stuff doesn't grow half as fast as it used to. I remember how my first wife ... used to say I looked distinguished because my hair was prematurely grey ... well, it's still grey, what's left of it, but it sure as hell ain't premature" (35). Somewhat more poignantly, he complains that his "legs feel like they're ready for the junk heap ... my mind'll probably go next, and then where will I be?" (*ibid.*). His grandson, loving and generous as he is, is considerably less affecting on the topic of aging when he refers to other retirees as "propped up in the lounge chairs like a row of dolls, staring straight ahead as if watching a playback of their lives" (16). He adds, "If I sound less than reverent toward my elders, there's a good reason: I am," as he has little trust in their wisdom, though this critique comes with the acknowledgment that he will one day be among their ranks.

For obvious reasons, mortality and human frailty are inevitable fodder for philosophical or existential horror in particular; everyone dies and, barring a religious commitment to the afterlife, ceases to exist. But while alive, there are other concerns. Loss of senses, limbs, sanity, sanctity. Another irony finds the leveling affect that pervades "Children of the Kingdom" reserving the most invasive of its consequences for females of all ages. The elderly woman in the retirement home first notices "dozens of sleepwalkers in her room" (49), whereupon she

3. White, Black and Other People

attempts to resist their assault as they beat her about the face, "'[turn] her on her stomach and [push] her face in to the pillow, and she [can] feel their hands on her ankles, hauling her legs apart—the nightgown [is] actually ripped right up the side—and then another one of them [pulls] it up over her waist...'" (50). Nearing the story's conclusion, Karen, too, is raped in their apartment and it is only after a number of years that the narrator has her permission to relate the event, with the implication of deep-rooted trauma. While it is difficult to imagine that Klein is exhibiting a fascination with rape, its presence in this text and in *The Ceremonies*, situated as it is at similar, climatic points, is significant. The correspondence pertains to the degree that "becoming-woman" can be an exceedingly challenging process when its opposition in the form of patriarchy (supernatural or otherwise) becomes reactive, a challenge that applies to everyone. This is not to diminish the very real abomination of female rape at the hands of very real and very disturbed men, but every person, Klein proposes, is subject to insidious violence, be it physical or political. Six weeks after the attack, Karen has an abortion, leading up to which the couple is given "a free lecture from a Right to Life group picketing in front" (68). It is a common scenario encountered by ordinary, sexually active women who choose to terminate a pregnancy, the exception being that the ignorance and hypocrisy of the picketers is especially pronounced in light of the "wretched little thing inside her" (*ibid.*). They perform their ideology that severely disempowers women with no regard for the personal history, or, for that matter, the potentially alien/demonic violation that the woman has undergone. They attempt to strip her of dignity as the chaos and self-orientations of life can sometimes do.[2] Everyone is vulnerable to literal or metaphorical rape. Another way of framing this, in keeping with Klein's general modus operandi, is evil does not discriminate according to gender, race, class, or sexual orientation, though it often has special "frolics," as Thomas Ligotti puts it with regard to a child molester's detestable actions, in store for those on the margins of dominant, normative culture.[3] Even Father Pistachio, the narrative's seer, disappears in the wake of the blackout.

The narrator eventually settles into his own aging—and thus increasingly disenfranchised cultural status—along with, perhaps, his wisdom following his grandfather's death: "*Wednesday, February 14,*

T.E.D. Klein and the Rupture of Civilization

1979"—"'Young men think that old men are fools,' a friendly retiree explains to him, "'but old men *know* that young men are fools.' She [purses] her lips doubtfully. 'Of course,' she [says], that wouldn't apply to you.'[He laughs]. 'Of course not! Besides, I'm not so young anymore'" (68). In fact, what he has begun to realize is that *all* men and women are fools, at least in light of our mutual susceptibility to the egotism that breeds ignorance, prejudice, solipsism, and opportunism. But the truth, as the narrator eventually discovers, is far stranger than mere foolishness—the inability to stretch imagination beyond the small world of a small life, the countless projections that govern perception, and consequently, relationality, religion, politics, small time philosophies. He discovers the "truth" of insecurity, ambiguity, provocatively rendered in his observations of a given locale: "a neighborhood can change in half and hour as assuredly as it can change in half a block. After dark it becomes a different place: another neighborhood entirely, coexisting with the first and separated by only a few minutes in time, the first a place where everything is known, the other a place of uncertainty, the first place of safety, the other—" (47). His insight, in keeping with horror's general horizon, centralizes around the notion that anything is possible, that the uncertainty of "the other" is forever close at hand, closer than breathing in some instances, and poised to intervene in the daily narrative of dominant culture.

And intervene it does, by the story's menacing conclusion, when the narrator, older, wiser, is walking in the city and notices a pile of pistachio shells near the opening of a sewer. He freezes upon sight of "something watching intently, its face pressed up against the metal grating, its pale hands clinging tightly to the bars" and detects "the gaping red ring of its mouth ... the face [is] alien and cold, without human expression, yet [he swears] that those eyes [regard him] with utter malevolence— and that they [recognize him]" (72). The "red ring" is further evidence of Pistachio's presence, along with the mutual recognition. In what is perhaps the ultimate sacrilege, a priest, or former priest, has become-monster; his malevolence indicative of what Machen's Ambrose would call "the infernal miracle" or "true evil" ("White" 116). That the figure vanishes "back to that kingdom, older than ours, that calls the dark its home" (Klein, "Children" 72) hardly ameliorates the story's tension or sense of doom. That kingdom is ever present, just beneath the surface,

3. White, Black and Other People

and can ascend at any moment. And of course, it does, in the everyday, if one is to graft the "infernal miracle" onto quotidian occurrences so as to diagnosticate over and above normative perception, that which is quick to dismiss "true evil" as par for the course, particularly when it happens to the other person, black, white, or otherwise.

Yet another horror trope further adds to the menace surrounding "Children of the Kingdom"—the presence of a book, in this case, Father Pistachio's book that tells not only of geographical origins but of "white people," and that remains in existence. Prior to the blackout, his interest in the narrator, and Karen in particular, revolves around her work at a publisher (unrelated to acquisition as her position is) with the hope of having the book published for the first time in English. His ambition has been to have it published in all major languages, to spread the gospel of what lies beneath. It is a vision that becomes forebodingly realized in Karl Edward Wagner's "Sticks," a story that precedes *The Blair Witch Project* in engendering forest stick configurations with truly sinister qualities. More importantly, Wagner's story focuses on horror fiction (and graphics) as a means by which to disseminate the presence of "true evil." In other words, a wide-reaching text is intended to return the repressed to life, to bring back what is never completely dead, only dormant, and thus to "take of heaven [and earth] by storm." Overtly Lovecraftian, "Sticks" follows a protagonist, illustrator of the macabre Colin Leverett, as he happens upon "insane [conglomerations] of sticks and wire" (Wagner 211) in a forest and soon encounters a creature whose "eyes that should be dead [are] bright with hideous life" (213). From this point on, try as he does to forget, nightmares bring the confrontation that "[can't] be forgotten" (217) back to the point of eventually generating, after an especially vivid dream, a "half-devoured heart he [clutches] in his fist" (223). In the meantime, he has produced numerous grisly illustrations for a new edition of work by one H. Kenneth Allard, a famed horror writer who, Levrett learns only when it is too late, is an emissary of the Old Ones; the book will be published as "an evocation so unthinkably vast that the 'pentagram' (if you will) is miles across" (224). More of the creatures Levrett battles at the beginning of the story assail him in the end, "lead him away, but he [cannot] awaken, [can] only follow" (*ibid.*).

Nothing can keep Wagner's protagonist from the inevitable fate (uncertain though it remains throughout the narrative) to which he has consigned himself via his curiosity. As Freud maintains in his "The Dissection of the Psychical Personality," "impressions ... which have been sunk into the id by repression, are virtually immortal; after the passage of decades they behave as though they have just occurred" (73). Beyond Levrett's newfound "wisdom," now countless others will be led to "follow" the inducement of the "evocation" that is itself "immortal," to become nameless ("all look much the same") lines in the "pentagram" that will stretch into "vast" existence. More importantly, however, the reader of Wagner's story is made privy to a "strange truth" indeed by virtue of the text being "structured to awaken ... imaginative possibilities deeply embedded in the human subconscious" (Introduction, "Sticks" 209), as one commentator puts it. While Levrett may be incapable of being awoken, his sleep parallels the "awakening" that may unfold by virtue of the imagination springing to ironic life. Once courted, it follows, always, as one must follow it. But is this "infernal miracle" one to eschew? Is "true evil" something to revile in a reactionary manner given what Lovecraft deems "the morbid introspection developed by an isolated backwoods life devoid of normal amusements and of the recreational mood, harassed by commands for theological self-examination, keyed to unnatural emotional repression, and forming above all a mere grim struggle for survival" in the (post)modern world?

Father Pistachio's transformation, be it foreordained against or in alignment with his will or a happenstance amidst the blackness of a chaotic New York night without electricity, can certainly be read as tragic, along with the murders, suicides, and rapes of Klein's own evocation. One might even feel sympathetic toward Levrett and the dire consequences of his morbid curiosity. And yet the question as to what, exactly, critical horror evokes and to what end(s) complicates the tragedy of becoming-monster/abject/disagreeably pale. Another way to frame the question: is it possible that we *need* the darkness of the kingdom, the thing that follows and demands that we follow its lead, that stares intently and accusingly at us from beneath the surface of our settled lives? The "infernal miracle" may be diabolical but the "normal amusements and ... the recreational mood" have an equally insidious, nefarious way of sanctioning unconsciousness; in contrast, the former provokes awareness, perception that is as stripped of projection as possible. Fear, of course, is largely fueled by the projection of an imagined future, though with heightened degrees of consciousness, its maze, like that at the core of Kubrick's *The Shining*, can be navigated with liminal intelligence, with advanced imagination, as opposed to the impudence and savagery of dullness.

"I somehow preferred the fear"

If its tenets are to be accepted, Harold Bloom's influential and exasperating *The Anxiety of Influence* is as, if not more, applicable to horror writers as to Romantic and other poets. His general claim of aesthetic and psychological battle waged between writers and precursors, with its inevitable anxiety for the former, might direct the historian of horror fiction to at least the 18th century, to Horace Walpole, if not considerably earlier, and onto Shelley, Le Fanu, Poe, Lovecraft, Jackson, and King, among other key figures. Lovecraft's debt to Poe is obvious, and the former's range of influence on the writers of the 20th and 21st centuries is considerable, particularly for the first-person narrator and horror writer of Klein's "Black Man with a Horn" for whom Lovecraft sets not only an influential literary precedent but remains a friend, forty years dead. In spite of the mortal gap and the reverence the narrator feels for "[his] friend Howard" (Klein, "Black" 135), he is wistfully clear that "even in death he had triumphed over me" (136). None of the six revisionary ratios that propel Bloom's theory apply to the second tier narrator whose self-proclaimed "life seems hardly to have mattered in the scheme of things. Surely its end cannot matter much either" (134).[4] Like his predecessor, he adheres to a pessimistic philosophy of "futilitarianism," the mocking terminology of which becomes comically and poignantly relevant when he recalls being honored at a conference only to have his "celebrated collection" misprinted in the conference schedule as *Beyond the Garve*" (138). In his old age, he is acutely aware of "lost opportunity" and having "lived out [his] life in [Lovecraft's] shadow" (167).

On the other hand, he appears to prefer the anxiety (of influence) over the delusion of originality, a preference that assumes the form of mystery-solving "detective" work concerning a disappearance, a murder, and a violent tribe not unlike the children inhabiting the dark kingdom.[5]

T.E.D. Klein and the Rupture of Civilization

Such work is of course inherently unoriginal; the dazzling epiphanies of Sherlock Holmes aside, it unravels the strands of a puzzle, or unpacks the layers of a narrative, as might the literary critic, or the psychoanalyst, an enigma that has already cemented its "influence," its inscrutable but no less historical sphere of action and consequence, especially when involving death. The sleuth merely compiles events, explores alleyways, blind or otherwise. The first sentence of Deleuze and Guattari's book on Kafka begins with the question "How can we enter into Kafka's work? The work is a rhizome, a burrow. The castle has multiple entrances whose rules of usage and whose locations aren't very well known" (*Kafka* 3). Despite its multiplicity and the "experimentation" that the philosophers state is necessary to unhinge texts from domination by semiotic conventions, mysteries yield meaning according to established incidents surfacing, becoming known, however much the entry points may lead to other thresholds. What is perhaps most telling about their opening question is the foregrounding of first-person (plural), the past tense of which, Klein's narrator suggests, offers "something inherently comforting" ("Black" 133). A self operating in a universe of criticism, investigation, philosophizing, critical thinking, and most importantly, alive to the moment of the text, the mystery, the life, whatever its restrictions or disappointments. The first-person provides the reader with the gift of vicarious safety: "'It's over now,' he says. 'I lived through it.'" "A comfortable premise, perhaps," the narrator goes on. "Only, in this case, it doesn't happen to be true. Whether the experience is really 'over now' no one can say; and if, as I suspect, the final chapter has yet to be enacted, then the notion of my 'living through it' will seem a pathetic conceit" (134). The first person, like many of Klein's characters, is confined not only to the shadow of another but is likely doomed to inhabit the multi-roomed "castle" where evidence emerges sporadically and, as in Kafka's fiction, death, literal or metaphorical, waits patiently and resiliently to strike.

Pathetic though it may be, the narrator finds himself having to face another of Klein's "strange truths," that of "living out another man's horror stories" (153). Lovecraft is essentially another character in this tale of "The Tch-Tcho People," or as the predecessor himself calls them in *The Shadow Out of Time*, "the wholly abominable Tcho-Tchos" (quoted, 152) with whom (the not surprisingly christened) Ambrose, a missionary

3. White, Black and Other People

the B-list writer meets aboard a plane, has had contact. The former soon vanishes, leaving the narrator to probe and go, ultimately, entirely too far. If Ambrose echoes Father Pistachio—in addition to Machen's character—in the context of Klein's oeuvre, the narrator is familiar territory as well, a retired NYC teacher with a keen appetite for the macabre. He has, in a sense, been territorialized by Lovecraft, by his influence as well as his cultural reach ("Ah, Howard, your triumph was complete the moment your name became an adjective" [137]), and the opportunity for deterritorialization via his own body of work has passed. What remains in the final years (hours?) of the narrator's time is the shadow of a conceit, that of comfort and safety, and of a life that he can call his own.

Whether in New York or in Florida, the two primary locations of "Black Man with a Horn," one commonality with the other Klein texts thus far is a heat-infested environment and the consequent "air conditioner, waging its lonely battle against the tropic night" (133). It is difficult to avoid the role of class in this regard, certainly after encountering Carol's compromised, thermal living space in *The Ceremonies*. But there is another environment in the current story, "Negri (sic) Sembilan"—"a land so humid that wallpaper [bubbles] on the hot nights and Bibles [sprout] mildew" (140, 141). There is a mild joy, a clever wink, in this last line that signifies decayed, or simply abandoned Christianity, at least the relatively proselytizing, indoctrinating version of the religion with its tendency to walk roughshod over other cultures, other traditions. Ambrose goes so far as to suggest that while venturing into the deepest recesses of the land, he "was pretty much on [his] own" (142), the insinuation being that it is a godless space, or rather, bereft of the Christian God. Sarr and Deborah certainly find themselves in such an environment, though it turns out, of course, to be their own land, their own cultural and domestic sphere—another irony that might afford a wink from the reader so constituted. As for the narrator, he at least has a "Father"/predecessor on whom to lean; that is until the shadow of the latter's "story" assumes the form of a potential "black face pressed to [his] window" (176), a malevolent horror creation whose presence spells death to the already aging narrator. Like Herman questioning his hairline or Jeremy, afraid of the many (relatively innocuous) implications that come with turning thirty, the second-class horror writer is doomed one

T.E.D. Klein and the Rupture of Civilization

way or another, contrary to the assertion on the sundial decorating his sister's Florida yard ("Grow old along with me, / The best is yet to come" [*ibid.*]). With or without a Lovecraftian demise, he is, like us all, subject to age and extinction, "the best," in his case, far behind in time, if it ever materialized in the first place.

The demoniacal "black face" at the window, in light of Lovecraft's history of racism and the story's title, in light of its many references to black, the color that negates or absorbs all light, is paramount. What is black? An aesthetically revolutionary square by Malevich. An elegant dress or suit for mourning, praying, judging. A hole in spacetime, a form of metal music. A relation to fashionable, Schopenhauerean (or Lovecraftian) pessimism or deconstructive cognitive limitation. Black also characterizes, for better and most certainly, historically, for worse, a person with dark skin. John Coltrane, who appears on an album cover blowing his horn and stops Ambrose in his tracks with what Lovecraft might call unfathomable dread, was black, as are the Tcho-Tcho People with their "pendulous [horned]" (151) demons, and a vast part of New York City's population, some of whom are impoverished, hungry, and therefore psychically and socially chaotic. The narrator is understandably afraid of a face peering into his window. It is not simply skin tone that warrants this fear; rather, it is a body, a gaze, a potentially malevolent other invading the (godless) space of his solitude, though given the degree to which "black" is foregrounded throughout the story, it is also impossible to overlook. Outside of this harrowing dénouement, however, the protagonist assumes a different attitude toward the otherness, or even the potential violence of black. When considering whether to move into a safer—and whiter—New York neighborhood, he realizes that "forced to choose between whites whom [he despises] and blacks whom [he fears], [he] somehow [prefers] the fear" (150). This is a tremendously important moment in Klein's fiction: an avowal of white privilege critique (including the subtly morbid "over there they read nothing but bestsellers" [*ibid.*]) and Bartlebyesque preference, when forced to choose, for darkness, for the black at the core of civilization's light.

This passage follows another admission, more intimate, endearing even, but pointed directly at the predecessor's notoriously inflammatory views. The narrator speaks openly to his old friend and literary father's deeply entrenched fear of the "alien hordes" of NYC when he asserts "I

3. White, Black and Other People

believed then, Howard, and I believe it still, that the nightmare was of your own making" (149). So even more than the concept "black," racism is a multiplicity and a construction, a "nightmare" that arguably fabricates as much negativity for its perpetrator as for its victim. It is a reaction to otherness based, ironically, on the active qualities of black, negation and absorption, that finds a parallel in Silverman's notion that "the ego consolidates itself by assimilating the corporeal coordinates of the other to its own—by devouring bodily otherness. The 'coherent' ego subsequently maintains itself by repudiating whatever it cannot swallow—by refusing to live in and through alien corporealities," what she finally refers to as the "self-same body" (Silverman, *Threshold* 24). This body, be it physically singular or culturally, politically global, practices the precise nature of black in its consumption and inevitable disavowal of the other. Consequently, it produces a variant of the anxiety central to Bloom's theory. On one level, the narrator of "Black Man with a Horn" manifests a reverent but antagonistic attitude toward Lovecraft; he suffers from a distinct form of anxiety that entails aesthetic influence as well as competitiveness with the "father." Racism, on the other hand, pits the "self-same body" against the other, leaving the self anxious not only about aesthetic failure or the "triumph" of a predecessor, but with the otherness integral to the self itself. In other words, black absorbs and negates—extinguishes—the light of life; it gestures, or holds forth like a cloaked, Swedish chess player, on the inevitability of death. The evil in Klein's narrative thus appears as "the black man, black horn to his lips, man and horn a single line of unbroken blackness" ("Black" 160) and is thereafter described as "Death itself" (161). Death may be deferred but it is ultimately unbroken. Everybody dies; everybody is black in the sense that death's "influence" is an impossible consanguinity, the forebearer who will not be beaten. We are all, the story suggests, in line with the knight of Ingmar Bergman's *The Seventh Seal*, "small and frightened and ignorant" in the face of our eventual demise.

Nevertheless, the "self-same body" endures as its own religion, or cult. Paradoxically, it is Lovecraft who, alongside the narrator's valuable insights, will call this body out, at least in its religious, evangelical capacity. He claims, in yet another quotation, "Missionaries are infernal nuisances who ought to be kept at home" (140). Granted sympathy for the plights of Ambrose and Father Pistachio, missionary work, when not

T.E.D. Klein and the Rupture of Civilization

committed solely to the material welfare of others, is disputably a kind of racist imperialism seeking to eradicate the otherness of "alien" culture and tradition. To frame it another way, missionary work is territorialization. From this perspective, the Tcho-Tcho People are practicing, however violently and horrifically, a form of deterritorialization when they punish the reverend, whose lung tissue turns up in his bedroom (156). On a related, and relatively pleasant note, it should be obvious that the other "black man with a horn," Coltrane, absolutely deterritorialized jazz. He was, in the view of many jazz enthusiasts during the era of his final, most experimental years (the 1960s), a "nuisance" to established forms and expectations. His blackness expanded to include other colors, sounds, mystical visions. To hear some of his band mates from this era speak of the perplexing onstage cacophony is to recognize a familiar reactivity to the potency of radical, critical horror.[6]

Ten years prior to Coltrane's musical innovations, another nuisance, less innovative, more missionary in her efforts, fought for her dominion in fiction, in every sense of that word; a grandmother who imagines herself an admirable matron in the light of old world nostalgia, attire, and racist proclamations. She even claims to exercise a "conscience" (678) in Flannery O'Connor's "A Good Man Is Hard to Find," the widely anthologized story of a lower middle-class family travelling to Tennessee, on the way to which they collide with a serial killer. The grandmother's racism manifests in language such as "pickaninny" and "nigger" (679), the violence of which is echoed in her grandchildren when, immediately following a car accident, they "[scream] in a frenzy of delight" and lament the fact that "nobody's killed" (683). In the story's ostensible search for a "good man," the first prospect enters as the owner of a general store/lunch counter who orders his server wife around and agrees with the grandmother that Europe is to blame for the many problems of 1950s America (681). Once the reader discounts him, the only man left aside from the largely emasculated grandson is the killer, the Misfit, who appears in a "hearse-like automobile" (684) and, with some degree of camp, wears a "black hat" (686). Once recognized by the grandmother, the Misfit is compelled to murder the entire family, calling his own "good" status into question, if this is not already an issue by virtue of his general occupation.

Even more than the holy men of Klein's narratives, however, the

3. White, Black and Other People

Misfit commands reverence, or at the very minimum, a modicum of respect. He is a contemplative (and even wears "silver-rimmed spectacles that [give] him a scholarly look" [684]) who testifies to the social "wall," "ceiling," and "floor" (687) that abound in his life, that have corrugated his direction into prison, and then out, by escape. He is a social product who is aware of the "civilizing" forces that have perpetuated his unsavory construction. In direct contrast, the grandmother, adding fuel to the fire of her bigotry, attempts to witness to him, to convince him not only that he is "good" but that he should "pray" (686). When her proselytizing goes too far, with a hand on the Misfit's shoulder, he "[springs] back as if a snake [has] bitten him and [shoots] her three times" (688). His final pronouncement about her, a eulogy of sorts, is, famously, that "she would have been a good woman … if it had been somebody there to shoot her every minute of her life" (689). Nor does he seem to enjoy the murder, as he confesses to a fellow convict: "It's no real pleasure in life" (*ibid.*). The grandmother is reduced to a coiled snake attempting to salvage its life and, equally important, its dubious identity as a "good" woman, her "goodness" limited to sentimental manipulation of the other in order to protect the "self-same body." The missionary should most certainly have been kept at home. The other, of course, is "black" in his overt recognition of what Jackson calls "absolute reality" (*Haunting* 3), a white man with a gun who resists the reality of walls and ceilings, of formal and metaphorical prisons, with the deterritorializing practices of a good, a perfect even, horror antagonist.

The Tcho-Tcho people do not appear contemplative or remorseful in their aggression. Unlike the Misfit, but very much in line with Kleinian monsters, they "grow" things in people, as they have done in Ambrose (Klein, "Black" 144). There is a ring of Foucaultian, interiorized fascism here, or Erving Goffman's notion of acting in such a way as to have one's interlocutor voluntarily, if not unconsciously, do one's bidding. There is also the blood, pulp, and protruded skin of a Bwada. Things grow in people regardless of how they eventually surface. Where "Black Man with a Horn" is perhaps most efficacious, and exhilarating in what is otherwise a relatively sedate detective narrative, is in its exposition of an anxiety that reaches beyond the ivied walls of America's top tier universities. How does one navigate localized and macro influences coming from every angle—from media, from our countless, addictive screens,

T.E.D. Klein and the Rupture of Civilization

our intimate thoughts always already informed by and around the mass construct of language, and of course, from our favorite poets and other writers? The answer may or may not lie in horror, though in the hands of Klein it certainly bubbles, infernally, critically, just under the surface of skin that is only barely impervious to what Lovecraft might call hideous, carnivorous eversion.

Chapter 4

Sorceries of Self-Negation: "Petey" and "Nadelman's God"

"Material affairs"

"It's such a nice party, I hate to leave it. It's such a nice party, I'd like to repeat it" (21), states a guest in T. S. Eliot's play *The Cocktail Party*, a desire that will come to fruition and challenge the reader to question what constitutes "nice" in the context of this or any bourgeois social gathering. The repetition communicates a sense of Eliot's critique in so far as repetitive language reflects redundancy in the lived life, not simply that of practical routine but in terms of manner, values, personhood in the service of automatism and unconsciousness, however clever the former qualities may appear. The drama unfolds over the course of two such parties and follows a separation between the privileged, married hosts, infidelities, absurdist preoccupations, and eventually a series of often caustic insights on the part of an unidentified guest who is later identified as Reilly, a psychologist. *The Cocktail Party* examines the prevalence of vapidity and superficiality amongst the upper class, "horrors" in and of themselves, but succeeds in magnifying the psychology of its focal plane, the character traits and compulsions that lead to what are essentially miserable lives. Lamenting the loss of his wife, Edward, the male protagonist (the wife, Lavinia, becomes equally significant) describes himself as "the dull, the implacable, the indomitable spirit of mediocrity" (Eliot, *Cocktail* 66). He is, according to Reilly, "nothing but a set of obsolete responses" (31) and, with one key exception, not including the psychologist, largely indicative of his social milieu.

So the critique expands out and into the bourgeois self, the one whose modus operandi is "[absorption] in the endless struggle to think well of [oneself]" (111), to the point where "at every meeting we are meeting a stranger" or the "affectionate ghosts" (72) who ultimately haunt with alienation as opposed to genuine intimacy. How can one know another intimately when thought is mechanically and more or less permanently directed toward self-congratulation (or flagellation, for that matter)? What makes the self-directed thought "obsolete" is its reactive nature, which is not to say that reactivity is a thing of the past, that it does not remain pervasive in the human experience; rather, the relationality that slowly emerges from relatively objective self-observation and cultural critique, that plays a significant role in shaping and informing the self, is the only valid present and future coalition of social selves. Without it, one may be reduced to the condition of "two people who know they do not understand each other, / Breeding children whom they do not understand / And who will never understand them" (140), a condition that produces its own form of isolationism. "What is hell?" Hell is oneself," states Edward, "Hell is alone, the other figures in it / Merely projections. There is nothing to escape from / And nothing to escape to. One is always alone" (98). "Hell is other people" because other people reflect the aloneness of a self and its delusions of both grandeur and insignificance.

The Cocktail Party is concerned with the psychological nature of Hell as a condition requiring profound introspection, a willingness to peer honestly into the portal of one's egotism, privileged or otherwise. And the play offers an antidote, prescribed, naturally, by the psychologist, but enacted most effectively by Celia, Edward's former lover. It is "a kind of faith that issues from despair" (141), he exclaims. Though it may be tempting to relate such faith to the Poroth's community and its role in the generation of evil, or to any number of grotesque, debilitating forms of faith-based ignorance, the central term here is "despair," that which emerges from productive introspection and seeks ultimately to diminish the self for the sake, paradoxically, of self-development. Deleuze, in characterizing Spinozist subjectivity, speaks of "individuating affective states of an anonymous force" (*Spinoza* 128), those one might attain only by way of the despair that comes of forthright and relatively uncontaminated self-examination. The "anonymous force" here is hardly an anthropomorphized deity, though it is suggestive of the degree to which its corresponding "states" preclude the conceit of self-absorption, the self-directed hell of aloneness. Between the two parties,

4. Sorceries of Self-Negation: "Petey" and "Nadelman's God"

Celia has travelled to a foreign land to do humanitarian work only to be crucified, literally, by a tribe (of Tcho-Tchos?), a grisly fate but one the psychologist describes as "triumphant" (Eliot, *Cocktail* 186) by virtue of her sense of inevitability, her voluntary acceptance of the call to self-negation.[1] The horror of Celia's demise is not necessarily Spinozist but its orientation is; the latter's consent to interiority, to the balm of "despair" in a milieu of superficiality and *precious* subjectivity is her triumph. Eliot may not be associated with genre fiction, though neither here nor elsewhere does he abstain from illuminating both the value and the horror of excavating Hell.

At one point, as a consequence of both his mysteriousness and his psychological insight, Reilly is referred to as having "some sort of power" and is aligned with "the Devil" (57). Another devil appears in Klein's "Petey," the story of a privileged couple who invite a group of friends, other privileged couples, to a Connecticut housewarming party, complete with cocktails. The "Little Devil" is a figure on a Tarot card they find in the large, rural home, isolated but "so close to New York" (Klein, "Petey" 84), out of which the original owner has been ousted and institutionalized for being mad (with "eyes like a sorcerer" [96]), thus making room for the new owners, urbanites George and Phyllis. One of the guests explains: "He's [the Little Devil] supposed to help the farmer tend the garden and clean the house, but he just causes mischief and eats up whatever's lying around. Including a few of the neighbors" (115). While Reilly's "devilishness" is ultimately directed toward psychological acumen, thus mirroring a Beelzebub figure bent not on destruction but on productive self-transformation, Klein's "Petite Diable" is, on the surface, a wholly exterior and malevolent creature whom, in addition to the foreshadowing of the card, the former owner has conjured and whose presence will become known by the story's startling conclusion.

"Petey" is, of course, the fiend come to life, and he is "H.U.N.G.R.Y." (111), as his maker explains by tapping letters in the wake of having ripped his own throat out. However, apart from being seen at a distance from the house, and rather disturbingly being misrecognized as a scarecrow, Petey only appears as "a grey shape [that fills] the doorway, blotting out the night" (129), as an unsuspecting guest turns to leave in the final sentence. There is irony here in that earlier Phyllis "[pauses] to draw the curtains, holding back the night" (92–93), an effort that is finally

T.E.D. Klein and the Rupture of Civilization

deemed untenable, as horror narrative is wont to argue, in so far as the shape obscures the night with its own dark density; Petey *is* the night. But this unfeasibility, terrifying as it may be in the form of a "sorcerer's" creation, also serves the story's second, and perhaps primary, function as cultural critique and thus links it thematically with Eliot's play. When two of the guests are questioning the manner in which George has acquired the house at such a low cost, one studies the visage of the other and observes "the endless cocktails of expense-account lunches, the daily betrayals disguised as good fellowship" (104). Inebriation may be unlocking a propensity for gossip, but the observation comes across as sobering in terms of what lies beneath the faces people are inclined to wear when performing or promoting themselves socially. Unlike *The Cocktail Party*, there is no antidote, no salvation in "Petey" given such façades and the turpitude that is invariably fomented by the impact of civilization. Nevertheless, there is "despair" in Klein's story, that which emerges from self-evaluation following misdeeds, or simply unconscious behavior. Despair and horror are contiguous in this respect; like the unidentified guest, they flirt (or consummate a relationship with) deviltry (or Hell) that exposes and reveals the underside. Horror typically makes "the night" an insurmountable barrier to salvation. The curtains blot out nothing but light.

The party's initial toast, with cheers and playful, teasing barbs from guests, in honor of George, their "esteemed host," along with Phyllis and her "stunningly coifed" "feathercut" hair style, is soon revealed to harbor numerous antagonisms (76–77). "To the reason we're all gathered here tonight, the cause of all our celebration—," begins one guest, until he is interrupted by his wife. "And jealousy," she concludes (77). When the house is referred to as a "museum," George becomes aware of the "envy" and the "bitterness" permeating the atmosphere (*ibid.*). As the night unfolds, another guest claims that the acquisition "makes [her] so angry [she] could positively scream" (87), while another glares at the hostess "with a touch of malevolence" (89), recalling Father Pistachio and his spiteful glower at the younger man who will one day be old, too. Like Baudelaire's incendiary poem "To the Reader" that catalogues an increasingly horrific list of "sins," these reactions to the great fortune of their friends with whom they share "good fellowship" progress from a form of daft covetousness to explicit enmity. There is no need for pistachio

4. Sorceries of Self-Negation: "Petey" and "Nadelman's God"

shells on the ground to alert the hosts to such pervasive animosity because it radiates from the community from behind the drunken smiles and well-wishes. In its hushed manner, it elaborates on the aggression and competitiveness indicative of certain civilized social dynamics. To civilize: to polish, make sophisticated. Klein is intent on making the grain beneath the gloss disclose its raw, but adulterated, texture.

On the other hand, the "it" of animosity follows George in particular, who is more sensitive to its machinations, not only as a testament to innate collective tendencies but as a repercussion of his own greed and sense of entitlement. All of the guests are privileged, evident when one of the Tarot cards forecasts a "commission to come," along with "skill in affairs—material affairs" (102), the divination of which refers to George, though another suggests "this kind of stuff could apply to anyone here" (103). George and Phyllis might be exceptional in their new residence, but they are all operating, as someone jokes, on the "playground of the landed gentry" (77), an amusing analogy that addresses the real condition that places them just under the aristocracy, such as it is in the United States, both financially and culturally; hence the common jealousy and malevolence. Still, it is George who has exercised his social influence "on the state highway commission" (82) and, as repeated soon thereafter, "with the highway commission" (83), the variant prepositions signifying dominance and collusion, respectively. Specifically, he has been tipped off about a highway bulldozing through the country area, notices for which have been sent out, though the project is eventually terminated. George is then offered the option of appropriating the country home for relatively little money while the owner is detained as unfit for society and therefore disenfranchised of his rights. The latter has a weapon, of course, the satanic figure who will seek vengeance by the party's end, though what is far more disquieting where the protagonist is concerned is his own guilty conscience.

It is certainly no accident that the new homeowner's surname is Kurtz. He is a colonizer. And like Conrad's enigmatic "Heart of Darkness" character, George falls ill, physically and psychologically, when confronted by the mirror reflection of his "friends" (who "[seem] almost interchangeable" [81]), those who would both secretly repudiate him and long for his recent success in "material affairs." He may "know the right people" (85) but this advantage does not make him impervious to

T.E.D. Klein and the Rupture of Civilization

what the "sorcerer" refers to as the rabid "feeding time" (86) of his creation, which is essentially a co-creation with the colonizer. Conrad's colonizer is infamously inclined, prior to his final days, to "exterminate all the brutes" of the Congo region in which he is stationed, an attitude with which Lovecraft may have had some sympathy but which Klein categorically and unambiguously renounces in "Petey" by having George succumb to the dehumanizing effects of his culpability. He drifts from the party to the isolation of a bathroom with queasiness motivating his steps and his self-reflection. He ruminates on having been a "schoolboy," when "the world had contained fewer secrets. Biology had been his special love; he had even dreamed, once, of medical school. How much he'd forgotten since then, and how mystifying the world had become" (115). Like the imperialist that he is, George has lost, or forgotten, his innocence that paradoxically affords knowledge—of self and the conscientiousness productively inscribed in the mutuality of fellowship—and given himself over to the mystification of an isolated (geographically and otherwise) subjectivity. It is this rendition of selfhood, motivated by greed and territorialization, that feels the deleterious effects of his choices. In the bathroom, he sits "crouching like some small hunted animal" (96), a sense that is reinforced by his Tarot card choice that is "disturbingly familiar" in so far as it "[arouses] the vague, half-buried apprehension" (103) that will remain ambiguous and yet readily apparent to the reader based on the horror he has more or less unconsciously self-generated. One could easily substitute haunted for "hunted" here as both terms illustrate the self-imposed conditions of avarice and portend the protagonist's (and most likely, his guests') inevitable demise.

Ideological systems, like any social entity, are subject to the vicissitudes of time and cultural re-mapping, especially as larger populations begin, however slowly, to assume responsibility for their collective, critical deliberation and relative liberation from alienating forces. While far right conservatives tend to deny or combat this manifest inevitability, seeking instead to garrison the isolated milieu, dominate culture, or self-identity, the system shifts, or collapses, it *becomes* in tandem with the strongest voice of its people, a fact that is doubtless recognized, and embraced, by the very general worldview of occultism. The Tarot cards inflect time, they fold what is an ineluctable alteration of future onto the present, as exemplified by "the top card of the deck [showing] a stone

4. Sorceries of Self-Negation: "Petey" and "Nadelman's God"

tower crumbling as a bolt of lightening [hits] it. In the background the sea [rages] furiously" (105). By the story's end, which is only a beginning of an end, George studies the card and begins to understand how the future is about to intercede in present preoccupations. "The Tower," he realizes. "Lightening [flashes], stone walls [crumble], and beyond them [rages] the sea" (128). The world in all of its trials, its marginalization of the poor, the mad, the abject other, rages beyond them, regardless of how fortified their towers, purchased at the expense of those who have no defense against the power of bureaucratic manipulation, may seem. And further, the "sea" that hosts cosmic mystery, unfathomable beings, some of whom prey upon those whose flailing in forgetfulness and conceit invites incursion, rages as a serpent that dwarfs the unthinking Gadsden reptile, as a little pink-skinned man, a white man, or a black man inseparable from his unmelodious horn, or Satan ("Yes, the grey shape [on George's card] probably [represents] Satan ... the Beast" [122], the guests decide). George is no longer mystified as he looks toward the entrance of their new home. Petey "[fills] the doorway, blotting out the night—and now, just as in the card, it [turns] to face him" (129) and the "Tower" is sure to collapse.

A key difference, then, between Eliot's elegant and buoyantly comic *The Cocktail Party* and Klein's "Petey" lies between the two devil figures, one being a literal incarnation of evil reflecting that of its human counterparts and the other a misunderstood psychologist whose function it is to redirect the superficiality of party hosts. There is no such healing character or force in "Petey"; rather, George and his guests are left with the turmoil of *unintentional* suffering, that which is sure to descend upon them with the ferocity of a raging sea. This absence leaves horror to fill the position for the reader. How does it do this? How might critical horror offset "civilized" ways of seeing and being? When one of the guests falls asleep at the party, he awakens from a troubling dream, and as he begins to recount it, George admonishes him to forget it. "No, man, you've got it backwards," the guest responds. "You're *supposed* to talk about your nightmares. Helps you get rid of em" (116). The most compelling writers create a conversation, a forum for examining the nightmare, be it stereotypically or surrealistically monstrous or abstractly guilt-laden in the aftermath of waking engagement in civilization's everyday iniquity. One "converses" with the character, the tension-building narrative, the all-important atmosphere by questioning not only what *will* happen but what *would* happen if one's own lived life converged with the circumstances of the narrative. Perhaps that convergence is more realistic than most would care to recognize on the margins of horror's mirror image. George, Phyllis, and their guests are garden-variety bourgeois subjects relative to their hyperbolic analogues in the Eliot text. Their concerns, their preoccupations ("Entropy had set in...; those most bored drifting to the bar like sediment to the bottom of a pond...; Sydeny Gerdts [is] holding forth to the Goodhues and the Fitzgeralds—the fall of the dollar, or perhaps the rise of crime..." [103]), their discourse, the manner in which they secretly (or not so secretly) despise one another, all amount to what Adorno calls the "general uncritical consensus" around the "culture industry" in its broadest sense, as an industry of complacent subjectivities. The reader of critical horror is typically faced with a severe disruption of this consensus and thus with the opportunity for self-reflection that is otherwise denied "the masses" (including the "Fitzgeralds" of the world) who may be "distracted from distraction by distraction" (120), as Eliot puts it in "The Four Quartets" long before the multitude of screens commandeered our lives.

To return to the mirror image, the most revealing moment for George is arguably not his epiphany concerning who or what is at the door waiting to get in; instead, it occurs in the seemingly innocuous instance of approaching a mirror. While leaving the bathroom and venturing further from the action of the party, he finds himself "[avoiding] looking at his image as he [steps] past it: an old fear, resurrected in the faint attic light, of seeing some other face stare back at him" (Klein, "Petey" 113). Literally, this dread is surely warranted in the context of uncanny horror, where monstrosity can have its way by consuming one's identity; and yet such literalism applies equally to the anxiety of beholding the self-same face only to realize in a split second of insight that the visage corresponds to neither one's ideal nor to one's lived, somatic or psychological reality. A fear, it is (un)safe to say, that does not discriminate according to subject-position and may be as old as the self who gazes upon its reflection. George may feel constrained by a long-standing childhood fear, however the disease with which he navigates the housewarming party, no doubt informed by the shady manner in which he has obtained the house, suggests that his fear is less an adolescent phobia

4. Sorceries of Self-Negation: "Petey" and "Nadelman's God"

and more a product of corrupted adulthood, of surrendering to what are in fact base instincts that can produce a grotesque self-portrait indeed.

Granted the power and scope of ambiguity, perhaps it is this fear that most accurately inspires that memorable and notorious line from the antecedent Kurtz, the one who is responsible for both placing other "faces" on stakes and thinking critically about his role in empire: "the horror, the horror" (129). The horror not of the other but of the self that is alien to itself. George is certainly closer to a Gatsby in temperament and cultural status, but Kurtzian horror may paradoxically be the more realist and common of the two when viewed from the standpoint of our individual and collective nightmares, those that seep into consciousness whether invited or not and require some form of expression in the larger, chaotic wilderness (or jungle) of our psychic and phenomenological formulas of existence. Or to frame such horror in an another way, one might consider scrutinizing the face of what one has become in the mirror of the screen, the Facebook page, the moment of really looking at that performance, those preoccupations, its "likes" and "dislikes," and realizing that it has nothing to do with a fundamental quality of experience, the "emancipation" that Adorno characterizes as "the development of autonomous, independent individuals who judge and decide consciously for themselves." Rather, it presents a horror show of sorts, the horror of too many faces reflected back—the spouse, the bar-hopper, the parent, the "foodie," the religious or political ideologue, the yoga expert, the music fanatic, the travel fanatic, the beer fanatic—an unending list of spectacles, none of which shed light on the self that emerges into the world as an infant, absorbs impressions, postures, information, and eventually dies without necessarily having learned what enculturation and mortality mean beyond a set of potentially corrupted or simply ignorant, dogmatic prescriptions. This is not to champion an essentialized self; on the contrary, it is to argue that critical horror, in undermining "uncritical consensus" in a manner that is more or less aligned with post-structuralist commentary on subjectivity, rips the essentializing tendencies of contemporary self-presentation apart. Any self that can be subjected to the psychological and physical violence of horror's rampage, however subtle, has no essential center; its porosity and fluidity (its multiplicity, as opposed its dogmatic indexes of identity) must ultimately prevail. Moreover, at the risk of overstating the obvious, this generalized self accounts for us all.

Of course, "Petey" is also pre–Internet, though George's crisis remains applicable to 21st- as well as 20th-century bourgeois experience. Like much of Klein's major work, it reflects what we might call the accurate face, the one just below the surface of everyday performativity, on and offline, that stares into the image of itself and discerns, if it is so inclined or acquiescent, a specter of a self that feels threateningly real. Here in this flickering moment, one is removed from the mirage of Lacan's mirror. It is that instant, extended, quite possibly, over a span of minutes in the consciously and methodically executed performance of Marina Abramovic's *The Artist is Present* in which she merely sits across from another and stares into his or her eyes with reflective neutrality. Why all the tears from countless, diverse others who occupy that seat in a spacious MOMA gallery, as depicted in the documentary covering the 2010 exhibition? Because most people are unaccustomed to being seen without the cultural filter of the "self-same body." Rubbing shoulders with the "right people," as one of George and Phyllis' guests puts it, implies co-mingling with a body-mind whose psychological and cultural filters are comparable to one's own, potentially judgmental and imperious but suggestive of a coherent self (limbs fully and consciously coordinated, solid bank account) nonetheless. The body artist invites only the accurate face that may or may not reveal itself in the immediacy of a neutral gaze. Critical horror exchanges such neutrality for sublime torment. Its mirror offers less an invitation and more an imperative to look, feel, and become.

"Material affairs" and Other Demons

"Petey's" George shares a fear with Lovecraft's "outsider," that of "[beholding] in full, frightful vividness the inconceivable, indescribable, and unmentionable monstrosity..." ("Outsider" 112) that may (or absolutely does) appear in the mirror image. Given the general critique of bourgeois values implicit in the narrative, it is evident that he fears the "monstrosity" of what he has become, which in some respects intersects with a (Anton) LaVeyan satanic sensibility that foregrounds egoism, material-

4. Sorceries of Self-Negation: "Petey" and "Nadelman's God"

ism, and social Darwinism. On the other hand, prior to his crisis of conscience, George is just an average guy, an upper middle-class white American male eager for comfort and the many privileges this status offers him with a little work and some under-the-table collusion with the "right people." In contrast, the protagonist of "Nadelman's God," the final story of Klein's *Dark Gods*, has, during his college years, explored occultism, or what he calls in retrospect "an adolescent interest in the outré" (185). By the time of the narrative's action, he has become another George, another bourgeois for whom "material affairs" and, especially in his case, sexual conquest constitute the height of fulfillment. He is relatively savvy, as though from a later era than his counterpart in "Petey," and yet their fates are sealed in much the same way as a consequence of committing to "uncritical consensus." In their own distinct ways, both men create an "inconceivable, indescribable, and unmentionable" god.

The story was originally published separately in 1979, though it is probably accurate to say that Nadelman has moved up in the world of a 1980s-style yuppiedom. He

> [lives] on the rich side of the river, in a two-bedroom co-op with a $240-a-month parking space in the basement garage...; he [belongs] to a health club near his office now, where he [sweats] away the extra pounds on steel-and-leather Nautilus machines, and the last thing [he's] written that [rhymes has] been a jingle for Jergen's Lotion. He [has] a wife [who has] just gone back to work for a computer graphics firm, a son in third grade at a special school for dyslexics, a $160,000 mortgage, and a dachshund. On Fridays after work he [has] guilty athletic sex in a Village apartment with a Yugoslavian divorcée from the health club [186].

Given his former preoccupation with occult matters, however distanced they have become from the material acquisitiveness of his adulthood, and his current sexual escapades, Nadelman is perhaps even more aligned with a hedonistic LaVeyan outlook. He is in the business of both attaining and, professionally, creating the need for possessions, including the right job, home, body, and mistress. In the past, however, his creativity has spawned an epic poem for a school literary magazine, "Advent of the Prometheans: A Cantata" (187), "a kind of allegorical recipe, for the construction of a servant in [a] new god's image" (191) that is supposed to "bring down God" (197). In reality, the poem merely represents a young man's "simple earnest desire to blaspheme" (198) in the context

T.E.D. Klein and the Rupture of Civilization

of his mandatory school worship services. Ultimately, all gods, he believes, are "amiable supernatural fictions designed to comfort childish minds," those that Freud's *The Future of an Illusion* attempts to correct, a process that feels "old hat" to him (*ibid.*). Until the major events of the story unfold, he is essentially atheistic: "There [is] no one in control up there. The office [is] empty. Nobody home" (200). Nadelman's blind spot in this regard is indicative of a common irony in atheistic lines of argumentation, those that *react* and endeavor to negate "childish" anthropomorphism and absurd exteriority, that focus their critique on a kind of cosmic property owned by a supernatural landlord, a sense of "up there" as opposed to the comparatively more complex and nuanced "in here." This oversight (or dereliction of sight) will cost him; will be far more expensive than his mortgage and his parking space. Because "maybe (and here [is] the germ of his poem) there [is] simply another god in charge, deranged and malign, delighting in cruelty and mischief" (ibid.), a "'furtive god,' the poem had said, 'a greedy god'" (201). As this maybe becomes a definitely, the protagonist, like George, loses his own control over the materiality of his life, such objects, people, preoccupations that secure an identity until one is bedeviled by the fruits of one's evocation.

"Nadelman's God" opens with the titular protagonist and his wife visiting an S & M club where they encounter a couple of swarthy and not particularly well-drawn characters, self-confessed witches who insist, on the subject of Lovecraft's work, "that stuff's not fiction!" (184). They may not be bright, they may be made of cardboard, but the aforementioned claim taps into what most any Lovecraft connoisseur would like to believe, that there is a Witch House, that Providence is haunted by unthinkable entities, and that a real *Necronomicon* exists in the vault of a nobleperson, or the attic of a Charles Dexter Ward. In spite of his youthful fancies, Nadelman is dismissive of the metaphysical until, years later, he receives a nearly illiterate letter from a fan of his poem, part of which has in earlier years been incorporated into lyrics by a successful heavy metal band. The writer, Arden Huntoon, has attempted to, and ultimately succeeds in conjuring the god who will eventually kill Huntoon and haunt Nadelman as his diabolical servant. And yet the latter is more than a stock Lovecraft monster, an unnamable fiend; he is known, as an early version of the poem has indicated (with no possibility of Huntoon ever having seen the name) as "The Hungerer"—"two small

4. Sorceries of Self-Negation: "Petey" and "Nadelman's God"

words" that "[punch] a single tiny hole in his [Nadelman's] universe" (218). He is made of garbage that apparently has the capacity to make phone calls, to evince "the soft, deliberate, liquid stir of mud—mud opening its jaws, yearning to speak words" (224). Embodied though the creature is, it also intimates Walter Benjamin's notion of detritus as "the once-fetishized object in its decayed and disabused/used form [that] exposes the collective fantasy or 'wish-image' that had once made it a valued object of social desire. On the other hand, this demystification or de*mythification* also points to the potential for change inherent in the obsolete object itself" (Mellamphy, "What's" 164). In other words, "The Hungerer" at once challenges "uncritical consensus" around commodification and consumerism and provokes the possibility of "change." In the context of Kleinian horror, of course, said change spells disaster for the protagonist but opens a space of *critical* thought around life choices, value systems, and relationality for the reader. Like *The Ceremonies*, the story concludes during the Christmas season, when Nadelman reflects on the fact that "most of his friends [complain] about the holidays—the pressures, the commercialism, the materialism—but [he has] always enjoyed them; they [are] one of the few times he [is] truly happy being a family man" (259). Perhaps there is something endearing in his pleasure, though the latter rests precisely on the "mythification" integral to object-fetishism, that which will be undone by the reconstituted detritus in the form of a revenge-seeking, servant of a demon.

Paradoxically, "The Hungerer" remains within the safe confines of poetic discourse during the exploratory college years and only becomes real (and highly dangerous) as the poet, again, like George, loses his curiosity. On his way to visit Huntoon, whose letters and phone calls have escalated to a point of consternation, Nadelman happens to recognize the woman of the couple from the S & M club who comments on the prospect of his revisiting his childhood home on the way. "You should. Believe me," she explains, "it's no good to lose contact with the past—bad things can happen. You get cut off from things" (229). "Things" implies ways of being, contemplating, acting, as opposed to material possessions of which Nadelman likely has a surfeit, along with a deficiency of the former. "All mysteries [pale] beside that of his own vanished past" (248) and "The Hungerer" has appeared to resuscitate this past in hideous glory. In addition to jaws of mud, the creature has a face that

T.E.D. Klein and the Rupture of Civilization

ostensibly appears in the seaside sky when Nadelman is a young boy, the very day that he begins to "sink into a hollow in the sand [... that opens] beneath him, then [presses] in upon him, [clutches] him, [tries] to draw him in. As if the earth were yearning to crush him, smother him, blot out the very memory of him. As if the planet, all nature, all creation, the very fabric of reality, were inimical to breeds such as his" (249). It is as though he receives a warning of what he will become, something that is antithetical to natural processes that trade in both life *and* inevitable death, reflection on which surely qualifies as a "thing" worthy of one's attention, rather than the "things," like the body itself, doomed to decay.

Nadelman may have a "tiny hole [punched] in his universe," but in the end his poem speaks to and generates the violation of a multiplicity rather than a mere singularity attempting to live a dream prescribed by his general reading material ("*Advertising Age* and *Fortune*" [212] magazines). According to the poem, the god is to be "shaped into 'a semblance of the monster in ourselves" (213). There is no clearer link between supernatural evil and the civilized self than this similitude. Nadelman "[feels] more guilty than angry, like the father of a psychopath, a father who [has] failed to warn the world" (250), and in keeping with the Promethean-inspired Victor Frankenstein, his example indicts "the monster in ourselves" that would breed hatred, economic disparity, and contempt over abjection. His guilt may humanize him, as it does George, but both George and Nadelman must nevertheless suffer the consequences of their individual choices. While the former is afraid of the mirror image for what it might expose, the latter is not given the option to avert his gaze. The final report on the creature that has been pursuing Nadelman—final for the reader, that is—witnesses the protagonist standing before a shop window in the night when he suddenly "[notices] a figure reflected in the [glass], ghostly in the dim light and intersected with the images of toys, games, and stuffed animals. For one crazy moment he [takes] the reflection for his own" (260). He then recognizes the god servant and flees into an Orthodox synagogue where he will wait for morning. The faces merge, it is clear, and the poem has proven prophetic. While not the sorcerers per se, both men create and unleash their demons. Neither is "crazy" beyond having recognized, quite late, the face of corruption born of privilege and the loss of a

4. Sorceries of Self-Negation: "Petey" and "Nadelman's God"

curiosity which, it is possible, aligns one with nature that is otherwise "inimical" to cultural and philosophical indifference.

"Nadelman's God" does not leave one feeling especially hopeful for the protagonist. The synagogue as a place of temporary respite notwithstanding; no religious institution is likely to help him given the trajectory he has paved for himself. When religious teacher G. I. Gurdjieff examines "intentional suffering," this is a different form of religiosity, born not of dogma or sacred architecture but of rigorous practice such as one might encounter in Zen Buddhism. A story such as Joyce Carol Oates' "Demon" offers more ambiguity than Klein's narratives where the individual psychology is concerned, thus complicating the notion of self-inflicted suffering. Here the "demon" has a dysfunctional family history, is identified as "not a demon-child but a pure good anxious loving child" only to catch sight of its "face floating in a mirror," whereupon "the demon has been released" (Oates, "Demon" 454). Specifically, the demon, a boy who grows into a man over the course of the short story, sees a pentagram in one of his eyes that has replaced in prominence a facial birthmark in the shape of a coiled snake. Everything about him screams "don't tread on me" despite his desire to belong. By the end, he has ripped the eye from its socket and observes angels embracing him, despite "his red-slippery mask of a face," to the point where, like Lovecraft's "outsider," he is able to join their ranks, potentially observable, "or a face like his, in a furious cloud" (456). It is impossible to defend the self-mutilation in light of the familial and social context of this "demon's" upbringing. That said, the "god" that he creates exhibits signs of otherworldliness; at the very minimum, he is characterized, repeatedly, as a "machine," one that "does not starve for what it does not know to name: *salvation*" (*ibid.*). A practice such as "intentional suffering" knows how to name salvation, the opposite of mechanical or automatic modes of being. Salvation may be understood as constituted by various forms of deterritorialization, or demythification, none of which register for the "demon" whose religious orientation appears to be horrifically fundamentalist in nature, the angelic abode of which would seem to have no other option than to be "furious."

To return to an especially captivating moment in *The Ceremonies*, when Rosie shows his true face to Carol in the muted light at the restaurant, it becomes rivetingly evident that the Old One is the embodiment of what Machen refers to as exceptionally "true evil." Rosie knows what

T.E.D. Klein and the Rupture of Civilization

he is; he embodies self-knowledge and is powerful in that awareness. Certain of Klein's protagonists, along with Oates' demon, on the other hand, exercise only a vague sense of themselves and the impact they have on others. They move through their lives more or less unconsciously, mechanically absorbing status quo prerogatives and ideological structures. As observed regarding Nadelman, "all gods [yield] before the implacable urgings of habit," at which point he returns to work following a disturbing visit to Huntoon, "his schedule unchanged, dutifully laboring..." (Klein "Nadelman's" 250). Klein is critical, then, of habits formed in the process of maturation, specifically those patterns that develop in accord with dominating, hegemonic forces that become interiorized, settle into the thinking and behavior of an individual, a community, and soon concretize to the degree that they are perceived as normative. Oates puts it this way: "to be away from what is familiar ... allows *something other* in. Or the *something other* has been inside you all along and until now you do not know" (*ibid.*). The "familiar" here might be conceived as innocence, or curiosity that may lead to insight, occult or otherwise, the loss or distancing of which creates fertile ground for territorialization. "Something other" is a symptom of adulteration in which the central modus operandi is reactivity rather than critical response; or, as Oates implies, one is always already territorialized and the process of deterritorialization is apt to be grisly. In the case of "Demon," as with Klein's narratives, the "*other*" is not necessarily culturally marginal or abject, but, on the contrary, an aggressive reinforcement of, albeit extreme, enmity and discrimination. It is the protagonist, such as Jeremy, who applies critical inquiry to otherness, be it in the form of sexual, religious, racial, or class difference, whom most successfully navigates territorializing forces while others perish under the weight of "habit." From this standpoint, horror is the "familiar" in so far as it is the infant, the child who must first come to terms with the perpetual otherness of a vast milieu—(ideally loving) parents and other people, geographies, sounds and visions—a progression that relies upon inquisitiveness and the probity of a necessarily curious past. Where critical horror distinguishes itself from the children's tale, of course, is in its intention to speak directly to the mature reader of crippling, authoritarian otherness with the intensity and brutality of a mirror's cold, unmentionable reflection.

CHAPTER 5

Goosebumps and the Haunting Conscience

The front cover blurb from the *New York Times Book Review* on my copy of *Dark Gods* reads, "A banquet for horror mavens." If Klein's general oeuvre is a banquet, complete with numerous, delicious courses, or layers of meaning, then this study is, in a manner of speaking, a series of speeches to celebrate his body of work and its potential impact on a public of "mavens." What is it about this relatively small collection of texts that warrants such attention? What makes Klein unique amidst an ever-growing field of genre writers? I would argue that it has something to do with emphasis on what he calls, in his extended essay *Raising Goosebumps for Fun and Profit*, "workaday horror" (36), the horror of the mundane, the average person in conflict with what appear to be supernatural forces. Of course, this average person, in the context of Klein's protagonists, tends to be white, male, and scholarly, but who better to terrorize than one who is socially advantaged? The marginalized receive quite enough brutality. Another way to put it is that Klein is invested in examining the real, the underlying social *and* occult realities that inform, provoke, manipulate, and, in some cases, destroy us as a consequence of participating in the rewards and discontents of civilization.

There is a curious tension in Klein's essay between the notions of horror as escapism and as an extension of malignant but common horrors in the everyday. At the beginning of his text, he refers to the genre's "medicinal effect" and, quoting Edmund Wilson, its quality that can "soothe us with the momentary illusions that the forces of madness and murder may be tamed and compelled to provide us with a mere dramatic entertainment" (2). He even references the now prevalent "roller coaster" analogy whereby "the pleasure of horror fiction depends upon the fun-

T.E.D. Klein and the Rupture of Civilization

damental unreality of the horror" (6). This view has been challenged, or amended, by numerous theoretical perspectives on why we crave horror, one of which includes Andrew Schopp's compelling analysis of *The Blair Witch Project* and the *Scream* franchise where he identifies what he calls the "safe space fallacy" that "assumes ... the horror consumer derives no pleasure from fear unless that fear is defused or lessened through the safety of narrative" ("Transgressing" 129). Though the cultural context of these films (and by extension, Schopp's argument) is separated by approximately two decades from Klein's work, the theorist's claim regarding "the safety of narrative" and films that "transgress" this safety in the form of critical horror certainly applies to the texts under consideration here. They all scrutinize "anxieties that our nation and culture are predicated upon a set of constructs that themselves provide merely an illusion of safety" (126). So when Klein speaks of narrative horror as "defanged, to be enjoyed in a spirit of play" (*Raising* 5), the sense that "we are not saved," from the conclusion of "The Events at Poroth Farm," to name one example, is stripped of meaning beyond its provocation of mere escapism. In this respect, S.T. Joshi's query seems entirely appropriate: "would any serious writer wish his work to be so 'defanged' that it would have no effect upon us after we put the book aside?" (*Modern* 98). And yet, Klein will eventually go on to reference the sublime as integral to a human condition that is otherwise submissive to the constraints of civilization, a sense of liminality that he equates with the "numinous," an emotional state that combines "fascination, terror, and religious awe when confronted by the otherworldly" (*Raising* 14). It as though he favors the safety of "play" over an experience of genuine fear while doing everything he can within the confines of his central narratives (and succeeding!) to foster the latter, as though a quality of wellbeing and enduring horror can somehow co-exist. I will address this beguiling prospect towards the end of the chapter.

Klein's argument becomes increasingly (and ostensibly) confused as it develops. He quotes Walter de la Mare on the imperative of horror generating "the gradual conviction that this workaday actuality of ours—with its bricks, its streets, its woods, its hills, its waters—may have queer and, possibly, terrifying holes in it" (29). There is an alignment between this conception of "actuality" and Shirley Jackson's bleak, alienated "absolute reality" in the form of Hill House and beyond, both of which

5. Goosebumps and the Haunting Conscience

point to the moment of Nadelman's creation "[punching] a single tiny hole in his universe." As this analysis has suggested, Klein's characters essentially co-create their monsters within and in more or less unconscious collusion with the limitations of civilized, American life. The holes are a result of both internal and external strife reflecting the degree to which critical horror, in response, must be "grounded [...] in reality" (33), so much so that "you don't have to travel to Transylvania to find the inspiration for a horror tale. In fact, you'd be better off staying at home. Chances are," Klein says cheekily, "you've got more than enough material already" (36). So where is the "play" in this ultimately acerbic critique of the real, that which manifests amply in the home, the forest, the fragmented self? Maybe there is something in the queerness of said holes, or to use more contemporary parlance, the queering of their inevitability by transforming or subjecting them to the dissection of horror narrative, that bridges the apparent gap between "play" and frightening realism. The campy (and for some, tremendously pleasurable) nature of certain horror tropes that has kept the genre from being taken seriously as literature and generally outside the literary canon is indeed playful at the same time that it is capable of producing satirical and searing, deeply disturbing criticism, as Klein's texts absolutely do.

Interrogating Actuality

The affinity between "workaday horror" and "workaday actuality" necessitates, among other things, an examination of actuality as it applies to the everyday, particularly in the American cultural climate that serves as the environment and atmosphere of Klein's narratives. The way de la Mare characterizes it is entirely phenomenological in terms of how a first-person relates to manufactured as well as natural objects; specifically, he proposes a kind of failed phenomenology, one whose porosity negates conventional association between individuals and the objects on which they set their attention, compromised as this attention might be in the age of omnipresent digital technology. Chapter one of this study has attempted to verify this approach, as both a precursor to and a methodology of horror. What remains is to consider how horror subverts actuality and, perhaps more important, how the latter subverts

T.E.D. Klein and the Rupture of Civilization

itself. Jacques Derrida scholar Jason Powell has paraphrased Derrida as claiming, at one point, that "the US is deconstruction in effect, it is what happens today ... because America is the place at which the West's tradition of exclusion is currently being undone and continued, the place at which the West of Europe has created both a satellite and a master for itself, an external mirror, which, like a simulacrum, is nonessential, and also as real as the original" (*Jacques* 97). The manner in which exclusivity is at once upheld and challenged is obvious, painfully so, to anyone who follows U.S. politics, at any given point in time, as is its status as a reflection of Europe, what it has been, what it is not, and what it is rapidly becoming. The U.S. is "nonessential" in the sense that it is always already in such tremendous cultural flux, that there is no real core, though its culture and the effects of its ideological formations, as played out in the lives of individuals and communities, are certainly real, lived, material actualities. But it is also a mirror to itself, a space where the Hegelian dialectic of thesis-antithesis-synthesis attempts to operate but ultimately fails to resolve in synthesis, where aporias punch divisive holes at every turn.[1] It is fascinating to note that despite his support and rich teaching experience in the U.S., Derrida, as Powell notes, finally turned back to Europe, becoming "ashamed of American arrogance and its lack of roots, its lack of a restraining, balancing memory of history and religious tolerance. Above all, its lack of tolerance" (98). Klein's own exasperation over such arrogance and ignorance should be readily apparent.

To be fair, no culture is completely bereft of arrogance or ignorant, ideological frameworks. The egoic tendencies inherent in the condition of being human guarantee disjunction, or holes to be metaphorically widened by critical analysis so as to expose and interrogate their depravity. Psychoanalytic theory has a great deal to say about why this is the case, as do certain religious traditions. As does Don DeLillo, throughout his oeuvre, and particularly via his protagonist in *Zero K*: "I maintain myself on the puppet drug of personal technology. Every touch of a button brings the neural rush of finding something I never knew and never needed to know until it appears at my anxious fingertips, where it remains for a shaky second before disappearing forever" (55). Contrary to its simulated infinitude, there is a danger of becoming arrogant and intolerant in relation to such technology. Its web casts a shadow world wide, much like Wagner's pentagram that is "miles [or continents] across." Performing

5. Goosebumps and the Haunting Conscience

the self online can generate self-absorption and the anxiety of the "neural rush" may lead to the intolerance to time itself, its varying speeds, its occasional disobedience, its intimacy with the mirrors of other people and death, its decomposition of all bodies. The many-faced screen stockpiles information for its users that bears little relation to what one who functions not necessarily off but between the grid(s) might call wisdom. The screen creates addicts, a wide world of depraved junkies.

As a "puppet drug," "personal technology" has a curious relationship with Derrida's elaboration on *différance* which Powell defines as "the absence within presentness" of language that is invariably "shadowy and trace-like, spectral," indicative of a "ghost reality" (*Jacques* 51). It is certainly too easy to link such terms to horror, and yet, their impact on how one occupies time, or to be more accurate, the auspices under which one fleshes out the everyday, is profound, and profoundly unsettling, especially for the individual whose relationship to time is dictated by digital simulacra of knowledge and intimacy. In an extended passage, Derrida develops the residual of his term:

> The movement of signification is possible only if each so-called "present" element, each element appearing on the scene of presence, is related to something other than itself, thereby keeping within itself the mark of the past element, and already letting itself be vitiated by the mark of its relation to the future element, this trace being related no less to what is called the future than to what is called the past, and constituting what is called the present by means of this very relation to what it is not: what it absolutely is not, not even a past or a future as a modified present ["Différance" 126–127].

In addition to the intricate commentary on the nature of discourse, this quote is striking as a reflection on the actuality of the "puppet drug"; how every "element" or piece of data not only finds meaning in relation to other data, and to the invasive process of exciting the "neural rush," but is immediately disassembled or "vitiated" as "what it absolutely is not"—which is a present from which one might draw what Derrida would surely be loathe to call immediate, originary wisdom, as opposed to the received, prefabricated wisdom of the Internet. There is, of course, "movement of signification" in the everyday. People communicate, face to face, or digitally. Ideas are exchanged, for better and for worse. But each of these exchanges is subject to compromise by the interpellative nature of language and "personal technology" and thus serves to constitute the self that might misrecognize itself as liberated through an infinitude of options, sites, images, sound bites, friends. On the contrary, it is the self that is essentially vitiated in this never-ending, holographic miasma of information.

The "trace-like" reality of the "something" one never knew and one never needed to know is "ghostly" precisely because it is instantly absent the moment it becomes present, both on the screen and, quite possibly, in the mind of the average consumer of "personal technology." It leaves a trace of itself, a ghostly presence that can only submit to and amalgamate with the blitzkrieg of the next something and the something after that, an ever-fading "element" of the signifying chain that is contemporary digital compulsion. Such is the nature of capitalism, as it happens, the beast that creates needs and leaves, more often than not, a spectral absence, the mere memory of having been temporarily satisfied that emerges from the past and attempts, in keeping with consumerist drives, to complete a future. An example of capitalist enterprise constructing the "ghost reality," as I am employing the phrase here, may be found in the current fascination with Digital Humanities (DH) and the tremendous sums of money supporting its many projects in an age of declining humanities (lower student enrollments being especially significant here). Humanities departments perceive a way to remain relevant by letting software locate and compile pertinent data, by producing digital installations that recreate a distant past, or by ensuring that no student gets out of a humanities degree without having fed his or her appetite for screen time. Granted creative potentialities (which generally fare considerably better in the hands of experienced artists, as opposed to desperate or bandwagon academics), what tends to be lost (or hauntingly absent) in this enterprise is sophisticated erudition. In catering to generations imprisoned by virtual stimuli, or simply ease of consumption, the DH agenda reifies the apparent obsolescence of rigorous philosophical engagement. Does this assessment suggest that digital civilization is less directed by aggression and more by mere ennui, or intolerance for assiduous contemplation and scholarship? Not at all, because the intentions of DH are by and large aggressively competitive and insidious; they are, in short, driven by power and money. And like so many cultural manifestations motivated by this twin engine, the results may range from amusingly insignificant to bizarrely mediocre.

5. Goosebumps and the Haunting Conscience

Powell argues that "Derrida's new Platonism calls one to leave the cave, and to come to a world as it is, and always will be, genuinely spectral and phantasmatic. The ghost appears and disappears as it wants to, but is never localizable, never inhabits a place or time, but is between life and death, like their in-between, yet neither" (*Jacques* 81). Perhaps there is something supernatural in Derrida via Powell's ability to have so astutely characterized 2014's *It Follows* long before this film appeared to reinvigorate the cinematic horror genre. The "it" that follows is non-localized, only vaguely corporeal, is present of its own mysterious volition, is neither dead nor alive—quite far from the gritty reality of venereal disease that also follows the contaminated body (by the scarring of memory if not by permanent habitation) and, without obvious precautions, down a line of other bodies, other selves. Despite this reality, the metaphorical conceptualization of the "it" supplies a far more powerful statement about one's inevitable entrance into the actuality of desire, sexual or otherwise. The world is "genuinely spectral and phantasmatic" in that its countless impressions, whether discursive, visual, sensational, or emotional, accumulate to form and inform a self that is always in flux, constitutionally porous and "haunted" by vitiating relations to time.[2] This is the actuality towards which Derrida points; its realization (in every sense of that word) offering an ironic quality of liberation from the delusion of static being, of monolithic, and thus misrecognized identity, and the egoism that might fuel such enterprises as the reduction of humanities scholarship to the screens of digital fanfare.

Film adaptations of Lovecraft's work are notoriously poor.[3] Klein's own foray into cinema, in screenwriting collaboration with Dario Argento on the latter's *Trauma* (1993), likewise warrants little attention. It lacks most of the visual and sonic strangeness of Argento's earlier work on such films as *Suspiria* and *Deep Red* and there is very little if any indication of Klein's literary style in the screenplay. That said, the film's focus on the titular subject matter makes it relevant to the present discussion and to critical horror's manner of leading the reader/viewer out of the Platonic cave of mere shadows and into the paradoxically actual, spectral world where traumas small and large become imprinted on the body/mind and may "follow" without any discernible anchor in a conventional comprehension of time or space. *Trauma* explores parent/child relations, between both a murderous, occult-preoccupied mother and her relatively innocent teenaged daughter and the equally curious dynamic between the daughter and a thirty-year-old man attempting to help and possibly sleep with her. Its "movement of signification," then, revolves around relationality, revenge (for the mother's son, lost to decapitation at birth), and the occult (she is a medium). Hyperbolic though it may be, the film succeeds in blending the supernatural with the mundane, the actual and the phantasmatic world, which are, at the levels of discourse, lived psychology, and critical horror, one and the same. It would be neither an Argento film nor a Klein text without both horrific exaggeration and some investment in the quotidian; trauma being, unfortunately, inherent in the latter. Horror performs trauma, aestheticises it, shifts predictable contours of the beautiful, and, at its best (which excludes *Trauma*), invites consideration of what might lie on the margins of the text given its revelation(s). As Della Pollock explains, "Performance is a promissory act, not because it can promise possible change but because it catches its participants—often by surprise—in a contract with possibility: with imagining what might be, could be, should be" ("Introduction" 2). The general aesthetic of horror, of course, necessarily relies on some degree of "surprise," but ideally with an intimation of becoming, for better and often for worse. Signing up for a "contract" with Klein's particular actuality offers precisely the possibility of broadening one's sense of oneself and of both the lowercase and capitalized other: the human being with whom one shares a bed, professional space, a planet, and the general alterity that is life and death.

Evocations of Happiness

Powell sums up Derrida's position on Marxism as "a ghostly system [that] will never be real, but will always haunt the world, as its conscience" (*Jacques* 195). A full-blown Marxist economic system may never materialize in the U.S., though the first two decades of the 21st century have seen it appear nonetheless as a shadowy and increasingly mainstream reposte to the vulgarity of far right, ideological absorption into and glorification of a distended capitalism. Or maybe Tea Party politics is an inevitable reaction to what most progressives would identify, for

5. Goosebumps and the Haunting Conscience

lack of a better word, as progress. Time and sequence begin to lose their credibility when considering chickens, eggs, and other dialectical relationships. What is relatively clear, however, is that the underside of seemingly concrete ontological formations that undergird identities and hegemonic power structures is haunted by conscience, however buried or camouflaged it may be in the culture, the person. This must be so because the individual, ever seeking his or her happiness, often subtly or overtly at the expense of others' well-being, or indulged in the egoic satisfaction of nihilism, belongs to community. Western civilization provides ample buffers to the probability that thriving on another's misery is ultimately generative of one's own desolation, but the sense of a shared humanity is there, in the shadows, and sometimes in the haunted house of a person, a tribe, the absolutely real that signifies both a common ground of alienation and the fact that such disaffection is partly, at least, a product of human will or the lack thereof.

"How do you recognize a ghost?" Derrida asks. "By the fact that it does not recognize itself in a mirror" (*Spectres* 156). A number of Klein's characters are terrified of this prospect, of beholding their ghostly pallor. "There is a mirror," Derrida adds, and "amid the commodity form is also this mirror, but since all of a sudden it no longer plays its role, since it does not reflect back the expected image, those who are looking for themselves can no longer find themselves in it. Men no longer recognize in it the *social* character of their *own* labour" (155). One can no longer observe the community in the self, the reason for one's being and one's labor, finding instead a monster, a ghost of a man or woman that labors under the delusion of unqualified singularity, or self-containment within the confines of a family or other unit that is ingurgitated into the self, absorbed into the "self-same" body, my identity, my impossible existentialism, my fear of being tread upon. Commodity-form haunts a person, like an object in a mirror that is closer than it appears, by instilling her or him with its own expiration date, but an expiration that will endure as a phantasm of use-value, neither in nor out of time, neither alive nor dead. "The commodity thus haunts the thing, its spectre is at work in use-value" (*Spectres* 151), Derrida asserts, the deadly implication being that the person is interpellated by a prescribed sense of value, a use that supersedes the immense value of an active, creative, compassionate conscience. The ghost has delegated his or her multiplicity to the exploita-

T.E.D. Klein and the Rupture of Civilization

tion of a prefabricated singularity whose death is at once prefigured and imminent, if not immanent, as reflected in the mirror image.

Critical horror is hauntological, to use Derrida's term, in the sense that its revelations, its ghosts, its cosmic foreboding, its mirror images all function as typically undisclosed conditions of the self and the great, consuming tapestry that is its home in civilization. It evokes a dialectic of fear based on past experience or knowledge of the past (Mrs. Poroth and Absalam Troet/Rosie/the Old One; Father Pistachio and the white people; George and his "Petey"; Nadelman and his God) but also situates an originary future of personal or cosmic devastation in the face of its reader. Another way of putting this is to say that it places the responsibility of the present, the future, and even the past in the lap of a given reader whose own monstrosity may surface and become a target of investigation. Critical horror evokes conscience and it does so with perverse pleasure, but not the moralizing variety of a conservative self-righteousness. It speaks to a gleeful hauntology as the precondition for ontology. Horror is fun, making nightmarish fun out of being. Hence the pleasure, the happiness even, that may emerge from its haunting, the recognition that conscientiousness in its myriad forms, that will likely create challenges and upsets in the lived life, is a necessary and favorable element of actuality. George may be far from happy and Nadelman's literal haunting, his abandoned curiosity, may have dire consequences, but the reader is led to relish these revelations.

Derrida tells us "the commodity, *is not so simple* (a warning that will elicit snickers from all the imbeciles, until the end of time, who never believe anything, of course, because they are so sure that they see what is seen, everything that is seen, only what is seen)" (*Spectres* 149–150). Nor is horror simple. Nor are people, communities, civilization, everything that nourishes and makes horror relevant, simple or reducible to sound bites or bumper stickers. Nor is happiness as uncomplicated as an "imbecile," or one on any side of the political or economic spectrum who is bereft of critical self-examination, might believe it to be. Is DH simply corrupt by its very nature? Might it be productively performing the traditional close reading it tends to despise on "other" texts, texts that may be intellectually valuable or, at least, that provoke critical inquiry? It is entirely possible. Is DH in fact the spectre of relatively traditional scholarship? No, the obverse is the case—the care put into close

5. Goosebumps and the Haunting Conscience

reading of *whole* texts is the ghostly non-presence haunting digitally-based scholarship that is always already in a process of dying, or being updated, which amounts to the same thing. If any question arises around this death, one might consider how long one's last smart phone lasted. Doubtless, some close readings are performed for the sake of adding a notch on a curriculum vitae, but they are rarely completely facile, and they need have nothing to do with technology beyond that of the book and the pen, pencil, or highlighter. Such scholarship yields an extensive, personal, exploratory process that is less interested in data analysis or reviving simulated phantasms of something called history and more invested in the propinquity or the immersiveness of a text. It is immersion that consigns value to scholarship and that critical horror absolutely demands for the sake of knowledge, liminal thrills, and polymorphous pleasures.

Klein's *Raising Goosebumps for Fun and Profit* title may be tongue in cheek but it makes a number of important claims that complicate "the How's and Why's of Horror," as the subtitle has it. His "banquet" reveals humor and irony around the notion of horror's profit motive (of course we all know that a select few of the genre's writers turn a healthy profit, cueing Augé's injunction on not "ignoring what [capitalism] does best"), though most importantly, it foregrounds horror as at once salutary and evocative, as this study has made clear, of challenging but promissory insights into the mundane. Critical horror may excel in the "taking of heaven by storm" but it does so with a kind of felicity. As one Lovecraft protagonist notes, "I experienced convulsions of fright. But that fright was so mixed with wonder and alluring grotesqueness that it was almost a pleasant sensation" ("Lurking" 17). For his part, to Freud's explanation of the uncanny ("that class of the terrifying which leads back to something long known to us, once very familiar" [Klein, Raising 10]) and George Satayana's hauntological claim that "real ghosts are [...] reverberations of the past" (*ibid.*), Klein responds with numerous commentators on the "medicinal effect" (2) of "pleasing terror," "delightful horror," and "fearful joy" (4). He considers the prospect that "a night cleansed of spooks turns out to be an unnerving, a discomposingly empty, place" (8), an actuality depleted of becoming and conjuration. Nadelman's example, doomed as it is, gives a sense of what it might mean to conjure before the fading of youth takes hold. In exploring his initial teenage forays into evocation, he comes to the conclusion that "he hadn't realized that his ideas had been germinating for so long" (Klein, "Nadelman's" 221); and mature these ideas certainly do. Or later, and more to the point, he arrives at the conclusion that "he [has] given the god life in the very act of naming it" (244). A question that may arise for the reader, then, regards the degree to which he or she remains capable of conjuring, of becoming something new, something productively, joyfully monstrous or subversive.

In spite of what is often his powerful adherence to the "final hours of gloom," Klein seems to favor a quality of happiness, or at least the happy resolution. Jeremy finishes reading Wilhelm Meinhold's "The Amber Witch" and muses, "would that all lives had such happy endings" (Klein, "Events" 331). Even in the wake of the events at Poroth farm, he "[remains], despite all that's happened, an optimist" (310). Klein himself "preferred [as editor of Twilight Zone] tales of a milder, more sentimental sort to the mailbags full of *contes cruels*, and [remains] to this day a sucker for happy endings" (*Raising* 27) and would probably align himself with Jeremy in criticizing Maturin's *Melmoth the Wanderer* for "[wanting] you to hate" ("Events" 319).[4] Apart from writer's block, Klein's devotion and great insight into the genre suggest that horror is integral to his own happiness and satisfaction; that a balance of critical commentary and literary pleasure serves as the primary engine of horror's evocations, as opposed to the barely concealed confessional of a sadist or misanthropist, a mere egotist whose infantile misidentifications continue to pose a severe problem before the mirror, and most likely, for others unfortunate enough to encounter this image.

With a few exceptions, including "The Events at Poroth Farm," Klein's *Reassuring Tales* collection, in the view of this writer, lacks the dynamism and enchantment of his major works. One such variation is "Well-Connected," the story of a couple on holiday at an old inn. Philip's mission, aside from a lovely few days with Margaret in the off-season, is to spend some time with his son Tony at a nearby private school. Before the latter can occur, the couple meets a man, Laszlo, who cajoles them into following him to swim in the indoor pool of a luxurious estate owned by a Mr. Hagendorn. Margaret has had a series of dreams about a nefarious "black man" whom she will eventually encounter, alone with Laszlo in the hills (Philip has stayed behind to await his son), and face

5. Goosebumps and the Haunting Conscience

the distinct possibility of being sacrificed. There are relatively conventional moments of foreboding, for example, when Philip has the realization that a phone call overheard between Laszlo and Mr. Hagendorn has been held without a telephone, just after his having discovered that the estate burned down in the 1930s. The "black man" has been a victim of said fire, charred rather than ethnically "marked," but a sinister, Lovecraftian trope nonetheless. As with a number of Klein's stories, the male protagonist is presumably upper middle class and, ostensibly like Mr. Hagendorn, "well-connected."

Where the story diverges from previous texts, however, is in the fact that Philip's privilege is not a target as much as his humanity is put on trial and emerges victorious. In what is perhaps the most sentimental moment in Klein's oeuvre, Philip is speaking to the stereotypically blasé teenager when Tony suddenly requests that his father read him a story when they meet. "Philip [feels] an unexpected rush of affection so strong it [embarrasses] him" and he assures Tony that he will "always have time for that" (Klein, "Well-Connected" 80). It is a remarkable moment in the context of Klein's work given its unembellished but emotive display of affection, as opposed to the paternalism one might expect from such a dynamic. This quality will come to define Philip by the conclusion when, not unlike the heroic Jeremy jumping through a wall of fire to save Carol, the former will charge through the hills to, it can be assumed, save Margaret from the clutches of the enigmatic black man and Laszlo. In other words, Philip exemplifies selflessness despite his privilege, leaving a shared life ahead, "days later and far away," a memorable story "to tell his son," and for the reader, the experience of having been brought to but ultimately "snatched back from the abyss while the other [goes] to meet his master alone" (92). If critical horror can be said to be "medicinal" and "homeopathic" (*Raising* 5), here lies the evidence of such features. It dangles one over an abyss in a liminal process of coming face to face with the sublime only to wrench one out before the ceremony turns into death. And even when it drops us into that cavern, or that inferno, that relational hell, it does so with a knowing wink and a sense that the sophisticated reader will benefit from what Eliot calls, in a different context, the "burning, burning, burning, burning" ("Wasteland" 46) of purgatorial salvation. Something called love triumphs and evil is left to its own malignant isolationism.

T.E.D. Klein and the Rupture of Civilization

Malignant may be a fair way to characterize the adopted philosophy (inherited, really, from his friend Howard) of the narrator in "Black Man with a Horn," his pessimistic outlook of "futilitarianism," though in keeping with Klein's general literary manner, the pessimism is qualified by a playful sense of humor here. Granted the decidedly unfunny doom that falls upon certain of Klein's characters, including a man and his child neighbor aboard a plane that, as of "Magic Carpet's" (another story from Klein's *Reassuring Tales*) final line, "[falters], [stops] dead, and [plummets] like a stone" (56). In this instance, the relation between adult and child could be the ill-omened (and real-invested) underbelly of the tender and, one assumes, relatively enduring relationship between father and son in "Well-Connected." But the "homeopathy" of horror is never far from Klein's proverbial pen, or his cultural mirror. Nor does "futilitarianism" quite describe a contemporary, competing vision of pessimism advocated by Eugene Thacker in his compelling *In the Dust of This Planet*, though the category of the human is ultimately presumed insignificant at best; insignificant from the essentially subject-less perspective of the Other, this "hideous," "hidden world," as Thacker puts it, "a blank, anonymous world that is indifferent to human knowledge, much less to our all-too-human wants and desires" (*In the Dust* 53–54). He goes on to speak of this world's "impersonal 'resistance' to the human *tout court*" (54), his many references to unrelenting global terrorism and climate change (that would appear to be the governing forces of daily life) bolstering the definitiveness of the "*tout court*." The overlap with Freudian and critical theory's general purview of the self and its communities is readily apparent in terms of "all-too-human wants and desires." On the other hand, his notion of "cosmic pessimism" that undoubtedly resonates with certain Kleinian narrative developments is finally a *projection* of cosmic nothingness and indifference, as opposed to a focus on the material self and its concomitant psychology that is so elegantly elucidated by a figure such as the 13th-century Zen monk Dōgen, whom Thacker seems to revere without consideration of the former's rich insights. Theorizing cosmology comes across in *In the Dust of This Planet* as a fascinating, erudite (and, I would argue, important) way of filling time, or books, to the degree that (Western) civilization is in dire need of rethinking and resituating to meaning. The various forms of mysticism Thacker explores, however, are essentially oriented toward

5. Goosebumps and the Haunting Conscience

collapsing or stepping outside of time for the sake of developing the kind of conscious attention that knows how to rest, and thus to remain vital in, the lived life, be it one of self-negation or otherwise. Klein is no mystic in the context of his fiction, but he is all-too-aware, with other writers of critical horror, including Jackson, Shelley, Oates, and Perkins-Gilman, to name a few, that "the demon is inseparable from a process of demonization" (quoted, Thacker 25), a process that may have cosmic reverberations but one that most definitely enacts a "workaday" intentionality on the face of this dusty planet, in the midst of quotidian, struggling, human beings.

In addition to struggle, humans (even, and in some cases especially, mystics) manage to locate pleasure, humor, laughter—happiness—and occasionally do so without jettisoning compassion. A final Woody Allen reference: in his film *Play It Again, Sam* (1972), protagonist Allan Felix ventures to an art museum to find a date and happens upon a lone woman in front of a Jackson Pollock. When he asks what meaning she finds in the painting, she replies with a litany of claims indicative of "cosmic pessimism" concerning "the negativeness of the universe," "the hideous, lonely emptiness of existence," and "a black, absurd cosmos." When he asks what she is doing Saturday night, she confesses to a date with suicide. Allan's next line is a jewel of dark comedy: "What about Friday night?" "Cosmic Pessimism" does not address pleasure, much less humor or happiness. But perhaps more importantly, it lacks Klein's sense of relationality's consequence in confronting what Thacker calls the "unground" (140), the indifferent abyss of Otherness.[5] Allan yearns for affection and belonging (and sex), for the strength of companionship, qualities of life that hardly preclude death and suffering but which demand a particular selflessness, a paradoxically enriching selflessness when undertaken consciously and conscientiously. In militating against optimism, in or out of horror narrative, it is as though an ideological (cosmic) pessimism is ascribing to the mandate against belonging and selflessness (and the happiness such qualities can invoke, especially in sexual congress) commonly fostered by the very fundamentalism it repudiates. It can appear that the cosmic pessimist is more aligned with a doomed and dour Mrs. Poroth and less with a Jeremy Freirs (who, at the every minimum, gets the girl, as they say, in the novel). In an ironic shift, we might return briefly now to James, the one who is so "goddamned labored" (and requires a largely rewarding labor from the reader), for an additional perspective on getting the girl or boy, on the centrality, the potentiality, and indeed, the horror of human relations as they contribute to or severely detract from the lived life.

Henry James' "The Beast in the Jungle" is neither comedy nor horror, but much of its language speaks to both a sense of non-being, of the world, of the self, and to a peculiarly Lovecraftian unknown, unmentionable, at the core of a man's life. Of course, Klein's Jeremy is right; the language is often worked over to a point of obscurity, though James' skill and insight give him, and by extension the reader, access to extraordinary nuance in human relations and individual psychology. The following passage is a case in point, revealing as it does the subtlety of intimacy between protagonist John Marcher and his friend:

> he wore a mask painted with the social simper, out of the eyeholes of which there looked eyes of an expression not in the least matching the other features. This the stupid world, even after years, he had never more than half discovered. It was only May Bartram who had, and she achieved, by an art indescribable, the feat of at once—or perhaps it was only alternately—meeting the eyes from in front and mingling her own vision, as from over his shoulder, with their peep through the apertures [H. James "Beast" 315].

An existential man, essentially, emotionally removed from the world, a "stupid," distracted world that exercises little power of observation and attention, and a woman who has mastered the indescribable art of selflessness required for "mingling" one's own vision with another. Unfortunately, John is far from selfless; he is haunted by "the sense of being kept for something rare and strange, possibly prodigious and terrible, that [is] sooner or later to happen to [him]" (309). The key component of their relationship is the fact that May understands the nature of John's haunting, the "thing" (310) that will crush him, and they spend the entirety of their adult lives, in addition to pursuing platonic pleasures, pondering and discoursing on "the beast in the jungle" (313). When May eventually dies from a blood-related illness, and without informing John of her insight into his lifelong condition, he is melancholy but stoic. "No passion had ever touched him," the narrator observes. "He had survived and maundered and pined, but where had been *his* deep ravage?" (338), he wonders as a consequence of "the great vagueness" (323) at the core of his existence.

5. Goosebumps and the Haunting Conscience

During a visit to the cemetery, John encounters another man hovering over a grave, clearly distraught, feeling something, and when the latter leaves his station and meets John's eyes, the something becomes arrestingly and tragically mutual. The man looks at him "with an expression like the cut of a blade" (337) and John suddenly sees, "in pale horror ... that *she* was what he [has] missed" (339). His ongoing teetering on the edge of his own personal "unground" has blinded him to the option of productive, selfless relationality. He is left only to contemplate "the escape [that] would have been to love her; then, *then* he would have lived. *She* had lived—who could say now with what passion?—since she had loved him for himself; whereas he had never thought of her ... but in the chill of his egotism and the light of her use" (339). The narrative closes with John weeping and throwing himself on her grave, the real horror, outside even of death, being the fact of an entirely preventable tragedy via the cracking open of the self and, pedestrian as it may sound, loving another for himself or herself. And yet there is nothing prosaic about self-effacement in relation to another (or others) who reciprocates or learns from a comparable magnanimity. John's only real victory by the end of the story lies in his having stared into the mirror of another and witnessed the "thing," his true face, as knife-sharp as his ego is cold.

What is perhaps lost, then, in Thacker's many absorbing and inspiring reference points is a groundedness in *why* examination of the "unground" is important, beyond the very real catastrophes of terrorism and encroaching climate change. In bridging the mundane and the supernatural, critical horror (and its extension of critical analysis) is concerned with precisely this question and offers, at its Kleinian best, an answer that removes one from the fetishism of projected indifference and heralds a humanism without the bourgeois human, one that accounts for material humanity and the centrality of human relations.[6] More specifically, it provides a series of responses in the form of ceremonies the intention of which is invariably to put the calculating, misidentifying, presumptive, fortified ego on trial with the hopes of it being at once entertained, educated, and, quite possibly, annihilated. The aim, contrary to Klein's own admission and, to a large degree, his practice, is not to "defang" horror. Rather, it is to add to its mouth of razor teeth so as to make the liminal, and productive, self-effacement all the more effective. From here, one might begin to grasp the depth of the "beast in the jungle" and the fact that it is always immediately present, not as a "surfeit of being" (*After* 217), as Terry Eagleton notes, but as a radical, subversive phantasm that haunts the ego, its recognition being a step towards "deep ravage" and diminishing the selfishness that would fail to embrace one's aptitude for remedial intimacy in its many, sometimes horrifying stripes.

Other Ceremonies

But regarding redemption, or an Eliotesque "burning, burning, burning, burning," let us not mistake the potentiality of salvation advocated in this study with Christian purgatory. Critical horror does not condemn or even necessarily conceive of sin; rather, it examines unconsciousness, cultural ignorance, and injustice at the same time that it celebrates abjection. In his analysis of the "how's and why's of horror," Klein evokes "the numinous," an "emotional state [that] is a combination of fascination, terror, and religious awe when confronted by the otherworldly" (*Raising* 14), and that is analogous to "religious humility" (15), but what is crucial here is the particular orientation of this state. It does not seek to bolster the self on oceanic waves of floating bliss, an ego informed by self-serving, self-congratulating pessimism, or smug, sticky, entitled optimism. On the contrary, "the subject perceiving this numinous emotion experiences a sense of 'creature consciousness,' of being 'dust and ashes,' and of sheer self-deprecation" (*ibid.*). "The numinous" that Klein considers indicative of horror's experiential platform, then, pertains to selflessness. As such it is more Deleuzean than orthodox Christian. Deleuze argues that "individuals find a real name for themselves ... only through the harshest exercise in depersonalization, by opening themselves up to the multiplicities everywhere within them, to the intensities running through them" (*Negotiations* 6). "Multiplicities" and "intensities" are the living material of critical horror, the inevitable aporias and extremities of a self as reflected in an aesthetic echo of that self in crisis, or ceremony. "Finding a name" for oneself means facing and coming out on the other side of that crisis, stronger for it but fully aware that the universe is replete with holes, fissures that may be as evil as one makes them.

Critical horror inspires a multitude of ceremonies that shift the ter-

5. Goosebumps and the Haunting Conscience

rain of personality. The most obvious is surely tucking in under the sheets or in a comfortable chair with a story or (the) novel by T.E.D. Klein. There is silence in your room, or perhaps quiet, mildly threatening music as soundtrack. Jeremy's example may find a parallel with cobwebs in your window corner, a shelf of other books, the lineage to which the Klein text is a robust and commanding contributor, or a figure standing still and menacing beyond the window, staring at you with the intrusive noise of an unspeaking, quiescent, and maybe unspeakable, "creature consciousness." Another ceremony may look like the weekly drive to the market for food where you pass a home proudly flying the Gadsden flag. The occupants admonish you not to tread on them but in a near comical turn of events, you had no intention of doing so in the first place. So you react, if so inclined, in the cavity of your thoughts, in rebellion against the dumbest form of arrested development. And then, to rise to the occasion of the ceremony, you assume responsibility for this reactionary mode of being and attempt to minimize the judgment, which proves exceedingly difficult. What is the image in the mirror amidst that sanctimony? Or another: you gather with your students for a film screening, with those who are not otherwise engaged and find cinema on a laptop abominable, that increasingly rare breed, eager to observe how they respond. The lights are turned off, the chatter begins to die down as the credits roll (the best horror films paralyze us as early as the opening credits, as in the original *The Texas Chainsaw Massacre* or *The Shining*), and tension builds steadily for approximately two hours. You observe their discomfort (the incessant screaming in TCM, the horrific transformation of Jack Torrance that gets under their skin) and wonder how their nighttime walk to the dorm will be, how resonate the crisis of self might feel as it comes alive in flickering shadows, a harsh and haunting exercise in reconfiguring the person. Only to reconvene the next day to discuss what they have seen, heightening, ideally, rather than diffusing the horror's impact. You keep it alive in the classroom and potentially beyond, that menacing figure, the horror, whose gun is pointed at you every minute of the life, as at an ignorant grandmother in some unholy, southern, American "backwoods life." A trajectory from screening to screaming to the relatively ebullient seminar room, culminating in a pedagogical ceremony the experience of which constitutes what any conscientious teacher of critical horror would surely identify as genuine privilege.

CHAPTER 6

"We are not saved": Critical Horror Today

What is today? What does that mean when the relativity of time encroaches upon one's sense of self and the temporal—and by extension, the cultural—context in which one operates on a moment-to-moment basis? At what point does today become an epoch? When exactly did modernism tip over into postmodernism, or are these categories still overlapping, in time, in the quagmire of competing values and lifestyles? Is the age of Puritanism really dead and buried? Is the individual who thinks compulsively of a past event, traumatic or otherwise, or of some event to come, occupying today? Is inhabiting a given moment of today, the immediate now, an antidote to trauma and neurosis? What might be the utility of contemplating horror both in and out of time?

The today of Klein's oeuvre is generally late 70s and early 80s New York City (and surrounding areas), before gentrification, when "sleeze" was a typical middle-America ascription to the city's face and the upper classes could still revel in a quickly fading but productive bohemia, or just get lost in the bright lights big city of cocaine and other diversions. This is not to say that such qualities and activities are extinct, that Sarr Poroth would not find the devil in every crevice of 21st-century Manhattan. But even he, if given the opportunity to view something other than "offensively ignorant programs," would have to admit that the digital sheen and inferior acting of Woody Allen's films since, perhaps, the mid-90s at the latest, do not compare to the golden age of the director's elegant, intellectually-engaging, and quite funny films that emerged precisely when Klein was well on his way to becoming a best-selling horror writer. This decline arguably mimics the sterilization of NYC. The "town" of Allen's Isaac (from *Manhattan* [1979]), who proclaims in dramatic fashion that "it was his town and it always would be," is relatively

6. "We are not saved": Critical Horror Today

white-washed and belongs to a different America in the 21st century, one that has even less time for challenging, thought-provoking cinema; for Bergman, Tarkosvky, Antonioni, Godard, Truffaut, directors whose work would have been shown to adoring, critical audiences at the Bleecker Street Cinema, now long since defunct.

That said, what continues to captivate, to freeze people in time, in moments of time, and in most every town, is horror. In horror's immediate provocation of gripping fear, or slow motion dread, for that matter, the genre stands, on one level at least, as a radical departure from the fundamentalist religion that Klein critiques in "The Events at Poroth Farm" and *The Ceremonies*. Though Frank Kermode identifies Christianity as the "most anxious" of major religious traditions, one that "has laid the most emphasis on the terror of death" (quoted, Strozier, *Apocalypse* 5), its fundamentalist varieties are, ideologically speaking, thoroughly focused on an apocalyptic future, as opposed to a present in which such terror might produce an exploratory sense of interiority and critical self-examination. One fundamentalist interviewee in Charles Strozier's illuminating ethnography, *Apocalypse: On the Psychology of Fundamentalism in America*, goes so far as to say that "psychiatry has destroyed us" in so far as "all our men are on the couch … wimps and helpless beings who could never repel a Russian invasion" (128). Analysis of the self is viewed here as lacking in the virility and machismo necessary to defend territory against those who might tread on one. To place this perspective in the context of M.R. James, the crown must remain in its proper, unexamined place, for curiosity shall breed only death and contamination by abject otherness. No matter that the inevitable anxiety born of such paranoia is precisely what psychological or psychoanalytic analysis seeks to ameliorate, not in a distant, mystical (if not mythical) future, but in the ongoing series of "nows" that constitute everyday experience of a life, fundamentalist or otherwise.

Through numerous interviews conducted over a five-year period, Strozier observed the common trait (and acute anxiety) of "broken narratives" having fueled, in part, the general turn toward fundamentalism. Such narratives, he asserts, "profoundly distort time.… The past is separated off, to be remembered only as an object lesson. You recall to forget." "The present, in turn," he continues, "is profoundly degraded and full of evil. God is furious, and about to end it all." And further: "There

T.E.D. Klein and the Rupture of Civilization

is no redemption in human purpose. Culture is rotten. The only hope lies in the mythical transformation of the future, in the remaking of the world during the millennium [Strozier's interviews were conducted in the late 1980s and early 90s] and the ultimate salvation in heaven after the final judgment," an orientation that "[reflects] the extent of trauma in the lives of fundamentalists" (45). Preoccupied with dark, apocalyptic imagery though it may be, this relationship to time, as a product of trauma, differs from aesthetic horror in its codification and closure of time, as opposed to the latter's collapse into a potentially revealing present that horror characteristically provokes, even as fundamentalism foregrounds the mundane as an antagonistic fount of evil. Like so many religious communities, then, fundamentalism is replete with damaged individuals. And yet, unlike traditions that extol the virtues of unqualified compassion and self-exploratory praxis, the fundamentalist purview, under the weight of a degraded present and an angry god, is likely to add further layers of psychological injury and dysfunction rather than enrichment and reparation. Time matters very much indeed in the many expressions of horror, be they critical and aesthetic or fundamentally delusional, embittered, and spiteful.[1]

Unlike critical horror, Christian evangelicalism, as an overwhelming consequence of its fetishizing a phantastical future, has little to no investment in social responsibility. From Strozier's standpoint, the notion of "the rapture lifts the faithful out of end time destruction" and thus "contributes to a tendency to opt out of involvement in political and social matters and into a privatized, separatist world" (120). It seems, even with a publication date of 1994, this argument is neglecting the "involvement" in the voting process that would have assumed a new fervor (in the form of the Moral Majority) as Strozier was preparing and executing his research and that has, of course, become a powerful force in the American political landscape of the 21st century. Nevertheless, he brings insight not only to separatist impulses but to the fact that there are exceptions and variations in social responsibility based on race and class. For example, he speaks of one Harlem-based reverend who both keeps up with current events and is "highly engaged and connected with life *now* precisely because of the imminent threat of collective death" (my italics 137). In general, there is a greater sense of social responsibility on the parts of those believers who are relatively marginalized versus

6. "We are not saved": Critical Horror Today

those who are not, as well as more urgency around the rapture for those who are less privileged. Likewise, attention given to the violence of the apocalypse is more or less graphic depending on class and gender, women and the wealthy tending to limit their focus on explicit carnage as opposed to uneducated males who were, in interview, often observed as reveling in the violence of endism. One commonality, however, is the sense that for fundamentalists in general, "nonbelievers are dispensable. If they intrude in the believer's world, the psychological conditions exist to make it possible for believers to accommodate violence toward nonbelievers" (90); "accommodate" being a fascinating term here. We might recall Freud's notion of aggression as an "instinctual endowment" rather than an act of consciously chaperoning violence into being. Perhaps "accommodate" as compliance with or harboring violence is the intention. What is certain is the fact that some ideologies abet violence more than others. Saar Poroth's education provides him with enough intelligence to treat Jeremy with respect despite his literalist beliefs, while others of his community are prepared to lynch the outsider.

What is equally clear is the degree to which biblical inerrancy and literalism, as a move "away from metaphor" and modernism, "[define] the religious experience of the fundamentalist" (95). Whether this move results in the support of bigoted, right wing politicians and ideological structures or incomprehensible terrorist attacks, the literalist proclivity is doomed to ignorance, a claim whose harshness is essentially corroborated by the many shades of violence that befall the psychology, the social relations, and most likely the body of one who fails to grasp the polysemous nature of language. Fundamentalists may succeed in evading modernity on the level of lifestyle choices, though it is arguably far more difficult to escape the insights of postmodernism, those that expose the cavernous and indeterminate quality of language, its tendencies to negate itself, to overshadow itself and reveal the severe limitations of rendition inherent in both the rendered and the renderer. That the average fundamentalist is probably without a working knowledge of Derridean deconstruction or Barthesian claims of dead authorship is inconsequential to the extent that Western culture at large—(post)modernity—has in the 21st century slowly and methodically constructed a bridge between the modern and the postmodern over which significant numbers of people ("the masses") unconsciously, reluctantly, or happily cross into a

T.E.D. Klein and the Rupture of Civilization

vision of reality that excludes intolerance born of inerrancy. Literalism is antithetical to this discursive, and indeed, lived reality. Though the latter is clearly subject to critique, its inevitable impingement on literalism as a breeding ground for cultish tribalism is an essential act of 21st-century humanist and religious progressivism.

Strozier prefers the term "totalistic core" (162) to cult in so far as the common term has too many variant connotations. He makes an admirable effort to treat his subject(s) with respect and impartiality, and yet the "totalistic" nature of fundamentalism is nevertheless indicative of literalism's insidious reach into the lived life of the believer. It corresponds with the cultish factors of the fundamentalist environment as summarized in the following passage that is worth quoting at length, factors including

> control of communication so that the balance between self and world is disrupted; manipulation of the individual around basic issues of trust and mistrust; the demand for absolute purity, which is contrasted with an outside world of pure evil; the obsession with personal confession as the vehicle for obtaining purity and merging the individual with the community; the maintenance of an aura of sacredness around basic dogma; loading the language with highly reductive, definitive-sounding phrases that can be easily memorized and repeated; the subordination of the individual to the claims of the doctrine; and drawing a sharp line between those who have a right to live and those whose lives can be dispensed with in the name of the movement [*ibid.*].

It is perhaps the final observation that is most disturbing to one for whom language, like the everyday experience that creates it for utilitarian as well as aesthetic purposes, is fluid. That "sharp line," one might say with a touch of melodrama, is one of two lines nailed together to form a cross on which an exceptionally wise individual might be crucified for the sake of an all-too-human belief system, one intent on perceiving language as an essentialist, ad hoc actuality.

At its best, fundamentalism is Sarr Poroth—educated and not entirely lacking a conscience but deeply ensconced in the scaffolding of a totalistic ideology; a man susceptible to what Mary Shelley, via her husband, politely calls "mutability" ("Man's yesterday may ne're be like his morrow / Nought may endure but mutability!") (quoted, *Frankenstein* 80) and thus vulnerable to becoming-monster. While it strengthens his fundamentalist resolve, Sarr's education and experience in New York City (which, incidentally, is the site of Strozier's interviews, as opposed

6. "We are not saved": Critical Horror Today

to the typical deep south demographic), is fraught with ambiguity in so far as it signifies a common intention to broaden his cultural horizons. The seeds of his demise are planted in the city in the form of a possessed feline and yet he has asserted himself over and against his mother's prerogative and consequently his culture. In a sense, Sarr becomes a man in the city. It is only afterwards, once he is wholly invested in the ethos and land of his religious ideology, that evil takes root and blossoms in his psychosomatic being. Mutability is the progenitor of this ambiguity, as it is for everyone, with the exception of René Descartes for whom his infamous claim about thinking and being, as Silverman observes, "projects a continuous presence behind its own exfoliation, a stable point of authorial origin. It offers us a narrator who imagines that he speaks without simultaneously being spoken, who believes himself to exist outside of discourse" (*Subject* 128). Post-structuralism (and thus postmodernism), on the other hand, maintains that "I" am thought, and therefore exist *in a particular incarnation* at a given moment according to the psychological make-up, culture, and discourse of that moment. Critical horror necessarily speaks to this malleability of the self, placing it in atmospheric, deterritorializing (or de-totalizing) frameworks that tend to leave ample room for hermeneutical processes of engagement.

The Last Exorcism: *Cuts and Ambiguities*

In contrast to what Strozier observes as "an unusual degree of ideological certainty, together with a marked suspiciousness of outsiders" (9) that characterizes one of the churches he attended for research purposes, lies his own ambiguity between faith and doubt. He claims that "the offering of myself for conversion was genuine. Otherwise I would have felt dishonest in the dialogue. I listened carefully to their pitch, and made every effort to let it enter my own spiritual imagination. Besides, how could I know for sure how the repeated evangelical onslaught to which I subjected myself would turn out? At some level I had to keep open the option that they would succeed" (19). To do justice to both his scholarly methodology and his humanity (along with that of his interviewees), he found it useful to make himself available to a deeply problematic and unreasonable belief system. This admission stands out as

T.E.D. Klein and the Rupture of Civilization

an odd, personal moment in the text, a tipping over from semi-objective scholarship (which includes the author's background) into the fallibility of shared humanity. To be more specific, it acts as a kind of cut (a narrative disruption; a cinematic breach) that reveals the *necessity* of ambiguity when engaging a more or less foreign ideology or individual/collective. The moment speaks to precisely the mutability that the fundamentalist sensibility seeks to conceal and asphyxiate, often, as Strozier's fieldwork suggests, to the psychological and physical detriment of the adherent. Scholarly and personal investment in the ambiguous nature of the subject (as person, as topic of investigation), contrary to simplistic logic, is not antithetical to personal integrity; rather, it fosters the productive cohesion of the many-layered self by recognizing patterns of mutability, or multiplicity, thus creating the potential of relative agency qua self-knowledge to the degree that the latter is more aligned with psychological cycles of the general human condition.

The value—and inevitability—of ambiguous becomings in the lived life applies equally to aesthetic productions. The cinematic cut, for example, develops a narrative at the same time that it may render a character (or a viewer, for that matter) powerless over his or her circumstances, particularly in the context of horror. In her seminal *Men, Women, and Chainsaws: Gender in the Modern Horror Film*, Carol Clover discusses the cut in, among other films, *Rosemary's Baby*, in which, to recap, a woman's husband has made a pact with a group of Satanists in which her child (surreptitiously fathered by the devil rather than the husband) is promised to the dark lord, as Lucifer's own spawn. As Clover explains, "Rosemary … is impregnated in just such a narrative gap: one sequence shows her growing drowsy and Guy tucking her in; the next her surrealistic dreams; and the next her waking in the morning and Guy's revelation, as he tucks in his shirttails, that he 'didn't want to miss baby night … it was kind of fun in a necrophile way" (76). This montage signifies, for Clover, a "cut into the woman…, into her unconscious psyche as she is impregnated" (*ibid.*). Moreover, the gap operates on another level, according to Clover: "where Satan is, in the world of horror, female genitals are likely to be nearby. The word *vulva* itself is related to *valve*—gate or entry to the body—and so it regularly serves for all manner of spirits, but the unclean one above all, in occult horror" (*ibid.*). Occult or otherwise, filmic or literary, critical horror interrogates such pene-

6. "We are not saved": Critical Horror Today

tration in all its abusiveness, be it at the hands of a male, a female, or a non-gendered other whose intention is to disenfranchise, to put it mildly. The narrative cut, then, may operate as an aesthetic, phallic weapon or an exposé on the machinations of power.

Like "The Events at Poroth Farm" and *The Ceremonies*, Daniel Stamm's film *The Last Exorcism* (2010) interrogates fundamentalism and does so by foregrounding the ambiguity inherent in what DeLillo calls "the poetry of alien places, where extreme situations become inevitable and characters are forced toward life-defining moments" (*Body* 31). Of course, any definitions that emerge are always already susceptible to tectonic shifts in the human or cosmic framework, variations formed by "a spiritual knife-edge" (*ibid.*) that inevitably cuts or forges new becomings, particularly in those moments when the codified self or identity is placed on the chopping block, so to speak. Or the cutting room floor. Though Baton Rouge is hardly Manhattan, it is from this Louisiana capital that a relatively polished but faithless, economically challenged evangelical preacher departs for a journey into the deeper south in Stamm's film. Accompanied by a documentary film crew of two, the protagonist, Cotton Marcus, is intent on performing a final exorcism for the sake of exposing its deception. The possessed (Nell), the teenage daughter of a fundamentalist, homeschooling farmer (Louis) whose religious zealotry has amplified in the wake of his wife's death, may or may not be genuinely inhabited by a supernatural presence. Her brother, who is initially hostile toward the outsiders, may or may not be evil. Louis may be guilty of having raped Nell, who, it turns out, is pregnant despite her saccharine innocence, or he is a genuinely decent man still battling profound grief. Cotton's own position as head of an upbeat, suburban family of three, is less equivocal but vulnerable to the demands of economic challenges. Religion may or may not be an illusion with a future, or an opiate for uncritical thinkers in need of hope, community, drama. What is certain, however, is that time, cuts in time, determine the poesy of places and the extremities that bore into otherwise mundane situations in which life and death are defined not by crosses but by blades and fire.

The interplay between one of the film's central binaries, static and fluid time, is informed in part by the found footage cinematic style, as inspired, of course, by *The Blair Witch Project*, released eleven years prior. As is the case with the earlier film, the viewer is given no insight into when and how this footage has been edited and presented, or by whom, and yet both films clearly foreground the act of filmmaking. *The Last Exorcism* is closer to a conventional film style in so far as it is ostensibly using a single, color camera and employs non-diegetic music in key scenes, though it overlaps with *The Blair Witch Project* to the degree that relatively urban, educated characters in both films venture to a rural location that appears to exist outside of modern time. In this regard, static and fluid are distinguished predominantly along the lines of class, education, and religion. To be more specific, the rural family is isolated in a fundamentalist, working-class, and relatively uneducated environment bereft, or so it seems, of cultural and economic modernity. In contrast, the urban family (including the filmmakers) participates in a community, is suspicious of superstitious religiosity, and is educated, presumably, in terms of both institutional degrees and modern, social responsibility.

Cotton's initial context for the documentary includes a brief theological commentary ("if you believe in Jesus Christ, you have to believe in demons" [*Last*]) that exemplifies fundamentalist dualism, and yet he is clear about having lost his faith and the necessity of foregrounding, instead, a kind of work-a-day pragmatism based on financial security. At this point, he believes in neither God nor Satan, which stands in direct contrast to Louis's faith and his intention to give his children a "fundamental" (*ibid.*) upbringing—two orientations that color not only ideological positions but everyday activities and relations. Their dynamic hits a number of crescendos, most notably in Cotton's initial explanation for what is happening to Nell, possession by a demon, Abalam, whose description and modus operandi is available (there does not appear to be a computer on the farm) only in a Latin demonology book. When Louis inquires about the language, Cotton asks "do you not read Latin?" to which Louis responds, exasperated, "No sir." "It's alright, I've got it for you" (*ibid.*), Cotton asserts, revealing his shtick as well as his urbane arrogance. It is a subtle moment relative to their eventual confrontations over Louis's intention to kill Nell if she is not properly exorcised, though it demonstrates the salient disparity of the two positions, a well-meaning conman and an unsophisticated provincial whose lack of access to an antiquated language may provoke sympathy from the viewer while producing a smirk over Cotton's cleverness. What both

6. "We are not saved": Critical Horror Today

men share, of course, what is indicative of their mutual humanity, is the fact that they merely wish to support the wellbeing of their respective families.

But time inevitably keeps them at odds. As Cotton and the filmmakers drive through the rural countryside, complete with run-down plantations, the exorcist notes how "ancient" the scenery feels, how it emanates a "stopped in time feel" that is a "perfect breeding ground for [the perception of] demons and evil" (*ibid.*). It is a landscape enveloped, in part, by a veil of ignorance in terms of irrational fanaticism on one hand, and the very real, lingering presence (the "demons") of slavery and bigotry, however dilapidated they may be, on the other. Cotton comes from a world in which time moves in keeping with the cultural shifts of modernity, a context he uses to manipulate his "clients," while Louis's milieu appears to be in a state of perpetual arrest, one whose strength lies in its monolithic timelessness as well as in the threat of a shotgun. But there is another level, or plateau, of the rural environment that emerges in the person of Nell and ultimately extends, ironically, to the local church community. When Cotton stops for gas before reaching the farm, a woman explains that they are headed to the very "gates to Hell" (*ibid.*). Her demeanor is, on the surface, that of a pleasant but credulous yokel. Nevertheless, her claim is born out by the film's conclusion, at least to the degree that others substantiate and enact the hell-laden mythos, whereupon "ancient" time assumes a new and distinctly ominous meaning.

In addition to playing hymns on her flute (the phallic nature of which may be read as either an ordinary "cigar" or what is conceivably the most destructive organ on the planet), Nell makes religious paintings featuring biblical scenes. These images turn ominous, however, when her demoniacal transition occurs, in their depiction of her family cat's bloody death, the foreshadowing of brutal murder, of the filmmakers, and Cotton's likely demise in a blaze of something resembling glory. The events occur in reality during the film's dramatic climax, when, following relatively benign resolution (Nell has simply been the victim of guilt over having fornicated), Cotton suspects they have been misled. Upon return to the farm, they hear noises, venture into the woods by the house, and discover a black mass in process. Louis is being held captive and is thus absolved from wrongdoing, Caleb (Nell's suspicious brother) is a

T.E.D. Klein and the Rupture of Civilization

Satanist responsible for decapitating the cameraman, a moderate preacher Cotton consults earlier in the film is leading his church flock in the ritual, and Nell, tied on a sacrificial table, gives birth to something that does not appear to be human. In other words, the supernatural, and specifically Satanism, is alive and well in the deep south. But in the larger context of the film's ambiguities, where does Satanism fit? Where does Rosie fit in the complicated universe of *The Ceremonies*? Two prior scenes provide answers: when Cotton begins vetting, and then exorcising Nell, of the family members it is only Caleb who is savvy enough to recognize the tricks. Only the Satanist is attuned to the gimmickry that dupes his fundamentalist kin. Secondly, after Nell's visual prophecy comes true and she, under the influence, so to speak, kills the cat, she begins speaking Latin, at which point the viewer is cued to recall the awkward exchange between Cotton and Louis around the demonology book. Not only is Satanism operative in rural culture, it is, paradoxically, unequivocally, palpably modern. Rosie, too, emerges from such an environment and is by far the most cosmopolitan character in Klein's novel. If the rural environment in *The Last Exorcism* is indeed home to the "gates to hell," its underworld, in contrast, or perhaps in addition to Sartre's dictum that "hell is other people," offers a distinctive vision. Hell is static time, where evil may ripen, over imperceptible centuries, and flourish.

Of course, Hell as mythical, cultural, and psychological condition casts a large shadow. And it is constituted by other people to the extent that we may project our own hellishness onto others who become either objects to subsume or mirrors to cover or break. In her possessed state, Nell is essentially undergoing a process of becoming-modern. In every such scene, she is eroticized, self-caressing, or reaching out to others in a sexual manner; she is educated in a language to which her uncultivated father has no access; in accepting the gift of Doc Martens boots from the female filmmaker, she clearly makes an advance over the drab footwear of an innocent, rural, Christian farm girl. And like Klein's Deborah, whose interest in current events beyond the boundaries of Gilhead, whose humor and outspokenness finally condemn her to monstrosity, Nell pays a price. Ironically, then, the central "cut" (to return to Clover's theoretical observations) in *The Last Exorcism*, when Nell's pregnancy is first discovered and the family's turmoil is incorrectly reduced to the

6. "We are not saved": Critical Horror Today

trauma of guilt, is striking. It is marked by one of several moments when the camera literally and abruptly stops filming and cuts to black. At this point, Nell, seemingly possessed, assumes command of the camera while the others are asleep. She positions it before a mirror so as to record herself pulling at and contorting her face. She then retrieves the camera, walks outside, strips nude, and proceeds to kill the cat. On one level, the scene constitutes a "cut into the woman…, into her unconscious psyche," in that she becomes fully demonic, erotically so, and thus dispossessed of her former self.[2] And yet she also becomes director and cinematographer (she is already an artist of sorts); a subject whose mirror image is not a horrifying epiphany but an empowering exaggeration, a performance wielded rather than passively and sickeningly revealed. Demon Nell transforms Lacan's mirror-stage into a Deleuzean plateau whereby the fragmented self *recognizes* and ("sings" and) celebrates itself. And what it assumes, you shall assume.[3]

Every such "cut" in the film (between the first time Cotton and company depart following the initial, faux exorcism and an especially unsettling scene in which Nell inexplicably ends ups up at their hotel, slipping eerily into another, nearly comatose personality, or between her being subdued after killing the cat and the second, sobering exorcism) makes Nell less ambiguous, more modern, though deeply ensconced in the ostensible dangers of modernism. When possessed, she is capable of bending time, of bringing the future into the present. She is not stopped in time. And yet the modernism of the generous, socially responsible, Doc Martens-wearing filmmaker, or that of Cotton, intent on rendering the falsehood of exorcism (not to mention evangelical dualism) apparent, co-exists with the modern adroitness of Satanism that, in *The Last Exorcism* at least, parallels (and far exceeds) the primitive, egoic aggression of fundamentalism. In this instance, however, Satanism's cunning, however emblazoned by the occult, is finally reduced to reestablishing Lacan's misrecognized self, the one on whom (an)other does not tread, or else, and to hurting people, especially, and paradoxically, those behind the camera.[4] By the film's conclusion, then, modernity is demolished. Be it at the hands of knowing Satanists or a grieving father whose only resource is a "pocket of ignorance," modernity as liberal humanism, or urbane aestheticism, is, like the cinematographer making the documentary, decapitated. All that is left of the modern is its valuable penchant for ambiguity and yet another viewing audience swept through a mounting process of thrills, intensities, and questions; a body without a rational, impermeable head, or a filmic "body-without-organs," to use Deleuze and Guattari's well-known (non)category.[5] The film provides a critical platform and it is up to the viewer to meet it, with his or her own inspired acumen, or deterritorialized body, where its cinematic and topical scopes unfold. At the nexus of filmic, supernatural horror, incinerated, beheaded modernity, indefinite time, and polymorphic ambiguity, lies a continuum of what horror and fundamentalism alike tend to call Hell.

The Infinite Legends of Hell House

What is Hell? To what are the many titles referring? *Hellraiser, Hellbound, Hell Night, Motel Hell, The Haunting of Hell House, Briefing for a Descent Into Hell, The Marriage of Heaven and Hell.* "Hell is other people." One looks and, in a moment of profound incursion, becomes acutely aware of being looked at, the gaze becomes all-too-real, a projection made hellish by virtue of reflecting the real. "Suddenly," Sartre via Silverman explains, "the voyeur hears footsteps in the hall or the rustle of leaves on the ground, and the first visual tableau gives way to a second. He is conjured out of nothingness into existence in the guise of an image for that Other who is evoked by the footsteps or leaves. The voyeur now vibrates with an awareness of himself as spectacle, and through that awareness a consciousness of self is produced in him" (*Threshold* 164). Footsteps and rustling leaves find their way into horror for precisely the reason that the other makes one aware of oneself. The resultant vibration can be infinitely pleasurable and rewarding, as in a meditative holy instant, or stultifying, as in a horror scenario that is drawing on quite ordinary social life (passing a dubious—always dubious—other on an otherwise isolated sidewalk; the other in the elevator, the waiting room). Or Hell is time, that which remains curiously and deadeningly static, at once insuring the dominance of agreeable patterns and a somnambulant "nothingness." Hell as time, as opposed to eternity that strips the ego of its somethingness, its excess of being, thus producing an awareness of self not as spectacle but as calm observer. Hell is self masquerading as

6. "We are not saved": Critical Horror Today

self. Hence Terry Eagelton's claim that Hell is "exactly the opposite" of Sartre's dictum: "it is being stuck for all eternity with the most dreary, unspeakably monotonous company of all: oneself" (*On Evil* 22).

Culturally, Hell may be understood as a dividing line between modernities—the literal hell of modern, fundamentalist, religio-political cosmology (bolstered, as most everything is, by technology) and that of liberal humanism that repudiates literalist adherence to supernatural evil and thus locates the "demonic" in injustice, hegemony, and unconsciousness, in any ideology that compromises democratic agency. Where the modernism of critical horror utilizes ambiguity to undermine the hell of closed meanings and veridical assumptions, fundamentalist modernism, or what Jason Bivins calls "religion of fear," fetishes apocalyptic fire, a notion of eternity very much rooted, one could argue, in the earthly time of what are essentially quotidian prejudices and self-serving mythologies. It goes without saying that this line floats, that the classic distinction between liberal and conservative horror, for example, is often blurred. And yet, even a modicum of self-observation and self-knowledge yields a sense of which Hell, if any, one is occupying, or promulgating, which modernity is informing one's life and those lives that have the fortune or misfortune of entering our sphere.

John Hough's 1973 film *The Legend of Hell House* may come across as dated (delightfully so for some pre-millennials) in its unhurried pacing through haunted, gothic corridors and dysfunctional personalities, though its legendary subject matter, like the pagan holiday of Halloween itself, is entirely modern and contemporary, forever being updated. I turn now to one particular revision of Hell that falls to the right of the line while nevertheless inadvertently marking itself with the sign of a current (some might say "with it") Devil. The fundamentalist Hell House phenomenon is the product of a fear-based Christianity that "not only reminds audiences of religious commitments [but] seeks to create (or reinforce) specific political commitments. Each panel drawn, lyric parsed, sin portrayed, and page written delineates the contours of hell, beckoning audiences to peer in deeply before pronouncing their rejection," as Bivins explains in his comprehensive *Religion of Fear: The Politics of Horror in Conservative Evangelicalism* (220). Emerging in late 20th-century North America, church-sponsored Hell Houses continue to thrive as

T.E.D. Klein and the Rupture of Civilization

> morality plays [that] illustrate to young audiences the dangers—not merely physical, but moral and salvific—posed by drug use, premarital sex, and other "illicit" activities or beliefs. Relying on intense and graphic dramatizations of car crashes, abortions, gun violence, and other incidents of shock, these productions use the techniques and narrative strategies of genre horror in order to explore a different kind of demonology, one which creators believe is erupting into social and political life [131].

The Hell Houses and their variants that take place on and around Halloween, as an alternative to what their sponsors typically deem yet another example of the occult flourishing in mainstream culture, are essentially an ideological (and to some degree, aesthetic) inversion of critical horror, though it is hardly as simple a matter as right vs. left orientations.[6]

While opinionated, to put it lightly, the project of Hell House is an inversion of critical thinking. Its condemnation of audiences—another fascinating term in light of audience theory and the notion that such a collective is fabricated via the rhetorical context of the "performance"— rests on indoctrination rather than on weighing the many factors at play in complex circumstances. Consequently, it is inherently bigoted in so far as it targets populations and activities based on what Bivins identifies as "brutal consequentialism" (140), on visions of consequence that leave little room for anything other than brutality. In other words, the gay marriage will inevitably end in AIDS, the abortion doctor will invariably be cold and monstrous in administering the procedure, the rave/teen party can only end in violent death and rape, and premarital sex, in unwanted pregnancy and deadbeat fatherhood. Furthermore, Hell House relies on shock in the way that what is commonly referred to as torture porn in the horror genre erects its narratives around depictions of extreme and highly realistic violence, without necessarily exploring substantive issues or ideas. Hell House is, to put it in a particular historical context, the technologically advanced (though theologically and intellectually inferior) equivalent of Jonathan Edwards Great Awakening sermon, "Sinners in the Hands of an Angry God," in which the preacher documents both the literalism and the horrific designs of Hell. Each example of fire and brimstone rhetoric is antithetical to critical horror that, like Zooey in J.D. Salinger's *Franny and Zooey*, is generally quick to dismiss the myth of original sin.[7] If critical horror could be said to offer a consistent "prayer," it may very well resemble, with no small

6. "We are not saved": Critical Horror Today

degree of irony, "forgive them, for they know not what they do" (*Berean Literal Bible*, Luke 23:24).

In spite of the distinctions between Hell House and critical horror, is it fair to say that the former is equally homeopathic? It employs the "poison" of mainstream (youth) culture to eradicate its effects and, crucially, offers an opportunity for salvation (Heaven) at the end of the performance in the form of wholesome, celebratory, redemptive socializing. Bivins observes that "Hell Houses consciously embrace the tools of the 'fallen culture,' redeploying them in explicitly political fashion as part of a perceived 'culture war'" (*Religion* 139). They utilize the hyperrealism of horror imagery and atmosphere for the sake of combating what their creators identify as culturally and spiritually toxic. However, regardless of emotionally captivating realism, "what is more palpable in these liberal pilferings from the culture of the damned is conservative evangelicalism's preoccupation with—and orientation to—the desires it condemns" (166). And herein lies the razor-sharpness of the dividing line: the modernity of critical horror, humanist or otherwise, necessarily recognizes and to a large degree validates desire and embodiment, aspects of the human experience that can doubtless lead to difficulties but remain central to somatic and psychological fulfillment. Hell is the disavowal of said fulfillment. In failing to recognize the value and importance of desire, the Hell of fundamentalism's "house" must contend with its own implication in desire without critical horror's "tools" of self-reflection, however obscured these might be by layers of narrative style, atmosphere, and the various tropes it may or may not incorporate to flesh out its relevance in the genre. To put it more broadly, in a "religion of fear's" "complicated dance with its enemies, there is the possibility that the categories of self and Other will bleed together" (220), a possibility for which one modernity is generally far more prepared than the other despite the latter's tech savvy and vague sense of youth culture perspectives. The dilemma facing the fundamentalist, of course, is not only an orientation to desire, a morphing of desire as didactic representation and carnal reality, but (to read the above quote from another angle) the inevitability of death; self and Other alike are susceptible to a potential bleeding out of life, a brutal exsanguination. Confronting the axe of a madman, the fangs of a vampire, or an amorphous It that follows until death or sex intervene, it matters not that one "loves the homosexual but hates the lifestyle" or habitually votes democratic and lives with absolutely no concept of a literal, horned figure lurking in every corner and crevice. In the immediate crisis mode of impending death, "self and Other will bleed together," a fact that may unfortunately be veiled for the fundamentalist by laminae of intolerance; unfortunate, because, like a father and son who realize the importance of being "well-connected," we more or less need one another.[8]

Hell is ubiquitous. For some, it is a feeling, an emotional and perhaps intellectual understanding of the challenges of contemporary life, especially as depicted by various media outlets and in the kind of call and response (or altar call?) that the media generates in a public that absorbs its sensationalistic narratives. In this sense, Hell is unconsciousness and sleepwalking through relationality, work, sex, politics, leisure, eating; it is everywhere, always already in the body, issuing from the mouth or the facial expression, communicating its subtle or overt violence. And it is most certainly in the mind. For others, operating out of a conservative evangelical tradition, Hell is not only literal, it is ontology. As Eagelton argues, "fundamentalists are basically fetishists. For Sigmund Freud, a fetish is whatever you use to plug some ominous gap; and the unnerving vacancy which fundamentalists hasten to fill is simply the fuzzy, rough-textured, open-ended nature of human existence. It is non-being which fundamentalists fear most. And what they plug it with is dogma" (*After* 208). Hell is indeterminacy, a modernist, John Cagean nightmare, an excess of being-in-time where the everyday often lacks clarity and conventional composition. For the horror enthusiast, Hell is also vacancy, but that which is illuminated on a motel sign on a rainy, California night when there is no where else to stay and the gentle, svelte young man who escorts you to your room and offers a sandwich in his parlor seems nice enough despite his eccentricity and apparent alienation. Hell is gripping narratives of psychopathology, film, and celebration.

A random video sampling of a Hell House (or not so random: in keeping with Klein's general milieu, a New York-based presentation is more appropriate than the usual southern fare here) satisfies both expectations based on Bivins's analysis and Eagleton's notion of dogmatic fetishism. The Youtube video entitled "Halloween New York City—Hell House," presented by Curious Travelers, tours a Hell House in Brooklyn,

6. "We are not saved": Critical Horror Today

complete with a sarcastic demon host, a rave ending in gang rape, suicide, an abortion scene, a school shooting, a gay wedding, the "brutal consequences" of premarital sex, drug addiction, and of course, the twin finales of Satan and Jesus, followed by a jubilant, light-filled party. Though visually captivating in terms of horror imagery and atmosphere, what stands out in the formula of Hell House is its language. The phrase "young love" (Curious, "Halloween") is used ironically to designate the source of abortion, as though the "fuzzy, rough-textured, open-ended nature of human existence," which includes youthful explorations of desire and affection, can only be contained by avoiding what comes most natural in body/minds young and old. In a related instance, the demon taunts a gay married couple, whose life can only end in AIDS, with the question "You want sexual freedom?" (*ibid.*) while one man comforts another in a hospital bed. Implicit in this rhetorical condemnation is the notion that there is no sexual freedom, that such freedom is at once illusory and unworthy of pursuit, particularly in the context of aberrant behavior. Eagleton states "above all, they [fundamentalists] cannot acknowledge desire, since to desire is to lack. Instead of holding fast to their desire, they stuff it full of fetishes" (*After* 217). The central fetish is an identity, a self in opposition to all that is Other, a dynamic that psychoanalysis and postmodern theory alike are generally quick to ascribe to common human experience. That said, the aversion to desire and freedom in desire deepens the vacancy inherent in the fundamentalist psychology; thus the fetish of self and its many puppet strands of dogmatism can never arrive at the actual value of horror. Horror makes a pilgrimage to the burial ground of the self and, when not averse to ambiguity, digs an even deeper grave, opens the space where death and non-being ultimately prevail—to the benefit of the living self whose freedom lies in acknowledging the open-ended play of human nature in all of its enormous complexity.

The "Jesus" in this particular Hell House, a bearded Caucasian male with shoulder length hair, a luminous smile, and, in all probability, a bountiful Hacky Sack collection, welcomes those who have made it through Hell with a first person rendition of Romans 10:9: "If you believe with all your heart that I rose from the dead. And if you confess with your mouth that I am Lord, you will be saved" (Curious, "Halloween"). What governs the ethos—and perhaps the pathos—of this passage is time, and specifically, an uncomplicated overlapping of time past and present. If you stake your life and belief system (your identity) on a historical (and, for the reader or the Hell House survivor, metaphysical) event, the scripture indicates, your salvation will be assured. Jesus makes many other claims in the Bible, none of which are necessarily legitimized or sustained by literalist interpretation, and this passage is no exception. Literalism is here conflated with history, a potentially dangerous amalgam, as any student of the philosophy of history knows. The risk here lies in the demarcation of the elect versus the damned based on belief in an event that is long since passed, relegated, if one is to assume its historical accuracy, to a history that can only be re-presented. In other words, the distinction between time past and present is upheld to the degree that time is cemented into linearity, as opposed to the eternity of a given now that is far more invested in the immediacy of psychology than in confession contingent on what is ultimately reducible to discourse. And it is from this discourse that Hell may be enacted and perpetrated.

By the tour's conclusion, very much in time, the celebration that welcomes participants to the possibility of purity and salvation via live acoustic guitar music, dancing, and shouts of "congratulations!" and "awesome!" is, curiously, also shrouded by time. Referred to as the "Gospel Hoedown," its title is referencing a form of folk dancing and singing that, while not entirely archaic, is clearly of another milieu than 21st-century Brooklyn. The music, at least in the brief clip from the video, is poorly played by young people dressed in white and the dancing of one adherent is more akin to a seizure than what John Travolta or Pina Bausch might call dance. Weirdly, and to the seeming dismay of the woman escorting the video's viewer, the event is essentially stuck in time, a time that is incongruent with the youth population that Hell House is attempting to convert. The community of Klein's Gilhead, the farm on which *The Last Exorcism*'s Nell has been molested by Satanists, the narrator of "Black Man with a Horn's" life in the shadow and "time" of Lovecraft, a white room in which exuberant young people erroneously conflate the meaning of "awesome" with blind, time-based faith—each of these occurrences and spaces serve to limit eternity, or what T.S. Eliot calls the "still point of the turning world" ("Four"119). Hell is time. The "Gospel Hoedown," to the hipster urbanite in search of amusement or

6. "We are not saved": Critical Horror Today

anthropological insight, is Hell. The hoedown is an inversion of "Children of the Kingdom's" blackout, in which "roaming whites" run rampant, so malignant as to make a monster of the peculiar but likeable Father Pistachio.

At various points, Bivins observes that certain of the most extreme positions in the cast of Hell House are highly coveted by actors, the figure of Satan topping the list. This tendency is perhaps further indication of the extent to which self and Other may "bleed together," in the conventional usage of that phrase. To get a stronger sense of this phenomenon as it may apply to relatively secular horror fans as well as to those who thump the Bible with the power of vicious inerrancy, I turn now to a contemporary short story by Laird Barron, "More Dark," that engages in both the atmospherics of horror and a critique of Ligottian antinatalism that stands, ostensibly, as diametrically opposed to fundamentalism. Though Ligotti asserts that "there is no satisfaction in a lonesome suicide," he is clear about the imperative of pessimism and large-scale, "death-drive" finality: "to depopulate this earth and arrest its rotation as well—what satisfaction, as of a job prettily done. This would be for the good of all, for even those who know nothing about the conspiracy against the human race are among its injured parties" (*Conspiracy* 161–162). Critical horror is hardly at variance on the pervasiveness of "injured parties," pessimistic or otherwise. What Barron will critique via satire, however, is the egotism of unmovable certainty around pessimism that ranges from goofy to ominously fetishistic. As this study has argued, it is precisely the precious, monolithic ego, in whatever variation of fanaticism, that debases civilization and shelters the banality of evil.

More or Less Dark

As many readers of a book on T.E.D. Klein will know, Barron is a popular horror writer of "today," with a literary style akin to Raymond Carver as much as to other influential genre writers. In a 2015 interview, Barron has this to say about religion: "I draw a line in the dirt at the codification of superstition into a belief system that is then inflicted upon hapless others" (Barron). He goes on to critique "a Ligotti-style

T.E.D. Klein and the Rupture of Civilization

automaton," as opposed to one who acts by going "inward deep enough to realize the internal vista is infinite" (*ibid.*). "More Dark" is a story that bridges these two assertions in so far as it parodies not so much Ligotti (known indiscreetly as "Tom L."), whose work Barron appears to admire, but the codification of his ideas, most notably antinatalism. It charts the course of another New York evening for several horror writers who attend a reading by the mysterious and reclusive Tom L. whose identity remains concealed behind a robe and a puppet, Mandibole, that captivates the audience with a violent, cosmically pessimistic narrative. The narrator, Mr. B., has alerted his reader to his intention to commit suicide back in his hotel, which he promptly does by the end without necessarily having been persuaded by the performance beyond its effective atmosphere. So what of the irony in criticizing the obedient adherence to a philosophy that negates the value of birth and concluding with a fatal gunshot? I will return to this point later, but there are several aspects of the story that help flesh out its predicament. The narrator is in a tough spot. His wife has just left him and it is not merely the ephemeral sensation of loneliness that is driving his sense of "self-destruction. Despair and grief, self-loathing and self-recrimination, failure and desertion … those [are] justifications" (Barron, "More" 273). His writing career, like that of "Black Man with a Horn's" narrator, is essentially dormant, though unlike the Kleinian character who simply waits for death to overtake him, Mr. B. will take matters into his own hands, though not before asserting numerous barbs at the culture(s) surrounding him.[9] The masses, including the bar crowd that follows the horror enthusiasts are "kissy-faces too enamored with one another, too intoxicated by their own adorableness … a swanky retro mass" (272), while a "kid with earphones [glances] at [him]" on the train earlier in the evening; "his earphones [resemble] the curved horns of a ram. His eyes [reflect] the void. He [smiles]. His smile [is] the void" (255). It becomes clear that Mr. B has very little hope of locating happiness in relation to others.

In keeping with what Barron identifies as the satirical aims of the narrative, however, there is pleasure to be found in its pages, at least for the reader whose appreciation of Ligotti does not extend to worship. The narrator's characterization of Tom L's audience is at once humorous and eviscerating. When the man of the hour takes the stage, it is as

6. "We are not saved": Critical Horror Today

though "a polar bear had breached itself upon an ice shelf with a heard of seals and the seals [bark] with joy, witless to their mortal danger" (264). The danger lies in succumbing to his power of persuasion—or hypnotism—concerning "consciousness [as] an abomination" (252). Mr. B's critiques of "the self loathing, chronically inebriated, perpetually persecuted set" are many; of course, he is describing himself here, but the insults become more focused and distanced from the narrator's own predicament. The audience is comprised of "seldom glimpsed wildlife that had crept from the forest depths to gather in the sacred glade and listen to Pan wheedle on his recorder by the dark of the moon" (261), a "roomful of wax dummies glued into their seats, heads fused, gazes fixed upon the podium" while Tom L's entourage does "the unsmiling thing" (267), a contrived, communicative brooding. Even John, Mr. B's friend who has brought his daughter's two puppets (one of which is called "Poe") as a form of homage, is transformed to the point of throwing the only remaining and seemingly molested "Poe" in the trash because, presumably, by the end of the night he has himself become a metaphorical puppet.[10] As Mandibole's vicious narrative hints that there is "something worse" behind even death, several of the listeners [join] in and soon it [is] like a church revival meeting with the parishioners chorusing the reverend's punch lines" (268). "Every person [is] slack-jawed, faces shining in rapt concentration while their bodies [fade] to lumps within the deepening shadow," Mr. B. observes. They are all "on some distant soundstage in Hell, hanging from the Tree of Anti-life" (266).

Hell is the opiate of hero worship. "You sway in the breeze like Jack O' Lanterns," Tom L. tells the audience via the puppet, "and cannot utter protest, or question your Maker, or petition your Accuser. You are muted by choking mouthfuls of gore. And this is Hell, my friends" (265–266). Hell is being pulled by the strings of Baudelaire's Devil; it is becoming a puppet at the mercy of a puppet. Even the room in which the ideologue utters his screed, the Kremlin bar, caters to "an audience that [buzzes] rather than [speaks]. A living, breathing, telepathically communing Yin-Yang symbol. Intimate and impersonal as an Arctic starfield" (261), thus resembling an inverted "Gospel Hoedown" in which adherents partake in the collective reverie, or group think, of obedience. Barron lacerates the audience bent on perpetuating phantasy and he does so in contrast to a Real that is hardly innocent of Hell but at least manages to petition

T.E.D. Klein and the Rupture of Civilization

the "Accuser" and sever, or loosen, the puppet strings.[11] A seeming voice of reason in the "Arctic starfield" is that of GVG, a renowned publisher who sees through the absurdity and the hypnotism of the event in so far as he is in contact with the concrete reality. "Wanna see horror," he asks, "come see what my three year old and a bottle of rubber cement did to the cat and a pile of slush manuscripts in my living room" (271). The Real is the "accidents" and "noises," the "small" things, such as what Mr. B. encounters on television back at his hotel room before committing suicide: "chains of American flags ... my wife's face in the faces of enemies and strangers, a Nazi aiming his rifle at another man's back.... Sufis keening in a temple, my wife again and again, and Mandibole cutting through it all, speaking in tongues except for one clear strain in the cacophony" (275).

So, in the universe of "More Dark," the Real is a face less of Hell than of horror, that which impinges upon the everyday. The earthly, quotidian realm in which people work and play and travel is the concierge of Mr. B's hotel "relaxing with a big stack of Jack Chick pamphlets" (*ibid.*), small cartoon tracts often left in various public spaces in an attempt to convert the lost. Thematically, they "insist," as Bivins observes, "that not only must one bow before the correct deity, one must fraternize with the right people, listen to the right music, and avoid certain habits of thought and practice in order to avoid the fiery depths" (*Religion* 41). They are highly dualistic and fundamentalist in nature, and therefore very much of the world, parochial admonitions attempting to raise, or codify, Hell. And their reader is apparently the last live human being Mr. B sees. But there is also his wife, "again and again," appearing on the television, and, just before he picks up the gun, "superimposed and [shimmering] there [on the face of a memory from the Kremlin], rippling with static, frozen in time" (Barron, "More" 275). The final straw for Mr. B has not been his waning writing career but his divorce, the primary image of which keeps him stuck in time, with a "function of repetition" that haunts, reviving as it does the face of a dead relationship. On one level, then, he, like most of us, wants to belong, but to an intimate other rather than a coterie of puppets, and suffers this lack to the point of suicide.[12] On the other hand, he has an acute sense of the core lack that desire seeks to fill, a void like that of a smile, or an un-smile. Here again (and again) is the Real, "rippling" with time.

6. "We are not saved": Critical Horror Today

In response to fundamentalism, Eagleton argues that at its center lies the ego, as in most centers of the self, though in this case, "the manic affirmation of self becomes a defense against its sweetly seductive emptiness. Evil is just this dialectic pressed to horrific extremes" (*After* 218). From a fundamentalist standpoint, the void is seductive because it ensures the repetition of desire, which prolongs the irresistible battle with Satan in his countless manifestations, from homosexuality to uppity women and non-white races, from educated people in the (relatively) non-digital humanities to the body itself, in all of its demanding, confounding corporeality. "Horrific extremes" can look like more or less legal efforts to deny rights to said others as much as they are planes smashing into buildings or a truck running down bodies on a celebratory street in Nice. "Hell," Eagelton asserts, "is the living death of those who regard themselves as too valuable to die" (*ibid.*). In contrast, Mr. B, given the particular time (as personal narrative and public milieu) in which he is living, opts out of this vision of Hell. But for "an interloper" and "a blasphemer" (Barron, "More" 261) against the antinatalist code (the imperative of living out one's pessimism), suicide is the logical extension of his life. What Barron accomplishes with "More Dark" is a blistering repudiation of consciousness-as-abomination and a satirical backlash ("Fuck you, Tommy L, fuck you and your little hand puppet too!" [272]) against the blindness of its figurehead's followers in the form of an abstract descent into death where, it seems, nothing is any different except for the fact that it—the fateful afterlife—merely "lasts longer" (276).

Minor Horror

"More Dark" is less apocalyptic endism than it is cultural (or anthropological) critique. And yet the two strands meet where the horror of "something worse" coincides with an almost religious devotion to Tom L's doom-speak. That the mesmerism of his performance develops in such a way as to mirror "a church revival meeting" is indicative of a striking correlation (or collaboration): that between cosmic pessimism/ antinatalism and fundamentalism. It should be clear that this alignment is one toward which the present chapter has been building in light of

T.E.D. Klein and the Rupture of Civilization

Barron's story and the earlier critique of Thacker, though it is an argument worth stressing, again. Ligottian pessimism guards against suicide, as does fundamentalism, as attractive as being out of this world and out of these originally sinful bodies may be; and it is this odd tension that fuels both the horror and the ideology of endism. Strozier defines the apocalyptic orientation as "the shadow side of our firm belief in renewal and second chances. It is our counter-narrative that competes with the boundless optimism we have in our future and our remarkable confidence in the capacity of our political system to correct itself for its own excessive enthusiasms" (*Apocalypse* 153). While critical horror is certainly intent on presenting "shadow sides" of life that sometimes end prematurely in death and on tempering the kind of "excess enthusiasm," or glib optimism, for that matter, that comes from political hegemony, it is not entirely averse to the possibilities of "renewal" and "second chances," or as Klein might put it, happy endings. The problem with the counter-narrative of both cosmic pessimism and fundamentalism is that it is anchored in duality. If not this, then that. This, not that, is absolutely true. Each orientation takes the presumptions of its narrative seriously, as though they have bypassed the finer points of postmodernism that categorically eschew, or severely challenge, Truth. The primary difference is that fundamentalism is reductive with regards to its violence as well, like Louis in *The Last Exorcism* on the verge of shooting his daughter because of something called Abalam. Cosmic pessimism is merely violent on the page and screen, shady puppet followers notwithstanding.

Outside the violence of shotguns and machetes, the "void," or Thacker's "unground," then, carry the same literal weight, the same assumptions as do unbridled optimism and the anthropomorphic god of evangelicalism. No one in touch with the former can deny that the cosmic pessimist is far less dangerous in his or her presumptions than the latter (which is not to say that literary or filmic narratives are bereft of the power to inform individuals and collectives—Barron's story speaks precisely to such power). That said, Thacker's notion of a "blank, anonymous world that is indifferent to human knowledge" caters to pessimistic inferences that are, at their most unsophisticated, based on fashion, hipster posturing, a sexy book title, or to an investment in literalism that runs the risk of transforming critical thinking into a chorus of mournful egos worshipping at the altar of Indifference. Fortunately, *In the Dust of*

6. "We are not saved": Critical Horror Today

This Planet is clear in its intent to avoid "disparaging" the world as "irretrievable and inaccessible." There is something of a celebratory nature to Thacker's methodology; it supports its cosmic pessimism with erudition and enthusiasm that (nearly) resists excess. On the other hand, when television shows and t-shirts commandeer a cosmology, danger is probably afoot. Adherents to the religion of cosmic pessimism are doubtless culturally shrewd relative to their fundamentalist counterparts, but even alternative religions must contend with inherently problematic language, not to mention the viral quality of the baser self/other dynamics in all of their potential insidiousness.

Critical horror does not discount cosmic foreboding. The genre mines it, identifies its force, and at times, promotes its necessity in the stand off against puritanical absolutism without giving in to the proclivity toward coveting capital "I" indifference. Critical horror wages war against the Hell of parochialism wherever it might manifest and ultimately sets its sights on those areas in which metaphor and allegory are shut down, misapprehended, or altogether despised due to their proportional complexity. In the depths of its disquieted atmospheres and endangered, organ-laden bodies stirs an evocation against what is perhaps the single-most vile culprit in the annals of human aggression and ignorance: ultimately, on one level or another, critical horror identifies literalism as *the* predominate disease of civilization. We encounter its devilry everywhere—in the sanctuary, the classroom, the desperate mind of the terrorist bent on destruction, in the desperate pathos that lies just beneath a façade of warmth in the fundamentalist household, in the voting booth, in art, literature, science, psychoanalysis, all perpetual, dehumanizing narratives of victimized and victimizer, in the hospital, the courtroom, in chat rooms, Digital Humanities projects, and in the torrent of social media information whose apocalypse would likely benefit humankind. But mostly it resides in the desperate mind hungry for meaning, attention, and purpose. Literalism makes monsters of those who would read (from Holy Bibles to blogs to news broadcasts) themselves, their inherited ideological foundations, into the text without an operative sense of discursive permeability as much as it does of the Poroths or Arden Huntoon, characters who literally read their monstrosity into being.[13] Such people (to revisit Eagleton's valuable observation) "have a surfeit of being," as opposed to the non-being or emptiness

T.E.D. Klein and the Rupture of Civilization

that undergirds the "open-ended nature of human existence." From this perspective, literalism is both the fetish and the disease that links its sense of ontological certainty to the equivalent of a coveted foot, breast, bank account, or compilation of words on a page. Obviously, the lifeline between self and that which can never be fully incorporated into the self (what Lacan calls the "*object petite a*" in his *Écrits*), or fully known, for the matter, is a flimsy premise for living and relating. Critical horror has much to say about this premise via its own language that is at once evasive and immediate.

In contrast to the impulse(s) to glut oneself with singularities of meaning is the imperative, for some, of defiance, or as others might call it, heresy. Whether this trespass assumes the form of religious apostasy or literary transgression, it is essential in any process of carving superfluous aggregates from the bloated body/mind—such a person who is novel, eccentric in the context of mass culture, deviant relative to bourgeois obedience and resignation. In so far as critical horror embraces such otherness, it is aligned with Deleuzean "minor literature" that is constructed "by a minority [people] within a major language" (*Kafka* 16). Critical horror is thus a kind of minor horror, a subgenre within the overarching field of horror that deterritorializes a genre that can be as intensely conservative as it is bloody; its defiance acts on behalf not of aesthetic formulas but of individuals who sense an imperative of darkness in life without the juvenile constraints of a stultifying, absolutist, cosmic stance. Moreover, in keeping with Deleuze and Guattari's category, minor horror "produces an active solidarity [between said individuals] in spite of skepticism" and consequently allows for "the possibility [on the part of the writer] to express another possible community and to forge the means for another consciousness and another sensibility" (17). Healthy skepticism, as the cliché goes, yes; ego-drenched cosmic pessimism, on the other hand, while a potentially absorbing performance, has little to do with health or happiness in Adorno's sense of the term. And happiness, really, is the final aim of "another consciousness" and "another sensibility," modes of non-being that thrive on and celebrate the empty space of becoming that can emerge from especially tenacious individuals, and in concert with others for whom the mediocrity of mass culture, including its trendy pessimism, is largely unacceptable.

Minor horror is critical horror that works toward breaking the man-

6. "We are not saved": Critical Horror Today

acles of literalism and so resembles "minor literature" specifically in its political milieu. The latter's "cramped space," as Deleuze and Guattari explain, "forces each individual intrigue to connect immediately to politics" (*ibid.*), which for the horror-inflected version means forging a cavity into non-being, an opening of the body that re-channels the obstinate aggression that raw literalism is tremendously efficient at arousing. The politics of deterritorialization uncouples that which is entrenched in both the body and the Word from its hosts. In other words, the "minor" aspect of critical horror extols the virtue and power of a productive void more akin to Buddhist emptiness than that which stares out from behind the eyes of a disenchanted young man, or into biblical Scripture with dead certainty.[14] Where does meaning go under these circumstances, then, when easy, conventional access to self and other are denied or obscured? It forms in and around what Deleuze calls elsewhere "a people who are missing" (*Essays* 4), what might be understood as the nascent agency of the individual/collective whose development, whose other "consciousness" and "sensibility" become multiple, life-defining moments. Such people are multiple in the sense that they are aware of their becoming, as opposed to reified, nature(s), and thus surface without the shackles of predetermined signification; they are "eternally minor, taken up in a becoming-revolutionary" (*ibid.*). The revolution is equally personal and suprapersonal. Both are political, as literalism and metaphor are political. Where this "people" differs from those who operate securely in bourgeois culture is in its capacity to be "eternal," or to be slightly less abstract, to participate in eternity.

"More Dark" concludes with a literal infinitude. Here, of course, Mr. B's eternity is simply an escape from the posturing, the self-performativity, and the "code" of pessimism, along with the trials of an average life. The eternity of minor horror in general, however, including the larger project of "More Dark," is one that necessarily stakes a claim in the eternal present of revolution. The genre is political not in Walter Benjamin's sense of art having to serve a political agenda (art for politics' sake), but in its inevitable push against cultural egotism, not to mention that which fuels a given individual's life. Barron's anthropological text, I would argue, is, at its base, a critique of egotism. Suicide is a profoundly informal critique of life, though the story is ultimately exhibiting the imperative (as all thoughtful satire contains an imperative) of removing oneself from the ensnarement of what is essentially fundamentalist thinking. The responsibility of doing so, of extricating the self from the cultural imposition of self, so to speak, requires both the time of immediate, political (and therefore personal) decision-making, and the eternity of death; the dying daily, to use a familiar trope, to the prefabricated impulses that coach the self in speaking, thinking, and acting on behalf of a culture whose Hell is neither eternal nor far from the surface of everyday life. Through its critical insights and horror aesthetics, a minor horror is revolutionary to the extent that it opens avenues into the person and into the *mise en scène* of his or her cultural, political community via personal, revolutionary acts of disobedience, be it civil or thoughtfully, exuberantly heretical.

"Congregation of the Enemies": The Perils of Salvation

Aside from uncommonly large spiders, malignant felines, demented couples, and leering young boys whose eyes are probably best left unseen, from what are we "not saved" if we are to take "The Events at Poroth Farm" as indicative, on some abstract, horrifying level, of civilization's discontent? Beyond the dizzying precariousness, if not menace, of literalism, fanaticism, steadfast ignorance, and boorish egotism, what persists in lording over us? Franz Kafka presents a number of ideas in this regard. Distant in lifestyle and sensibility as he may be from the average person working an unremarkable job and carrying on ordinary relations with others whose lives are equally standardized, Kafka's hunger artist grasps the nature of his—and our—essential aloneness. He celebrates this condition as solitude rather than mere loneliness. Naturally, Kafka will qualify this celebration with the fact that ultimately isolated beings need other solitudes with which to commune, others to acknowledge, however delicately or nonchalantly, our ephemeral presence. Nevertheless, even when loving others are in abundance, we are not saved from a core aloneness. "A Hunger Artist" teaches us this. Secondly, for one who cannot accept what the culture offers to fill the void of one's remote subjectivity, he or she is not saved from the vulgarity of this culture, producing as it does "a whole world of non-understanding" (Kafka,

6. "We are not saved": Critical Horror Today

"Hunger" 250), "indifference and inborn malice" (254), qualities that might elicit profound "dissatisfaction" (246) or even "nausea" (247). The "amusement-seekers" (250), of course, will always manage to thrive, supported as they are by an assortment of media outlets and, for those who can buy in, consumerism. They will always evince "a positive revulsion from fasting" (*ibid.*), from the insistence on aloneness, the refusal of reducing the "book" of one's time and inner depth to a "face." And yet, they are we and we are they in so far as everybody dies; something else from which we are not saved.

Like Barron's Mr. B, the hunger artist chooses premature death. And why not, as opposed to the megalomaniacal "living death of those who regard themselves as too valuable to die," who gorge on the "food" that is given then as a panther in a cage, "furnished almost to the bursting point with all that it [needs]" (255), without seeming "to miss [its] freedom" (*ibid.*)? The hunger artist becomes a "suffering martyr" (248) for the cause of introspective dignity and cultural dissent. He eschews "the world" and therefore elevates the relative indignity and desperation of Mr. B's far more personal, neurotic demise, valuable though it may be as a negation of philosophical negation. There is freedom in death, to be sure, albeit one that does not fulfill beyond its immediate relief. Arthur C. Clarke's "The Nine Billion Names of God" complicates liberation with its portrayal of Tibetan monks who use a couple of red-blooded American engineers to unknowingly precipitate the world's extinction in the secluded ramparts of a monastery. Before they realize what is happening ("without any fuss, the stars were going out" [Clarke, "Nine" 422]), they manage to criticize the monks' curiously primitive but mysterious project, along with fundamentalist endism, in addition to yearning for the "freedom and sanity" (*ibid.*) of home. With the story's famous last line, the reader is invited to weigh the value of human life as most Americans know it.[15] Maybe the monks are privy to a plateau of freedom called emptiness that exceeds common understanding? Perhaps the American vision of sanity ("the way he felt now, even the sight of a TV commercial would seem like manna from heaven" [419]) is juvenile? The ease with which "freedom and sanity" can be conceptually and corporeally interchanged with impotence and insanity is a fact that those who would deny death are not prepared to entertain. Martyrs are an essential opposition to such people. And still, we are not saved from self-serving renditions of mainstream American liberty and mental health.

Adorno maintains that "the categorical imperative of the culture industry no longer has anything in common with freedom. It proclaims: you shall conform, without instruction as to what; conform to that which exists anyway, and to that which everyone thinks anyway as a reflex of its power and omnipresence" (*Culture* 90). It is fascinating to consider how this statement could be equally applied as right or left wing religio-political ripostes to what it deems abject in popular culture. Adorno is obviously concerned with how the machinery of capitalism becomes interiorized in consumers, though the fundamentalist reaction to the culture that exists on the margins of its walls, from Elvis to *The Exorcist* to Martin Scorsese's *The Last Temptation of Christ* to contemporary horror film and metal music, also speaks of blind conformity, and certainly of the devil's omnipresence. Both positions are disturbed by the curtailing of freedom and sanity but on vastly different fronts. From the angle of critical horror or metal—the latter, one imagines, being especially vile to the cultivated but sensitive tastes of Adorno—there is often a similar antagonism at play toward what exists or is thought "anyway." Both art forms, the overlap of which is not difficult to decipher, are highly specialized in their genres and subgenres and require a certain commitment on the part of the reader, viewer, or listener. They push back against conformity and hegemonic power structures, most notably as the latter emerge from the far right.

The 1980s PMRC (Parents Music Resource Center) debacle is, in retrospect, a laughable swelling of conservatives and fundamentalists who came of age in the 1960s without, it would seem, having identified with what was potentially beneficial about that era. Ultimately, however, it was more sinister than this, as yet another flourish of Calvinist reactivity in American history that began with puritan diatribes and prohibitions against anything smacking of occult otherness, up through the Great Awakening of the 18th century to the presidential jeremiads in its wake to Jerry Falwell's Moral Majority in the 1980s.[16] Spearheaded by Tipper Gore, the PMRC was responsible for the notorious Parental Advisory labels that appear on albums and CDs, along with identifying "The Filthy Fifteen" songs of the time (including a bizarre range, from the overtly satanic Mercyful Fate to Cyndi Lauper) and, crucially, fortifying

6. "We are not saved": Critical Horror Today

the right wing in its attempts to implement censorship. Beyond merely interrogating song lyrics about the Devil or masturbation, the PMRC participated in a McCarthyist witch hunt that destroyed the lives of many innocent people (i.e., people who may or may not have been interested in the occult matters but had the right to do so, along with the right to express those interests artistically). As Stacy Rusnak puts it, "acting in the name of 'national security,' important moral entrepreneurs framed this cultural crisis as a diabolical conspiracy by a powerful underground network of Satanic cultists intent on undermining the moral fabric of American youth" ("Scapegoat" 173). Those "entrepreneurs" on the hunt were essentially enforcing a capitalism of morality by selling, with an injunctive incentive to buy, the products of Moral Majority values that included bigotry, homophobia, economic and spiritual entitlement, and paranoia. Another way to put it is to say that the satanic panic of the 1980s was yet another demonstration of the culture industry at the hands of which, as in every such example, "conformity [had] replaced consciousness" (Adorno, *Culture* 90).

In other words, there was (and always already is from the perspective of a minoritarian, critical horror) a cultural war between progressive and reactionary positions, the former critical of dominant ideological structures and the latter emblematic of tradition and orthodoxy. Rusnak goes on to observe the manner in which

> the American dream came to be defined through the 'good old values' system, which excluded others through racism, sexism, and classism. If you worked hard, investing your energies in the family and in your job, then the nation would secure the social and economic conditions wherein your hard work would pay off, and you could live a dignified life. This philosophy tied the strength of the nation to private fortune which, by nature, was already exclusionary because the American dream is a fantasy inaccessible by the economically disadvantaged ["Scapegoat" 173].

This narrative has a history that extends much further than bourgeois but militant Christians near the end of the 20th century, though the outcomes specific to its contentions around "freedom and sanity" affected (and continue to affect) individuals and communities in distinctly unpleasant ways. In recounting the harrowing story of the West Memphis Three, teenagers who were imprisoned for nearly twenty years for murder on the basis of having been interested in metal and the occult,

T.E.D. Klein and the Rupture of Civilization

Liisa Ladouceur notes, regarding their eventual release in 2011 due to new DNA evidence, that such injustice "is the legacy of Tipper Gore, of tabloid TV specials, of the 'occult cops' and the Filthy Fifteen. That is the power of Satan" ("Filthy" 170). When dominant narratives come to specialize in demonization, they prompt alternative chronicles of subjectivity and becoming. Unwittingly, of course, they also prompt demons.

A band such as the aforementioned Venom has been clear that their Satanism was for entertainment purposes only, that it was not grounded in practice beyond the shock rock imagery (the usual suspects of pentagrams, goat heads, inverted crosses). Nonetheless, Venom represent an initial, explosive response to fundamentalist persecution and cultural oppression that sought to retaliate by giving "moral entrepreneurs" the Satanism they were attempting to locate where it generally did not exist (on albums played backwards, in the lives of young people in search of meaning and small-scale revolution, in cartoons and commercials). No need to play the record backwards or put the toothpaste advertisement under the microscope—it is all right here, on the cover, in the song titles and lyrics (the first track on Venom's freshman effort, *Welcome to Hell*, is entitled "Sons of Satan"), it shouted. Representations of overt Satanism have persisted, of course, in Black Metal and with bands whose Satanism surpasses adolescent amusement; a name such as Greece's Rotting Christ is arguably a product both of Venom setting the course and, paradoxically, groups such as the PMRC parading their histrionics. "By the end of the 1980s," Rusnak concludes, "the 'good old values' only served to reinforce the internal fragmentation of the United States. Frustration, dissatisfaction, anxiety, greed, and neuroticism over the national image still prevailed" ("Scapegoat" 198), and this neurosis has hardly abated, especially where right wing politics dovetails with the fire (and the avowal of a literal Satan) of evangelical ideology. Venom's title "In League with Satan" signifies quite differently from what was likely the band's intention when considered in relation to the (im)morality capitalists who believe what they sell.

In the immediate wake of Venom's eruption, Switzerland's Hellhammer, which eventually became Celtic Frost, pioneered their own brand of influential, low-fi metal that culminated in their final album *Monotheist* (2006). To explore the cultural and aesthetic consequences of politically and religiously-inspired censorship and other misjudg-

6. "We are not saved": Critical Horror Today

ments "today," a track such as Celtic Frost's "Synagoga Satanae" proves informative. At nearly 14½ minutes, the composition ranges from walls of guitar feedback and primitive but highly exigent, detuned riffs, to choral tones and a surprising spaciousness around one variety of the track's vocal work, as a spoken, solitary voice, in German. The rest of the vocals (in English and Latin) are comprised of vocalist Tom G. Warrior's characteristic angry growls, though they are not those of the conventional barker or jock, death metal singer; Warrior's voice is personal and confrontational in its directness and odd sense of intimacy, enriched, I would suggest, by a longtime history with and understanding of heavy metal. Most important for the purposes of this study, however, is the lyrical content and the liner notes' commentary. The lyrics could very well have been penned by Klein's diabolical Rosie/the Old One/Absolom Troet, a horror-inspired tribute to Satan, the infernal Lord to whom allegiance is a dark and monumental honor.

But before we become mired in the thought of a literalist's Satanism, it is necessary to consider the opening line of the track: "Internalized conflict externalized as war" (Celtic Frost, "Synagoga" 2006). In spite of what follows, the lyrics begin with psychology and the inevitable exteriorization of the conflicted, fragmented self, whether this "war" is physically or emotionally aggressive. This statement is followed by a set of decrees, if not invocations: "In darkness. Thou shalt come unto me. In darkness. Thou shalt worship me. In darkness. Thou art mine eternally" (*ibid.*). There is confusion as to whether this is a hymn to Satan or a personal testimony, though what finally becomes apparent is that the two—the narrator and Satan—are one. "They" are then referred to as the "Scapegoat" and "a monarch enthroned upon my throne of guilt" (*ibid.*); the "scapegoat" who suffers both "a whole world of nonunderstanding," as Kafka puts it, and the morbid, fallen angel whose guilt is legion. "I am hell," the writer proclaims, "a barren shrine to decay and neglect," and concludes the English portion of the lyrics with "in the end when thou art mine thou will be like me" (*ibid.*). "Thou" is also subject to "internalized conflict" and "war," to "guilt" and social persecution; the reader/listener is also Hell in so far as he or she neglects the decomposition of self at the hands of scapegoaters, those who would territorialize for the sake of their infernal, or terrestrial, power, their grim visions of "freedom and sanity."

T.E.D. Klein and the Rupture of Civilization

With the commentary, Martin Eric Ain, Celtic Frost's bass player and co-architect, explains the deterritorializing quality of the track's lyrical content and intentions. An extended passage begins, as it happens, with an assertion regarding the metaphorical nature of Hell:

> Hell is a concept concocted by followers of the "Christian Faith" to anticipate a netherworld, where the enemies of Christ will be punished for all eternity. By their definition, I am one such "enemy." "Synogoga Satanae" stands for "Congregation of the Enemies." In the exegesis of the term coined by John the Revelator, the heretic, the schismatic, the superstitious, the hypocrite, and the infidel, make up said congregation. Which by this definition would actually include the majority of the human populace on this planet. I have therefore tried to refine my place in this "Church of Satan," and by doing so, I have taken the liberty to blaspheme some things sacred and to sanctify others more profane [*ibid.*].

It should be clear that the quotations around "this Church of Satan," and around other words and phrases—"Christian Faith"; "enemy"—are meaningful. In each case, they call into question not only the literalism of the language (the "Satanism" of the writer's "church," the monolithic nature of Christian faith, and the status or disposition of an "enemy"), but the directionality of its power. Another way to frame this is to say that Hell is deterritorialized (and defamiliarized), stripped of its fire and its brimstone for the sake of elucidating the horrors of oppressive dualism and literalism. And in keeping with its horror sensibility, the track's ethos includes a sense of revelry, celebration, without succumbing to the dumbed-down forces behind the familiar territory of self/other polarities. "Enemy" is unhinged from its identity-politics, re-appropriated as a form of conceivably productive, ecstatic transgression in defiance of literalist condemnations. The "congregation," of course, consists of most people, some of whom are more aware (for worse and certainly for better) than others of the rich potentiality of their diverse community and its commonsense eschewal of the hellish visions that would drag it to a world under the relatively refined surfaces of sanctity, intelligence, and joy.

As much as I would like to conclude this study with the full musical and lyrical experience of "Synagoga Satanae," some comments on "freedom and sanity" from the perspective of critical horror will suffice to bring the track's own critically horrifying aesthetic into further calibration with the subject at hand. What is blasphemed in Ain's commentary

6. "We are not saved": Critical Horror Today

is not simply Christianity but a literalist vision of Revelation's Hell. Hell is mythology that becomes real, a temporary or chronic rip in the fabric of conscientious relations, when heresy is politicized, or personalized, or simply imagined. Hell is fiction, the kind that evolves not from the penetrating minds of canonical or marginal writers but from the self that is divided between delusions of grandeur and inferiority alike. What is sanctified is "the majority of the human populace on this planet," those who might venture into the music of Celtic Frost or the fiction of T.E.D. Klein as well as all others for whom the attribute of "other" would surely be enforced outside the ecumenical and comparatively tolerant "Church of Satan." To distance the latter from its provocative invitation to literalism, we might think of its correlate, the "Congregation of Enemies," from the standpoint of critical, minor horror; such horror that creates the possibility of "another community," a "Congregation" whose recognition (however protracted or lacking in methodology) of non-being qualifies them for access to "freedom and sanity" based on a combination of horizontal collectivism, self-reliance, and a capacity for grasping the power of metaphor. The diametrically opposed alternative is ideological inerrancy. Whether it is fundamentalist or politically far right, the cult of self whose very identity depends on intolerance and paranoia misreads both the limits and the continuum of its "freedom and sanity." Here freedom assumes the form of a barricade against modern, moving time, in favor, as George Lakoff explains, of "the situation prior to the expansion of traditional American ideas of freedom: before the great expansion of voting rights, before unions and worker protections and pensions, before civil rights legislation, before public health and environmental protections, before Social Security and Medicare, before scientific discoveries contradicted fundamentalist religious dogma" (*Whose* 5). The "sanity" of such freedom is a losing battle with self, one whose fantasies around upward mobility inevitably flatten along the horizontal line of democratic progress that is itself lifted, vertically, through a series of ever-expanding plateaus, as a collective populace slowly, begrudgingly, and sometimes quite happily observes kinship and solidarity among its many, diverse faces.

For Klein, "freedom and sanity" are like "truth," a female in Father Pistachio's estimation, who is "far more strange" than most would think. But to be more specific, we might say that freedom is the grandfather

T.E.D. Klein and the Rupture of Civilization

in "Children of the Kingdom" who can "move in either world," on either side of a class divide, as much as he prefers communing with the lower class. He appears to perceive a relative authenticity in their ranks. Moreover, along with his learned friend, he is able to recognize that "all men are homeless," the "truth" that leads to compassion, if not equality in slow-burning, existential malaise, or revelation. All men and women are without a permanent home in life, for death will inevitably counter our presumptions, our hard, ideological truths around which we construct affected selves in paper castles. Sanity is acknowledging "a semblance of the monster in ourselves," as Klein's Nadelman is forced to do, without sinking into the ignorant abyss of a despotic, hypnotizing notion of original sin that colors the life and death, the "home" of the fundamentalist in pathetic union with his or her own saccharine—or vicious—dream of divine providence. Sanity is also listening to the "man on the bed" when he tells us to "R.U.N." ("Petey" 109). It entails being open to the insights of the "sorcerer," even when he or she appears to be a "creep" *par excellence*. Life and death may depend on these visions that transcend bourgeois cosmologies and ferreting, earthly avocations.

"Petey's" portents are, of course, indicative of the fact that despite propositions of freedom, sanity, and even happiness, critical horror nurtures an inherent ferocity, without which it would be merely a body of "reassuring tales" with no hint of irony. Critical horror never loses sight of Satan's power. It is forever fascinated by the diabolical, the demoniacal, and it is as quick to point out the reprehensible flaw of taking such power literally as it is intent on scaring its audience into a healthy vigilance. It coaxes us into occult portals, bloody scenarios, damaged, stolen lives, but most importantly, into awareness of the reader/viewer's implication in the activities of those unhallowed spaces. Critical horror thus bestows the gift of a graduated mirror stage in which the mirror reflects not only monstrosity but a self *in potentia* having nothing to do with fiendish hunger or pitiable misidentification; rather, this becoming-self is made acutely aware of its limitations, knowledge of which is the only possible course to "freedom and sanity." It produces radical, productive "enemies" of majoritarian strongholds while diagnosticating the "congregation's" own vulnerability to reactionary thought and behavior. And it does so without sparing us from a deeply pleasurable, far from innocuous peril.

We are not saved from a destructive, psychologically debased

6. "We are not saved": Critical Horror Today

human condition whose attempted dethronement would be tantamount, as Kurt Vonnegut might put it, to stopping glaciers. Contrary to all overwhelming evidence, we may be saved, however, with the right guidance and inspiration, from ourselves as individuals and minor collectives. There is immense power in self-knowledge born of honest, intelligent self-interrogation. While it seems ridiculous to imply that now more than ever, American culture—always already insistent on its exceptionalism and consequently susceptible to every dim-witted misdeed—is in need of such salvation, the more digital and mechanical we become, the greater the impact our cultural texts must make on our febrile minds and bodies, excited by every popular sensation as they are. In a culture intoxicated by the dirty money and consumerist oblivion of virtual reality, Jackson's "absolute reality," that *The Ceremonies*' Jeremy both laments and sanctions, must be an emphatic voice sounding throughout the cultural wilderness. It howls in the hope of awakening a minor disturbance, or agitating the sleeping-walking certainties of a nation, critical in its delineation of social failures and paramount as a blackened, macabre atmosphere that seeks to descend upon the parade of colorful apparitions, those spectral proponents of piety inured to interiority's wisdom and cheated, with open arms and gullible hearts, by the false messiah of all that is truly, literally evil.

APPENDIX I

Reassuring Words: An Interview with T.E.D. Klein

PHILLIPS: *I'd like to begin by asking a question to which I'll return, in part, later. What does horror (fiction or film) mean to you in 2016?*

KLEIN: Thomas, I'm somewhat abashed to admit this, as it suggests a lack of serious commitment, but I have far less interest in horror fiction (and horror films) than I used to. In fact, I read very little fiction of any kind these days; like a lot of men my age, I prefer reading nonfiction—generally 20th-century history and some easy popular science. I'm sure this has something to do with mortality breathing down my neck.

PHILLIPS: *Your response makes sense on a number of levels, Ted. For one thing, it also suggests that what we* do *commit to carries weight. To what, we might ask, are we committing when absorbing the imagery, be it literary or filmic, of horror? The issue begs the question as to the value of what we allow into our lives, particularly given how brief these lives ultimately are. But on that note, I wonder (and please don't feel pressure to get too personal): does the proximity of mortality precipitate an interest in the relatively pragmatic disciplines of history and science, or does your lack of interest hinge more on a general aversion to horror?*

KLEIN: Normally I'd reply that in reading history and science, I'm attempting to make up, late in the game, for my woeful ignorance after a lifetime of avoiding nonfiction. I used to complain—still do, actually—that majoring in English in college was a mistake, since it's left me envying people who actually *know* things.

But that doesn't explain the almost physical satisfaction I get, these days, when settling into some big fat history book—whereas books that set out to make my skin crawl ... well, that's just not a sensation I particularly crave anymore. Maybe I'm becoming an old lady.

Appendix I

Speaking a bit more broadly, after a lifetime of reading fiction for pleasure, I suspect I'm becoming a bit jaded; I find I'm increasingly critical of, and impatient with, the fiction I've been reading lately. The contrivances, the labored attempts to shoehorn in—or shovel in—exposition, the withholding of vital information, the overelaborate set pieces, all seem too obvious. (Mind you, I'm not pretending I can do any better. I see these failings in my own stuff as well.) I feel the same about the movies. I used to be a passionate filmgoer—I actually have an MFA in film—but in recent years I certainly don't feel the wild enthusiasms I once did. Again, I think it may come down, at least in part, to having seen so damned many movies.

I certainly share your reticence around fiction/film, especially that which has appeared in the 21st century. Some of the recent novels to come from the French publisher Les Éditions de Minuit, however, have gone a long way to revive my literary enthusiasm. Somehow I can imagine you enjoying Christian Gailly's An Evening at the Club *or Jean Echeno's* Piano, *to name two examples. But on the English major topic, please allow me to share a quick anecdote. A student recently made a similar point in class discussion about Philip K. Dick's* Ubik, *claiming that non-fiction offers information and knowledge, while fiction provides us with "lessons." Fair enough, though I suggested that the rather clever manner in which Dick exposes and repudiates racism, and further, ascribes to his protagonist—and possibly the genre of science fiction—the role of "professional agitator," would seem to be a "lesson" we (still) can't do without. That said, I certainly know the experience of being a humanities professional and feeling at odds with a techno-savvy, STEM culture.*

*On a related note, I recall your having mentioned the correlation between yourself and Jeremy from "The Events"/*The Ceremonies. *This may very well be a stretch, but I wonder if Jeremy's immersion in gothic/horror fiction prepares him in any way for the heroism of the novel's dramatic conclusion?*

That's an interesting thought. In fact, his heroism, such as it is, bothered me so much that when I recently reread the novel for the first time in 30 years, with an eye to revising and correcting it, I rewrote most of that final scene. But I'm not sure I managed to make his actions any more convincing.

Reassuring Words: An Interview with T.E.D. Klein

I guess you're asking, in part, if a steady diet of horror fiction might make the supernatural seem a little more familiar and hence less threatening; and I suppose it could, just as a lifetime of reading military histories and tales of bravery might conceivably make someone behave more courageously in battle. Yet I suspect that immersion in horror fiction—especially the work of someone as gloomy as, say, Le Fanu—might just as easily have the opposite effect, affirming one's sense of helplessness and futility vis-à-vis the supernatural, the way a diet of antiwar fiction might demoralize our hypothetical soldier.

In another interview, with Carl T. Ford in the 1987 special issue of Dagon, *you claim "there's horror in these [Lovecraft's] tales, but there's beauty as well." Can you elaborate on the beauty of horror in general? Does it have to do with the particular atmospheres horror evokes, or is it more complex in your estimation, a product of the sublime, for example?*

That's an interesting question, but I'm not sure what you mean by "the particular atmospheres horror evokes." Maybe you yourself can elaborate a bit?

For whatever it's worth, I've argued in the past that supernatural horror logically has a bright and shiny flip side, so to speak, since a universe with room in it for malevolent forces presumably contains benign ones as well; the existence of demons presupposes that of angels. But now, I have to say, that notion strikes me as a bit glib; I guess I've made my peace with living in a universe where science rules, where magic spells don't actually work, and where no houses are really, truly haunted.

By the atmosphere of horror I mean, with reference to Lovecraft's claim on the subject in Supernatural Horror in Literature, *that horror has a way of provoking especially striking and visceral "sensations," as opposed to merely entertaining, or even deeply engaging plots. A fantastic example from* The Ceremonies *is that incredible moment when Carol catches Rosie glaring at her malevolently, showing his true face in the flickering light, at an otherwise pleasant dinner table. Astonishing. Or when he emerges as a "bundle," and then "a gaunt and wrinkled old woman" on the verge of killing Carol's roommate. But let's move on to the next question that may take us further into the appeal of the genre.*

Appendix I

Thank you (if I may interject). I'm always curious as to what works or doesn't work for a reader.

What might it say about the generalized "us" that a provocative and often quite violent form of beauty is so popular?
Sorry, not sure I follow.

Sure—how about I reframe it in this way: despite most evidence to the contrary (or simply a lack of compelling evidence), many people want houses to be haunted. What might this say about humanity, particularly given that we seek representations of hauntings, among other unsettling events, on such a large scale in fiction and film? Do you think we need horror, at least at certain points in our lives, as a medium for transcending, however briefly, what might be otherwise banal and not necessarily "beautiful" lives? Or does it come down to Stephen King's notion that we're all a bit mad and need to nourish the unconscious in relatively safe ways?
I agree that there's a desire to transcend the banal. A world in which houses can be haunted is definitely a richer, more exciting place, and in fact a more *meaningful* place—though not necessarily one I'd prefer to live in.

I find that there's a great deal of cultural critique in your work, particularly "The Events at Poroth Farm"/The Ceremonies, "Petey," and "Nadelman's God," in terms of religious and class ideologies. How important is such critique in your overall project of writing horror?
Well, I'm a little conflicted about this. On the one hand, it's hard to disagree with the common assumption that art which carries a message is bad art. And this surely goes double for fantasy; as a general rule, I'd say that political messages and, as you put it, cultural critiques have no business in fantasy fiction. Whenever I sense some sort of agenda in a story, I resent it. I accept the notion that insofar as art is political, it isn't art. But that's speaking in the abstract. I also happen to be a fairly opinionated fellow, even about stuff I know nothing about; I like to argue; I spend a lot of time (maybe too much) reading the news; I'm quite politically engaged, not necessarily in ways you'd expect from someone living on the Upper West Side of Manhattan. And it's hard to resist taking

Reassuring Words: An Interview with T.E.D. Klein

advantage, so to speak, of the humble platform that a work of fiction affords me. When I'm writing, I fancy myself as a truth-teller—I mean, don't we all?—and it's a pleasurable indulgence to inject some opinions into my work. As to whether they belong there, I'm not sure I can say.

On a related note, you mention Edmund Wilson's notion of "homeopathic horror" and similar descriptors in Raising Goosebumps for Fun and Profit. ***I understand that this term speaks to the (important) entertainment value of the genre, but is the provocation of critical analysis in some horror the homeopathic poison, so to speak, that provides a possible antidote to cultural ills (including but not limited to the raw egotism of individuals and collectives)? What does "homeopathic horror" signify for you?***

Was I really that insufferably pretentious? I've looked through *Goosebumps*, and I see that, yes, I guess I was—although I seem to have quoted Wilson explaining that notion ("injections of imaginary horror, which soothe us with the momentary illusions that the forces of madness and murder may be tamed") without actually using the phrase itself. Looking back at Wilson's essay, I see he agrees that "a political element ... seems clumsy and out of place in a ghost story." Unfortunately, he also suggests that horror has a special appeal to readers during wartime ("Gestapo ... tank attacks and airplane bombings, houses rigged with booby-traps"), which seems to me quite doubtful, and he thinks highly of "The Turn of the Screw," which I find the most overrated ghost tale ever written.

I don't believe, on reflection, that a passion for horror fiction and films has much to do with current events, the world situation, etc. Our fascination with the genre starts when we're quite young, don't you think?—long before we have the slightest interest in the day's news. Historians and critics used to maintain that the revived-dinosaur and giant-bug-and-lizard movies of the '50s were, quote unquote, a response to the real-life terrors of the Atomic Age, the uncertainties of the Cold War, blah blah blah—but that strikes me as silly. True, "atomic testing" supplied filmmakers with a handy explanation for how these creatures got so damned big; but I was crazy about those movies when I was growing up in that era, and believe me, their appeal had nothing to do with any concerns about the Bomb, because such concerns never entered my mind, nor the mind of anyone I knew.

Appendix I

Oh, I absolutely agree that such fascination begins when we're young! Those mid-70s Saturday nights with Chiller Theater were quite formative for me. I do think, however, that the genre often calls its reader out—on the convenient illusions of suburban safety and immortality, for example. But I also find your critiques of the Gilead community in The Ceremonies/*"Events" or of George's financial and other improprieties in "Petey" to be not only insightful but organic elements in the respective narratives. Perhaps there's an inherent impulse to seek (and possibly destroy) human presumptuousness without necessarily negating the potentiality of what you called "benign" forces in life in the act of creating horror scenarios. Any further thoughts on this quagmire of an issue?*

I think you're quite right about "Petey," but in fact, when you mentioned cultural critique, I thought you were alluding to the other three stories in *Dark Gods,* all set in New York City and all, at times, a bit snarky.

I was initially drawn to writing horror for the sake of both fun and what always feels like genuine experimentation relative to other forms of writing, including so-called experimental fiction. There's something tremendously compelling in creating an alliance between such disparate modes of writing as the nouveau roman, for example, and horror. Have you generally felt unimpeded by tradition or stylistic convention when writing horror or are there particular constraints that inform how and what you write?

When I hear the words "experimental fiction," I reach for my gun. I live among thousands of books, but have I ever read any experimental fiction? Beats me. Did I ever publish any in *Twilight Zone*? I doubt it. Have I ever dabbled in it myself? I don't believe so. I'm not even sure what it is.

Your writing style comes across to this reader as effortlessly literary, by which I mean it pushes well beyond attempts to emulate Lovecraft or conventional, post-MFA writing that's peppered with the usual similes and attempts at hyper-realism, surrealism, or some kind of baroque arcana, etc. Rather, it seems to ride a fine line between exceptionally graceful, sophisticated prose and the grittiness that is more or less integral to horror. To quote the Ford interview again, you suggest that "a

Reassuring Words: An Interview with T.E.D. Klein

work of fiction is more than just a series of events set in such-and-such a time and place; it is also about language." What is it about your particular relationship to language that both sets it apart from others and has inclined you to give it voice in the horror genre?

You're very kind, first of all. I only wish my writing were so effortless. It doesn't come easily at all, which is one reason I've done so little of it. You know, I've recently gone over the full text of *The Ceremonies* and two of the tales from *Dark Gods*, making hundreds of tweaks and small revisions, wincing (and occasionally cringing) at what struck me as embarrassingly clumsy writing. I hope I've improved it. I'm not sure exactly what it is that I'm after when it comes to style—certainly it never works out, on the page, the way I imagine it's going to—but I have to tell you, I've always been inspired, to the point of imitation, or at least attempted imitation, by the writers I most admire. And they're not necessarily writers in the genre.

Just a comment here: I believe that reading horror alongside (or even behind) writers outside the genre is tremendously useful. Among the most fascinating parallels I've happened upon in this book is between "Petey" and T.S. Eliot's The Cocktail Party. The overlap is mostly to do with content, though the two texts can illuminate each other in very, very interesting ways.

Thank you; I'm honored—though candidly, all I remember of *The Cocktail Party* is that, offstage, some woman ends up getting improbably crucified in Africa. Permit a free association: There's a scene in a Patrick White novel I read many decades ago in which an aging writer is leafing through his youthful notebooks and comes across an Eliot poem that, as a young man, he'd admiringly copied down, albeit without attribution. The old writer doesn't recognize the poem, takes it for one of his own, and thinks something like, "Gee, I really turned out some good stuff in those days."

Well, despite the irony in this delightful and poignant example, and at the risk of overdoing the praise, I for one think that you've undoubtedly "turned out some good stuff." Regarding The Cocktail Party, perhaps where horror ends and where Eliot begins (thematically, that is) is where "Petey's" George gets what's coming to him and the crucified woman,

Appendix I

and in yet another irony, locates redemption (albeit a painful one, to put it mildly) in the context of what is otherwise a drearily confused existence. Here's where your fiction really shines to me: in its ability to land the reader in some serious murk, cosmic or otherwise, and often on a rather dark note, without necessarily eschewing the value of humanity.

You are obviously a fan of cosmic horror, which often ends badly for protagonists, though you've also stated that you enjoy happy endings. Some critics have reacted negatively to what they perceive as a discrepancy here. What are your thoughts about this reaction, and more broadly, about what appears to be an underlying imperative or ideological position concerning the related notion of cosmic pessimism?

Hmm, "cosmic pessimism" certainly sounds like the sort of philosophy I can subscribe to! (I wish it were otherwise.) But yes, I continue to prefer happy endings—as happy, at least, as the demands of the work will allow. Do you mention, in whatever precedes this interview, anything about my titling that little collection of mine *Reassuring Tales*?

I'm fond of something the late Robert Bloch once observed: that the fantasy genre is "one of the few areas left in which good can still triumph over evil. And that's one of the reasons, I'm afraid, why it's called fantasy."

Oh yes! In fact, I look at "Well-Connected" as an example of your work that provides reassurance not only of being "snatched back from the abyss" but of the possibility of tenderness in the human experience (in this case, between a father and son). That said, it's impossible not to be aware of the title's irony given certain of the collection's other stories. I suppose the difference between your vision and proponents of "cosmic pessimism" is that they don't seem to "wish it were otherwise." Rather, they come across as strangely and paradoxically religious about their adopted cosmology to the point of criticizing others who dare to allow for any semblance of optimism.

Yes, interesting thought. It reminds me of a collaborative horror novel I read years ago by two young writers I'd published in *Twilight Zone*, John Skipp and Craig Spector. I don't recall the details, and I'm paraphrasing what follows, but something unexpectedly shocking and gruesome happens to one of the minor characters, and after describing the carnage, the authors remark, "God's funny that way."

Reassuring Words: An Interview with T.E.D. Klein

Meanwhile, in the godless universe we actually inhabit, I'm convinced we have far too many "village atheists," despite the fact that I share their outlook. The late philosopher Sidney Hook used to say that, though he himself was an atheist, he was not about to argue with a mother who, grieving for her dead son, found comfort in the thought that she would eventually be reunited with him in heaven.

Laird Barron's controversial story "More Dark," a satire on the antinatalism of Thomas Ligotti and his followers, is quite caustic in its critique. You, too, have made critical remarks in the past regarding the general demographics of horror readers and, through your fiction, occultists. Is there anything that contemporary horror can do to productively counter the "fantasy, play-acting, and delusion" of "creeps," as the protagonist of "Nadelman's God" puts it, while maintaining the genre's intent to unsettle?

Once again—forgive this refrain—I'm not entirely sure what you're asking. If you mean, is there some way of wresting supernatural horror from the goths and the occultists and their ilk, I'm not sure how we'd accomplish that, and I suppose I should hate to lose a portion of our audience. I must say I'm intrigued and amused by that type—by their earnestness—and a teeny bit contemptuous of them (okay, more than a teeny bit), and sometimes alarmed.

Going slightly off-topic for a moment, have you ever noticed that sports fans seem to have barely any interest in fantasy, and vice versa? That's certainly the case among friends of mine. (And sorry, whispering the phrase "fantasy football" is not an argument!)

I often go back, even today, to a remark a therapist once made, and which I quoted approvingly in "Nadelman": I was telling him about how a girl I knew believed she'd been a Pharaoh's mistress in a previous life—not a slave, mind you, but a Pharaoh's mistress, maybe even a Pharaoh—and how she'd walk out onto her apartment building's roof once a month to pay elaborate homage the moon. And he nodded as if he'd heard it all before and said, "Reality is never enough for some people."

I suppose my question is ultimately more about the genre than its readership. Of course, readers arguably inform a given genre as much as they are formed by it. While few writers or artists wish to alienate their

Appendix I

audiences, I wonder if horror (and this takes us back to a number of points made above) is an appropriate or even necessary venue for engaging the "reality" that isn't sufficient for some, a project that has the capacity to disrupt certain identities or identifications, even and perhaps especially those that deem themselves marginal? In other words, perhaps horror, despite its supernatural components, is an especially effective mode of grounding one in "reality" that appears to care very little if at all about our precious egos. Would you agree with that?

If you mean that a work of horror can serve as a reminder of the cruelty or at least indifference of the universe, I'd agree that it can. But then, unfortunately, so can many a history book.

Absolutely—and herein lies the essence and ongoing relevance of cultural critique as far as I'm concerned.

As for sports fans and fantasy, there's something compelling there! I imagine it has a lot to do with varying modes of embodiment, among other things. In an Emersonian world, we would all be more or less functional as athletes, engineers, scientists, historians, and maybe even English majors, or at least minors …

Ted, I can't thank you enough for sharing your thoughts. It's been a sincere pleasure.

Appendix II

The Singular Ceremonies

The first sentence of Don DeLillo's *The Body Artist* is "time seems to pass," an observation laden as much with the girth and powerful relativity of "seems" as with the ostensibly monolithic phenomenon of "time." Life, in its quotidian and its cosmic perceptions alike, is always already composed of impressions, images (the falling leaf, the furrowed brow) and ideas (why? how?) that stir one into a sense of things at the very same moment that they belie their quality and their meaning. The signification of a sparrow or a philosophical construct—what is that in the span of its being, or its immediacy? Fleeting. This much we know. We are also acutely aware of the fact that relativity is a luxury—one well worth pursuing, but a luxury nonetheless—in the face, the often stern visage of deadlines and world-heavy pressures. Student essays to grade. The necessary follow-through with projects. The clothes that hang on our consciences, our bodies, to affect a very odd creature indeed. The burdened man, the faceless scarecrow on whom daring black birds perch, the one whose eyes open in a moment of quick, unsettling horror, as in Frank De Felitta's 1981 *Dark Night of the Scarecrow*. The woman lost in time, dragging her daily suitcase of errands, hauntings, and impediments. Barbara Hershey in Sidney J. Furie's 1982 *The Entity* (also penned, as it happens, by Felitta).

That is, until summer arrives, for the teacher whose income is stretched across the year, the sound of which constitutes a silent distention for the quietly focused, head down, committed scholar, his pleasure in research and reading without thought for bewildered students now given free reign to advance and spill over into all hours, including dreams. As it does for Jeremy Freirs, the protagonist of T.E.D. Klein's "The Events at Poroth Farm" and the story's expanded novel form, *The Ceremonies*, a book about books. As it does for the one whose summer

Appendix II

has just begun in the wake of a more or less successful semester, another academic eager to read for pleasure. *The Ceremonies* at the top of the list and finally—finally—within his grasp. The bulking hardback having rested on a coffee table for too many months, its cover design, a vision of the earth being engulfed by some snake-like creature, perhaps an unfortunate caricature of Klein's unparalleled discourse and of the weight, heavier than time, its language is capable of giving to evil.

 The scholar enlivened by his or her discipline paws for time when the latter is given short shrift during an academic year (a period supposed by some, cretins and philistines, plodding, clownish reactionaries, to be largely bereft of effort or value). A particular scholastic, one of whose core research topics might best be defined as "darkness," joins Jeremy in the summer hours that no longer feel like eternity (oh no, that time, the time of youth, of sparkling camaraderie and ice cream and television, warm air at once stifling and bolstering play when school wraps up in June, is long since vanished). Though he determines to explore the novel, to meet it where its language, if the preceding story is any indication, speaks to the elongated now of extant, urgent narrative. His dissertation long since complete, along with the horror seminar in which he teaches the short story, it is time for discovering where the novel elaborates upon and pushes the evil, how it penetrates, evokes disaster, disruption of the fanatical self. Perhaps it is this wounding quality that has compelled his students to respond so positively to the story, the manner in which it baits and antagonizes religious zealotry, self-righteous morality, even as Puritanism informs the non-believers, students on the fence (where else should they be as students?), with its enduring program of cultural and psychological illiteracy. We all more or less enjoy being ruptured in the secrecy of our interiorities. Some seductive reversion of the Real, the Omega Point, the call not of Cthulhu but of the splintered self we know ourselves to be beneath the layers of words and pictures. The remote prospect of integrity the barest frequency in what Emerson might call that "resounding tumult."

 The book waits. A material object having little or everything to do with the predicament of being human. It strikes him as somehow intentional in its mere presence. He awakes in the morning, moves through his ritual of contemplation, breakfast, tea, music that dots rather than fills the space of an otherwise calm living room, and it is always there,

The Singular Ceremonies

on the table, conversing with the ritual in a low hum, luring him into its bedeviled universe. And beyond the morning, well into the evening hours. A grimoire. This is how he comes to perceive the book over the course of weeks and months. His knowing just enough of the conspicuous "events" that populate its pages to be seduced by its inevitable night, over time. What is time? The thing that has burrowed within, from the beginning and before that, deceptive in its weightlessness in the chest, the quietly desperate mind. And without, enshrouding us in those key moments, like the eyes of Dagmar Lassander in Lucio Fulci's *The House by the Cemetery* (1981), in close-up. A ghostly presence, the thing in the basement, what is in fact concrete in the chest, and the distinctly other, stabbing eyes urging one whose sensibility has opened a cavity in his being to pick it up, move through it, unravel the seams, crack the book. Read.

He turns to what is regrettably Klein's only novel on the first full night of his summer—it's his, the warm air and that time belong to him now—at an hour that is still early enough to accommodate the walkers, people he likes to observe taking in a leisurely stroll by the park. His home an apartment on the edge of a green, child-friendly island. The window by his comfy chair prime for observation, especially during the day when strollers can't see in due to the glare. Women joggers in scant shorts and tank tops. A book long since out of print, he folds the hardcover back, gently fondles paper as thoughtful adults do with treasured books and familiar bodies and discovers on the title page a stamp above *The Ceremonies*, the word DISCARD. A mutilation. A heresy at the hands of a former owner. Or an incitation, to the reader of a particular sensibility, to proceed with the ceremony, one bereft of morning serenity. Lose your complacency. A disciple of the grimoire coaxing and daring, passing it on. Or simply a librarian following protocol at the end of an unwanted book's tenure; though her name may be Carol, he will consider in retrospect, and she may be urging the reader, from another time, forecasting this moment in an intuitive collapse of time, to run. Go to sleep. Dispose of the book and run back to your morning light that nourishes and makes of darkness a shadow hobby, a sexy, scholastic endeavor. Please do this. But it's so much more, or less, than that, he thinks. The temperature has already begun to rise, it's feeling oppressive out there now, tonight. All is quiet in the park and he flips pages, careful not to make a crease, and lands on the prologue: "Christmas."

Appendix II

"It was outside nature, and alone." Page one. Referring, of course, to the inevitable evil. And yet, evil is said to be legion, its paradoxical namelessness a multiplicity. And it resides, in context, among the charred, graceless ruins of a forest, "black against the blackness of [a] tree," an old child of some nature at once beyond and kindred with our own, at one and the same time arborescent and the rhizome whose roots proliferate laterally, like the fire that has sent a forest ablaze. So what's really at stake here? Perhaps "it" is the lone reader himself or herself. She wanders the barren landscape of a turgid culture while remaining grimly static; he deceives himself with technology, the countless screens and virtual portals to progress, when the entropy of a cancer, his bare inattention and subsequent complacency, eats him alive.

But not this reader, no. He is resolved to abstain from the dismal surface life. A critical thinker, a purveyor of liminality, largely untouchable by the hands of consumer-vision progress, yes. Progressive, sure. "*Soyez réalistes, demandez l'impossible!*" But not bullied by market fundamentalism, junkie reactivity. With Jeremy, he finds something refreshing in the Poroth's Luddite ways at the same time that he disdains the remarkable crudity of their cultish religious order, its inerrancy and butch patriarchy. Especially the demeanor of Saar, the husband. The strong, quiet type. Easily unsettled by a break in orthodoxy. He bristles malevolently when his cosmic, and therefore personal vision is ruptured. How much happier he would be, thinks the reader, if he embraced the darkness for what it has to teach regarding relativity ("*Il est interdit d'interdire!*"). Or at least opened himself to mischievous laughter on occasion, like his wife Deborah, who, if the protagonist is correct, wears nothing under her long black dress. A "handsome" woman. A young couple whose recently purchased farm lies tranquil and hushed amidst their remote community, a mere thirty miles plus from Times Square. Young enough to require extra income to supplement their devout work ethic. They are far from George and Phyllis of Klein's "Petey," a bourgeois pair of Kurtz's who have no real ethic and essentially steal their country house. So they, the Poroths, rent a converted henhouse for the summer to Jeremy Freirs, whose semester of teaching is over, unlike his dissertation, very much in progress. Time for reading, notating ideas. In the company of the Poroths and their cats, one of whom, Bwada, is destined for flesh-tearing possession. A condition that will not be relegated to a feline as the ceremonies unfold, no, not at all. "It" is aiming to consume the world.

Now the book lives atop a small stack of other texts: a clever and psychoanalytically rich French novel, something hefty about the demise of capitalism, or the spiritual ruin it brings to people, and one of the *Commentaries* by Maurice Nicoll. Books that shed light, to be read in collaboration with the sun. Klein also sheds light, as long as we understand the verb to mean casting off rather than radiating. The darkness by his chair.

Bwada is a female. Jeremy is a male who desires both Deborah and Carol, the virginal librarian from the city whose trajectory is arranged by the Old One to align, catastrophically, the reader surmises, with Jeremy's. Everybody desires in this book, one of its many nods to the kind of mundane, earthy realism that Klein marries so skillfully to cosmic foreboding. Comfortable in his large reading chair, he—he—is inclined to ponder his own implication in wondering what's under the black folds of the dress, or in rooting for Saar when the husband allows his humanity to assert itself with the prospect of sex in a field. In chuckling when Jeremy remains hopeful about fucking the virgin despite all indications to the contrary. Healthy disturbances, all, though a feminist lens, that vision that reroutes the male gaze, or splinters it so as to insure at least partial self-reflection, may suggest otherwise. Saar's mother, a solemn, morose seer whom the other Brethren of the Redeemer esteem while remaining at a careful distance, is noted at one point as being "the only truly dark thing in the landscape." Not unlike an advanced-in-years Goodman Brown who, Hawthorne observes, "was himself the chief horror of the scene," even amidst devil worshippers and, of course, Lucifer himself. She fears the devil, whose name is legion, but the conscientious reader can only wonder if one such name is Desire, especially when her consternation over Carol's arrival at the farm is insinuated to stem from a grievance with sex outside of holy matrimony. From this perspective, her *Dinglichkeit*, her thingness, is truly dark indeed, grounded as it is in the notion of a natural world corrupted by libido. She was never introduced to the insights of Wilhelm Reich. She carries the flag for a holiness bent on neurosis. Deborah, who embraces her own sexuality with curiosity and good cheer, will be among the first, after the cat, to succumb to bedevilment. Her body initially conceived by her husband as "His sacred

Appendix II

instrument." His, meaning God's. But Klein begs to differ. The woman is hijacked, territorialized, by more than one dark thing, by less than sacred tendencies, reductions, all too human blasphemies.

Jacques Lacan chooses the word *lamelle* to signify the crossroads of narcissism and desire. A juncture of the self whose self-love is compromised in a thousand different ways, who desires to maintain her ideality, his close-to-the-vest identity, in the same moment, or unending series of lifespan moments, that a host of others are intended, and invariably fail, to constitute and fortify that love. We love our opinions and our static thingness, but we also crave companionship. The reader contemplates this intersection as it might relate to the routine unconsciousness and everyday automation that fuels evil. The immediacy and vitality of perdition propelled forward, but slowly, over time, bending time to meet its needs. Until it breaks the self in an instant of quick, cracking fatality. The violence of unconscious emotion, dubious prohibitions. The reader slowly melts into Jeremy. He glances out the window, into the night. He prides himself on possessing the book, a scholar undertaking serious study, utilizing time that others spend with the dumbest possible culture. Television, a book of faces, abortions of the human experience. And he proceeds to acknowledge that he needs these others. For company, recognition, smelly sex, self. He observes the crossroads in the night sky, proliferated and multidirectional. The darkness telling him to—look—as one might observe the lesion-infested image of a brain scan, or a spear of summer grass that is in fact the thin, weedy strip of your shabby consciousness. Inside, look inside. The night seems to him one of quiet howling.

There remain several hundred pages to go, and an estimable quantity of summer hours in which to read them. Suddenly, as though stricken in that conventional instant of horror, he stops reading. He becomes aware of his body, from the outside. He senses the many fissures and longings of a worshipful self, the being prone to lethal rumination, frightful concerns. Perhaps he should have discarded. Please do this. He flips back to the beginning. He returns to the first page of *The Ceremonies*. "It was outside nature, and alone." He senses a quickening in his limbs and a silent, anesthetizing howl in the close distance of his corporeal life. It is the thing in the attic, the creep on the roadside in the dark, waiting, the material property that embodies your seasoned, internal Hell. He manages to turn his head with great halting effort and look into the darkness of the night, the window open, the screen has collected moths and webs, he looks in search of revelation, maybe something akin to celestial support as the hardback weighs heavy in his lap. It's still relatively early, the moon is young. A walker has stopped walking, on the other side of the window by the park. He squints and focuses and wants to recoil, for some reason—why are we so afraid?—but can't, can't not look. An ambiguous figure, a shadow in the night. Is she a cloaked, elderly woman, a seemingly feeble little man in black? A boy with eyes of blood? The other is staring directly at him. Him, whose body is draped over a chair, novel in hand, but propped and looking, a motionless torso askew and illuminated by lamp light. A more than competent academic. A thoughtful man, desirable and desiring, committed to the night and fully in view from the road on the park. The figure is staring directly at him, remains staring, at the thing in the chair. Everything is different now and it all begins and ends with the word suddenly. The grimoire is staring to work.

    It all plays out in an imagination schooled by gothic turns of mind, critical, maledictive words, the language of others eager to unhinge as much as to entertain, perhaps these are the same process, the imagination that lives atop a body sprawled over a chair. And from here the action we crave emerges, floating mist, smoke from a fire, events, objects materializing. He thinks of and to himself. Alone by the window, the night is closing in, no more joggers, just the one, *le regard*. "A person may feel scrutinized by someone whose eyes and physical being are invisible."[1] He thinks well of himself, loves his work, most of the time, the work that makes summers off all the more fulfilling; though here, now, the unrest that has drifted into being makes him yearn for the company of others, students, other faculty, however pedestrian or oblivious to the literature that gets inside and stays. He once thought about a librarian, he loved her love of him; he, such a thoughtful man, exceptional in the scheme of people following and worshipping, he feels the look from beyond as much as he sees the non-face, the entity outside, hating and hateful, full of hate. Suddenly it begins to swell. And beckon. If it has a mouth the mouth opens, and shrieks like metal on metal. Or guttural hell. Like Donald Sutherland at the end of 1978's *Invasion of the Body Snatchers*. It could be 1978, he's losing track of time in the swirl of

Appendix II

unknowable horror encroaching upon the warm summer night, upon the fortress of his otherwise precious home and the little, isolated sense of self and wellbeing.

It collapses. The black clothes falling too slowly to the ground, still screaming, maybe they're frothing from the hole in what should be a face. And then the mist is real, *The Fog*, 1980, but not aglow in the dark, barely illuminated by a street lamp, coiling up and hovering over the street. There's no visible green in the park. No life except the outlines of crooked, angry tree limbs that should be livelier against the barest gleam of planetary luminance. It hovers, waits, for what, what. For him. With nothing between them but a common sidewalk, the incline of a front yard, physical, nothing realities that only mean something when one pays attention in the face of occult devastation. He can think only of the distance between them now, how pitiable it is, how earthly, even the concrete, how inadequate in the helix of events, objects, darkening out everything but themselves as they linger, only to act, and act.

The *lamelle* as "something extremely flat, like a blade, which can be displaced and go anywhere."[2] This is how it acts. Its unfathomable ability to contract and flatten, still hovering as he watches with giddy revulsion, but a line now, or a disk. The shapeless miasma configures into a clear surface over the bundle of dark clothes in the street as over pods in a dead, *Alien* ship, 1979, hundreds of them, here only one. He watches and waits and thinks of the psychoanalyst and how he got it wrong, on libido and the animation of life. The line in the air, poised to strike, he knows, animates death, living death at the crossroads of self and other person, thing, vapor. He knows it's about to happen, the riptide through time and space, the sprawling over and enveloping of the window, the seeping in through cracks, where insects enter and eat to stay alive, to sever body from life, and it does.

Though darkness may be necessary to penetrate our waking sleep, to axe through the bathroom door of our stupidity and our righteousness, it is useful to be aware of how far the time of skin might give before it punctures and oozes. He leaves thoughts of earthen nebula to better writers than himself. He sits up in the chair. The unnamable figure is still, actually, there, has not moved, its hidden, still gaze enough to penetrate. The thing in the chair becomes aware of its body, from the inside, something is happening on the margins of imagination, while the other,

The Singular Ceremonies

it need not move closer, it's already here. In the home, in the body, propagated seed, the infestation of spiders and a window of nerve net cobwebs. Imagine the ordinary sensation of being watched. You attempt to flee but can't. Avert the eyes but you can't manage this simple reflex. It's your only company, the evil with a purpose inside nature, inside, it may as well *be* you in the darkness of night. The figure is so still as to move, forward and in. The book is staring into you. The thing in the chair, a lone scholar who couldn't imagine being anywhere else now, is struck by the discomfited reality of the time of his life, not eternal, not now, and there are so many pages yet to go.

Chapter Notes

Introduction

1. A current exposition of pessimism such as Eugene Thacker's *In the Dust of this Planet* offers a compelling argument that flirts with the "treason of the artist." I will examine some of its assets and assumptions relative to Klein's "optimism" in Chapter 5.

Chapter 1

1. "In [Melanie] Klein's concept, phantasy emanates from within and imagines what is without, it offers an unconscious commentary on instinctual life and links feelings to objects and creates a new amalgam: the world of imagination. Through its ability to phantasize the baby tests out, primitively 'thinks' about, its experiences of inside and outside" (Mitchell, Introduction, *Selected* 23).
2. Frederic Jameson refers to the Lacanian category of the Real as "simply History itself," and specifically, "the history of the subject" (*Jameson* 106).
3. Any reference to Freudian liberation, of course, must be qualified by its infamous and reprehensible negation of female sexuality as fuel for broader theories of familial and cultural dynamics. See Anne Koedt's influential essay "The Myth of the Vaginal Orgasm" in this regard.
4. Consider Stephen King's claim about the nature of horror as being, at its best, at once "reactionary, anarchistic, and revolutionary" ("Why" 3). I will examine the immense value of this popular genre in the following sections and chapters of this study, particularly where the critical or "revolutionary" quality is concerned.
5. See chapter two of my *Liminal Fictions in Postmodern Culture: The Politics of Self-Development* (New York: Palgrave Macmillan, 2015).
6. "The only thing I could think of ... was how to hit upon the spot where the crown was supposed to be" (James 568).
7. Which is not to say that such matriculation is easy or even possible, though one would hope that years of Lacanian analysis might serve to transform the "alienting identity" in a productive, healing manner. "Curiosity" or progressiveness is at least positioned to become aware of said identity and thus to tinker with its psychological and cultural technologies. If this fails, mystical traditions are generally happy to accept the baton.
8. It is important to note, however, the magnitude of pleasure that overrides generalizations around ideological alliances. Reactionary tendencies are equally capacious and some pleasures, I would argue, are relatively innocent in their aboriginality.

Chapter 2

1. See Michael Moynihan and Didrik Søderlind, *Lords of Chaos: The Bloody Rise of the Satanic Metal Underground* (Los Angeles: Port Townsend: Feral House, 1998).
2. Notorious BM band Mayhem's first full length studio album is entitled *De Mysteriis Dom Sathanas* ("About the Mystery of the Lord Satan") (1994).
3. The one exception is Sarr's mother, Mrs. Poroth, whose ancestor is in fact Absolom Troet, who disappears from the remote community after a fire consumes his family and their home. She has unique knowledge of the coming evil based on a collection of drawings from her childhood; she

Notes—Chapter 3

is severe and reserved in manner, unloving, but serves as a counter-force to the Old One's malicious intentions.

4. Consider, in contrast, Harlan Ellison's relatively abstract AM in his story "I Have No Mouth and I Must Scream," the massive computer that has subsumed and destroyed all human life save five individuals and whose hatred for them is unremitting. Even here, however, the "evil's" mission to torment the humans for eternity is a consequence of the impossibility of its need to belong. The Old One is perhaps all the more frightening by virtue of its seeming intention to precipitate total extinction, unlike a Lovecraftian "Outsider" who spends its own eternity cavorting with other ghouls.

5. Consider the final line of John Donne's sexually suggestive "Holy Sonnet XIV": "Nor ever chaste, except you ravish me," the speaker beseeches God.

6. The male position here will be complicated by the fact that Jeremy is largely "at [his] ease" throughout his time on the farm, a topic for the next section of this chapter.

7. For a rich account of Jackson's life and possible clairvoyant abilities, see Judy Oppenheimer's biography *Private Demons: The Life of Shirley Jackson* (New York: Ballantine, 1989).

8. Consider Eleanor's common thought process in *The Haunting of Hill House*: "Perhaps Hill House has a tower, or a secret chamber, or even a passageway going off into the hills and probably used by smugglers—although what could smugglers find to smuggle around these lonely hills? Perhaps I will encounter a devilishly handsome smuggler and…" (32). The cognitive halt and the adverb signifying lack ("perhaps") are obviously not the only links between the two passages. There is much to be fulfilled in the lives of these heroines who must suffer at the hands of both terrestrial and paranormal events.

9. During one of Carol's initial encounters with Rosie, he mentions the phrase "binding straps" as part of a ritual and she suddenly imagines "a night sky, a mound aglow with flames, and a girl very much like herself bound naked to a kind of altar. Something long and white emerging from the shadows" (75). Moreover, in light of the fact that Carol has recently completed "a sophomore course in the Mystics, [and has] wondered if she might not be one of them herself" (65), this masochistic vision for which she is indeed bound is all the more prescient.

10. An important concession here is the current tuition costs of The New School that are so exorbitant as to be exceptionally prohibitive.

11. Maugham's narrator in *The Razor's Edge* considers how "the devil, looking at the cruel wars that Christianity has occasioned, the persecutions, the tortures Christian has inflicted upon Christian, the unkindness, the hypocrisy, the intolerance, must consider the balance sheet with complacency. And when he remembers that it has laid upon mankind the bitter burden of the sense of sin that has darkened the beauty of the starry night and cast a baleful shadow on the passing pleasures of a world to be enjoyed, he must chuckle as he murmurs: give the devil his due" (208–209). This passage clearly speaks to the aggression that certain expressions of Christianity can evoke as well as to the languishing, despondent egotism inherent in the attribution of "sin" to the human experience.

12. A passage like the following from *The Ceremonies* could easily finds its way into a Lovecraft narrative, especially in terms of its vision of evil: "She saw now what it was: a plump white worm, thick as a baby's finger—a plump white worm, that, as she watched, uncurled, raised its unwrinkled head, and glared at her. A plump white worm with a human face" (39).

13. Machen's young heroine in "The White People" "[wants] to make faces and twist [herself] about in the way that [the white people do]." She "[makes] faces like the faces on the rocks, and [she] twists [herself] about like the twisted ones…," following which point she comes upon a "big round mound…" (122).

Chapter 3

1. See *A Thousand Plateaus*, pp. 275–277.

2. A comparable event occurs in Jackson's *The Haunting of Hill House* when Mrs. Montague, a ghost hunter of sorts, insists that she has spent countless hours "in purest love and understanding, alone in a room and yet never alone," asserting that "there is no danger where there is nothing but love and sympathetic understanding" (196), all the while treating her husband and his guests at Hill House, the people standing before her, as op-

posed to the virtual beings, with utter contempt and disrespect. An unborn fetus is certainly not virtual (as in the case of a ghost), though its lived life may as well be so to those pro-lifers for whom the child born is no longer their concern, no matter its circumstances.

3. See Ligotti's "The Frolic" in *Songs of a Dead Dreamer* and *Grimscribe* (New York: Penguin Classics, 2015).

4. The ratios, including "clinamen," "tessera," "kenosis," "daemonization," "askesis," and "apophrades," all speak to the trajectory, as Bloom sees it, of a poet's inevitable anxiety over influence by preceding poets and its eventual resolution whereby the earlier work is evaluated in relation to the contemporary work.

5. And even here, Lovecraft has beaten him to punch. As the predecessor exclaims in one of several epistolary comments, "I, too, was a detective in youth" (156).

6. See Stanley Crouch, "Coltrane Dethroned," *JazzTimes*, September 2002, http://jazztimes.com/articles/19805-coltrane-derailed.

Chapter 4

1. A parallel may be drawn here with G.I. Gurdjieff's notion of "intentional suffering" whereby one embraces and observes, through a particularly acute and exercised lens, tension arising from feeling the conventional parameters of identity challenged, thus generating new insight into the common impediments to self-development. See Gurdjieff's *Beelzebub's Tales to His Grandson* (New York: Viking, 1992), p. 223.

Chapter 5

1. That the U.S. continues to debate equal pay for women as of the writing of this book (2016), despite the significant progress in civil rights, is but one example of a cultural hole, the abyss of which critical horror both exposes and characteristically denounces.

2. It is useful to note the relative timelessness of *It Follows* here, its milieu being situated somewhere between the 1970s and the 21st century decade of its release.

3. There are exceptions, including, possibly, *The Evil Dead* (1982) and *Dreams in the Witch-House* (2005), among others.

4. As mentioned earlier, Jeremy is equally critical of Shirley Jackson in this regard. And yet, his own critiques of the Poroths and their community, an extreme rendering of current day fundamentalists, is hardly without spite. At his best, Jeremy is a relatively curious Luke Sanderson from Jackson's *The Haunting of Hill House*, a savvy, humorous, and sometimes faintly mischievous young man.

5. Another way of putting this, in the always remarkable and sometimes awkward language of Lovecraft (as rendered by Thacker in his *Tentacles Longer Than the Night*), is "indifferentism," "an indifference registered by the human in the utter apophatic blackness of incomprehensibility" (125–126). In addition to the Woody Allen scene, I am reminded here of an anecdote from David J Haskins' memoir *Who Killed Mister Moonlight*, on his tenure in Bauhaus and his many experiences with "off-white magick" (10), as he puts it, in which he makes an amusing but astute observation regarding "the fine line between high magick and high farce" (161). My intention is not to dismiss the potential (and as this study has argued through and through, *critical*) value of presenting alternative visions of civilization or the cosmic vortex in which it manifests. It is, however, intent on recognizing the degree to which such "blackness," as manifesto, as ideology, though culturally and theoretically sexy, to be sure, may allow one to forget, as Terry Eagelton notes, "the grossly inconvenient news that our forms of life must undergo radical dissolution if they are to be reborn as just and compassionate communities" (*Culture* 208). Adherence to a mystically oriented "indifferentism" is convenient on a number of levels, while the pairing of "radical dissolution" and social responsibility, of which critical horror is an extension, requires a challenging investment, however compromised, in materialist, humanist culture. For example, it is not a great leap from "indifferentism" to Lovecraftian racism; the former carves space for the latter by projecting alienation and hostility (Klein: "I believed it then, Howard, and I believe it still, that the nightmare was of your own making"), while critical horror produces a kind of aesthetic ethnography of these qualities

or tendencies for the sake of both literary pleasure and confrontational, critical examination.

6. To be clear: are people often loathsome? Of course. Is the common strain of self-help books that Thacker (and Thomas Ligotti) repudiate steeped in insipid superficiality and mediocrity? Absolutely. But most people are loathsome because they *need help* without necessarily knowing it. Is horror the best therapy for our collective and private woes? Probably not, though critical horror may at least fill in some blanks as to why one might need help amidst the turmoil of civilization, even as it raises delightful goosebumps.

Chapter 6

1. The critical distinction between time and eternity is worth considering in this regard; the former being conventionally rooted in the past and the future, while the latter is understood as eternally at hand in the present. See Joseph Campbell's popular but insightful *The Power of Myth*, p. 223.

2. During a second exorcism, sans props, she cries, "I don't have any control over what happens to me."

3. See the opening stanza of Walt Whitman's "Song of Myself."

4. It is important to note the difference between the self-centeredness of a by now classic LaVeyan Satanism and a current, nontheistic organization such as The Satanic Temple, whose mission statement revolves around political and social justice issues; here, the tropes of Satanism are used primarily to undermine the hypocrisy of fundamentalist Christian injustices.

5. From *A Thousand Plateaus*: "The BwO is what remains when you take everything away. What you take away is precisely the phantasy, and significances and subjectifications as a whole" (151). The ambiguity of *The Last Exorcism* leaves the BwO flailing in fire and death, though the viewer is left with the obvious—one hopes—course of "[inventing] self-destructions that have nothing to do with the death drive. Dismantling the organism has never meant killing yourself, but rather opening the body to connections that presuppose an entire assemblage, circuits, conjunctions, levels and thresholds, passages and distributions of intensity, and territories and deterritorializations measured with the craft of a surveyor" (160).

6. Though not the first of its kind, Hell House was created and is marketed by Keenan Roberts as the most recognizable (and notorious) brand of the phenomenon.

7. Salinger references the Jesus Prayer, from *The Way of the Pilgrim* ("Lord Jesus Christ, have mercy on me") and has Zooey "thank God" that the book leaves out the "miserable sinner part" (*Franny* 111).

8. It may be instructive to consider the chasm between the bigoted and sensationalistic realism of a Hell House presentation and the "absolute reality" of Jackson's Hill House that points to a relatively poignant and profound sense of alienation. While the writer of critical horror identifies and examines what can be a severely damaging experience common to the human condition, Hell House ultimately perpetuates this experience for both the one who is struggling with desire and one who erroneously assumes he or she is impervious to its force. Klein's Deborah is an example of a woman who experiences each side of this "dance."

9. Quite different from being a puppet whose voice and actions are dictated by another.

10. "He [Tom L.] wants what's best. What's best. We're coming out of the cave. Got to, can't go on like this. Go to come out of the dark" (21), John says in a soporific tone never before heard by his friend.

11. From Lacan: "The phantasy is never anything more than the screen that conceals something quite primary, something determinant in the function of repetition" (*Four* 60). The Real, in contrast, "may be represented by the accident, the noise, the small element of reality, which is evidence that we are not dreaming. But, on the other hand, this reality is not so small, for what wakes us is the other reality hidden behind the lack of that which takes the place of representation" (*ibid.*).

12. It is important to note in this regard the degree of his longing, his hoping to meet someone at the bar, as well as the general aura of female objectification that peppers the narrative. The boys club of drunken horror writers laugh, or brag, about witnessing topless women engaged in a "coconut lotion rubdown" (4), to name one example. On the other hand, Mr. B recounts the story of an-

other writer, Mark S, who has "worshipped at the altar of L," "good ol' woman-hating S," until he is killed by another writer, a woman, after having stalked her repeatedly (7). In calling out misogyny, the narrator speaks to the gender climate and culture of genre writers (not without dark humor) and does so in the context of commonplace desire, some expressions of which are less damaging than others.

13. In spite of being moderately educated and sex-positive, the Poroths, especially Sarr, cultivate a lived aversion to the evils of secularism and thus plant the seeds (albeit in cursed soil) of that antipathy all around them. Deborah's good nature is, of course, something to be contained by literalism's patriarchal dominance. Huntoon makes the simple mistake of misrecognizing metaphor and the limited power of youthful defiance with grave consequences, for himself and the ill-fated poet philanderer.

14. As Buddhist scholar B. Alan Wallace explains, emptiness implies the lack of "intrinsic nature" in all phenomena; thus, "reification is the root of all our ills, dividing our sense of self from everything else. Once that division is made, the next step is attachment to 'my' side, to what I mistakenly believe is inherently mine" (*Tibetan* 182), a step that intones don't tread on me. "The antidote," he goes on, "is to experience the emptiness of all phenomena, and to recognize their nature as dependently related events" (*ibid.*). Be they at Poroth farm, in the space of a hellish, Brooklyn anomaly, or at the reading of a malevolent author/puppet, said events, however precarious or conventionally "real," are the products of projection, in this view, that serves merely to substantiate the self as Lacan's "*moi*." Silverman's notion of "textual intervention" speaks to the potential of critical horror's ability to foster (indirectly or otherwise) experience of this condition.

15. "Overhead, without any fuss, the stars were going out": this is no typical fire and brimstone apocalypse.

16. For a fascinating example of the jeremiad principles, see Emory Elliott, "The Legacy of Puritanism," Divining America, TeacherServe©, National Humanities Center, http://nationalhumanitiescenter.org/tserve/eighteen/ekeyinfo/legacy.htm.

Elliot includes the following: "we must beware of enemies who plot to destroy us; we must acknowledge the gap between our ideals and current realities; and we must reject corruption, greed, and selfishness, and other sins; and finally, we must work together to restore our superiority among the world's nations. With God on our side, we shall continue the American Dream and fulfill our sacred Manifest Destiny." Obviously, 21st-century manifestations of right wing fundamentalism face a conundrum in terms of "corruption, greed, and selfishness, and other sins" given the celebration of capitalism that dominates American culture, though Elliot asserts that this was the case for puritans as well: "From early on, the Puritans had difficulty keeping God's grace and business profits separated."

Appendix II

1. Ragland-Sullivan, *Lacan* 94.
2. *Ibid.*, 80.

Bibliography

Adorno, Theodor W. *The Culture Industry: Selected Essays on Mass Culture*. Ed. J.M. Bernstein. London: Routledge, 1991.

Allen, Woody. *Side Effects*. New York: Ballantine, 1980.

Asimov, Isaac. *Nine Tomorrows*. New York: Doubleday, 1959.

Augé, Marc. *Someone's Trying to Find You*. Trans. Chris Turner. London: Seagull Books, 2015.

Barron, Laird. "The Internal Vista Is Infinite." Interview with Jon Padgett. *Thomas Ligotti Online*.

———. "More Dark." *The Beautiful Thing That Awaits Us All*. New York: Night Shade Book, 2013.

Barthes, Roland. *The Pleasure of the Text*. Trans. Richard Miller. New York: Hill and Wang, 1975.

Bivins, Jason. *Religion of Fear: The Politics of Horror in Conservative Evangelicalism*. Oxford: Oxford University Press, 2008.

Celtic Frost. "Synagoga Satanae." *Monotheist*. Century Media, 2006.

Clarke, Arthur C. "The Nine Billion Names of God." *Collected Stories of Arthur C. Clarke*. New York: TOR, 2000.

Clover, Carol. *Men, Women and Chainsaws: Gender in the Modern Horror Film*. Princeton: Princeton University Press, 1992.

Conrad, Joseph. *Heart of Darkness*. https://www.aub.edu.lb/fas/cvsp/Documents/reading_selections/204/Spring%202020 13/CS-204-ReadingSelections-Conrad-HeartDarknestDarkness.pdf.

Deleuze, Gilles. *Essays Critical and Clinical*. Trans. Daniel W. Smith and Michael A. Greco. Minneapolis: University of Minnesota Press, 1997.

Deleuze, Gilles, and Felix Guattari. *A Thousand Plateaus: Capitalism and Schizophrenia*. Trans. Brian Massumi. Minneapolis: University of Minnesota Press, 1987.

———, and ———. *Kafka: Toward a Minor Literature*. Trans. Dana Polan. Minneapolis: University of Minnesota Press, 1986.

DeLillo, Don. *The Body Artist*. New York: Simon & Schuster, 2001.

———. *Point Omega*. New York: Scribner, 2010.

———. *Zero K*. New York: Scribner, 2016.

Derrida, Jacques. *Specters of Marx*. Trans. Peggy Kamuf. London: Routledge, 1994.

Eagelton, Terry. *After Theory*. New York: Basic Books, 2003.

———. *Culture and the Death of God*. New Haven: Yale University Press, 2014.

———. *On Evil*. New Haven: Yale University Press, 2010.

Eliot, T.S. *The Cocktail Party*. New York: Harcourt, 1978.

———. "The Four Quartets." *The Complete Poems and Plays*, 1090–1950. New York: Harcourt Brace and World, 1971.

Freud, Sigmund. *Civilization and Its Discontents*. Trans. James Strachey. New York: W.W. Norton, 1961.

———. "New Introductory Lectures On Psycho-Analysis." *The Standard Edition of the Complete Psychological*

Bibliography

Works of Sigmund Freud, Volume XXII (1932–1936).

"Halloween New York City—Hell House." *Curious Travelers*. Online. 1 October 2016.

Haskins, David J. *Who Killed Mister Moonlight? Bauhaus, Black Magick and Benediction*. London: Jawbone, 2014.

Jackson, Shirley. *The Haunting of Hill House*. New York: Penguin, 1984.

James, Henry. *The Altar of the Dead, The Beast in the Jungle, The Birthplace and Other Tales*. New York: Charles Scribner's Sons, 1922.

———. *Tales of Henry James*. Ed. Christof Wegelin and Henry B. Wonham. New York: W.W. Norton, 2003.

James, M.R. "A Warning to the Curious." *Collected Ghost Stories*. Hertfordshire: Wordsworth Editions Limited, 1992.

Jameson, Fredric. *The Jameson Reader*. Oxford: Blackwell, 2000.

Joshi, S.T. *The Modern Weird Tale*. Jefferson: McFarland, 2001.

Kafka, Franz. "A Hunger Artist." *Franz Kafka: The Metamorphosis, In the Penal Colony, and Other Stories*. New York: Schocken Books, 1975.

King, Stephen. "Why We Crave Horror Movies." http://humbleisd.net/cms/lib2/TX01001414/Centricity/Domain/2669/whywecravehorrormovies.pdf.

Klein, T.E.D. *The Ceremonies*. New York: Viking, 1984.

———. *Dark Gods*. New York: Bantam, 1986.

———. *Raising Goosebumps for Fun and Profit*. New York: Footsteps Press, 1988.

———. *Reassuring Tales*. Burton: Subterranean Press, 2006.

Lacan, Jacques. *The Fours Fundamental Concepts of Psychoanalysis*. Ed. Jacques-Alain Miller. Trans. Alan Sheridan. New York: W.W. Norton, 1998.

Ladouceur, Liisa. "The Filthy Fifteen: When Venom and King Diamond Met the Washington Wives." *Satanic Panic: Pop-Cultural Paranoia in the 1980s*. Surrey: Fab Press, 2015.

Lakoff, George. *Whose Freedom: The Battle Over America's Most Important Idea*. London: Picador, 2007.

The Last Exorcism. Director Daniel Stamm. Lionsgate, 2010. DVD.

Ligotti, Thomas. *The Conspiracy Against the Human Race*. New York: Hippocampus Press, 2010.

———. "Professor Nobody's Little Lectures on Supernatural Horror." *Songs of A Dead Dreamer and Grimscribe*. New York: Penguin, 2015.

Lovecraft, H.P. "The Outsider." *The Lurking Fear and Other Stories*. New York: Ballantine, 1984.

———. *Supernatural Horror in Literature*. New York: Dover Publications, 1973.

Machen, Arthur. "The White People." *The White People and Other Weird Stories*. Ed. S.T. Joshi. New York: Penguin, 2011.

Manhattan. Dir. Woody Allen. United Artists, 1979. DVD.

Maugham, W. Somerset. *The Razor's Edge*. New York: Vintage, 1972.

Mellamphy, Dan and Nandita Biswas Mellamphy. "What's the 'Matter' with Materialism? Walter Benjamin and the New Janitocracy." *Journal of Interdisciplinary Studies in Literature, Continental Philosophy Phenomenological Psychology, and the Arts* 11 (2009).

Modleski, Tania. "The Terror of Pleasure: The Contemporary Horror Film and Postmodern Theory." *Studies in Entertainment*. Bloomington: Indiana University Press, 1986.

Oates, Joyce Carol. "Demon." *American Supernatural Tales*. Ed. S.T. Joshi. New York: Penguin, 2007.

O'Connor, Flannery. "A Good Man Is Hard to Find." *The Longman Masters of Short Fiction*. Ed. Dana Gioia and R.S. Gwynn. New York: Longman, 2002.

Play It Again, Sam. Dir. Woody Allen Paramount Pictures, 1972. DVD.

Pollock, Della. "Introduction: Remembering." *Remembering: Oral History Performance*. Ed. Della Pollock. New York: Palgrave Macmillan, 2005.

Bibliography

Powell, Jason. *Jacques Derrida: A Biography*. London: Continuum, 2006.

Rosemary's Baby. Dir. Roman Polanski. Paramount Pictures, 1968. DVD.

Rusnak, Stacy. "Scapegoat of a Nation: The Demonization of MTV and the Music Video." *Satanic Panic: Pop-Cultural Paranoia in the 1980s*. Surrey: Fab Press, 2015.

Schopp, Andrew. "Transgressing the Safe Space: Generation X Horror in The Blair Witch Project and Scream." *Nothing That Is: Millennial Cinema and The Blair Witch Controversies*. Ed. Sarah L. Weinstock and Jeffery A. Detroit: Wayne State University Press, 2004.

The Seventh Seal. Dir. Ingmar Bergman. Perf. Gunnar Björnstrand, Max von Sydow. Svensk Filmindustri, 1957. DVD.

Shelley, Mary. *Frankenstein*. New York: Signet, 2000.

Silverman, Kaja. *The Subject of Semiotics*. New York: Oxford University Press, 1983.

_____. *The Threshold of the Visible World*. London: Routledge, 1996.

Strozier, Charles B. *Apocalypse: On the Psychology of Fundamentalism in America*. Boston: Beacon Press, 1994.

Thacker, Eugene. *In the Dust of This Planet*. Winchester: Zero Books, 2011.

_____. *Tentacles Longer Than the Night*. Winchester: Zero Books, 2015.

Wagner, Karl Edward. "Sticks." *The Dark Descent*. Ed. David G. Hartwell. New York: Tor, 1987.

Index

Abramovic, Marina, 90
Adorno, Theodore 17, 18, 31, 88, 89, 142, 146, 147
aggression 14–16, 24, 25, 40–41, 42, 119
aging 25–26, 68, 75–76
Alien 172
Allen, Woody 6, 59; *Manhattan* 116–117; *Play It Again, Sam* 111
anti-intellectualism 55–56
The Anxiety of Influence 73, 77, 177ch3n4
Apocalypse: On the Psychology of Fundamentalism in America 117–121, 140
Argento, Dario 1; *Trauma* 103–104
Asimov, Isaac: "The Last Question" 30
Augé, Marc: *Someone's Trying to Find You* 55, 107

Barron, Laird: "More Dark" 135–139, 143, 163, 178–179n12
Barthes, Roland 30
Baudelaire, Charles 16; "To the Reader" 84, 137
Baudrillard, Jean 28
Bauhaus 6
"The Beast in the Jungle" 112
Beelzebub's Tales to His Grandson 177ch4n1
Benjamin, Walter 93, 143
Bergman, Ingmar: *The Seventh Seal* 77
Bivins, Jason: *Religion of Fear: The Politics of Horror in Conservative Evangelicalism* 129–132, 135, 138
"Black Man with a Horn" 73–78, 79–80, 177ch3n5
Black Metal 35, 58, 148
Black Metal 35
The Blair Witch Project 71, 98, 123–124
A Blaze in the Northern Sky 35
bliss 30
Bloch, Robert 162
Bloom, Harold: *The Anxiety of Influence* 73, 77, 177ch3n4
Blue Velvet 36

The Body Artist 34–35, 123, 165
Buddhism 13, 143, 179n14

Campbell, Joseph: *The Power of Myth* 178n1
capitalism 17, 52, 53, 55, 56, 104
Carver, Raymond 33, 135
Celtic Frost 148; "Synagoga Satanae" 149–151
The Ceremonies 1, 5, 34–64, 95–96, 120–121, 126, 153, 156–157, 165–173, 175–176n3, 176n6, 176n9, 176n12, 177ch5n4, 178n8
Chick, Jack 138
"Children of the Kingdom" 65–73, 135, 151–152
civilization 3–4, 10–17, 19–24, 26–28, 30, 32, 36, 44, 46, 56, 59, 63
Civilization and Its Discontents 11–16, 24, 32
Clarke, Arthur C.: "The Nine Billion Names of God" 145
Clover, Carol: *Men, Women, and Chainsaws: Gender in the Modern Horror Film* 122
The Cocktail Party 81–83, 84, 87, 161
Coltrane, John 76, 78
"Coltrane Dethroned" 177n6
Conrad, Joseph: "Heart of Darkness" 85–86, 89
consumerism 54–55
cosmic pessimism 110, 111, 139, 141–142, 162
critical horror 2, 3, 14, 20, 60, 61, 63, 64, 72, 78, 87–88, 89, 90, 96, 106, 107, 109, 113, 114–115, 122–123, 129, 130–131, 133, 135, 140–143, 151–152, 177ch5n5, 178ch5n6
Crouch, Stanley: "Coltrane Dethroned" 177n6
Crowley, Aleister 49
culture industry 17–18

Dark Night of the Scarecrow 165
Darkthrone: *A Blaze in the Northern Sky* 35
De Mysteriis Dom Sathanas 175ch2n2
de Chardin, Pierre Teilhard 29, 49

Index

De Felitta, Frank: *Dark Night of the Scarecrow* 165
de la Mare, Walter 98, 99
Deleuze, Gilles 32, 82, 114, 127, 143
Deleuze, Gilles 2, 32, 39; and becoming-woman 65; and BWO 178*ch6n5*; and deterritorialization 39, 62, 63, 78, 96, 143; and Kafka 74; and minor literature 142–143; *A Thousand Plateaus* 176*n*1
DeLillo, Don 5; *Point Omega* 29–30; *The Body Artist* 34–35, 123, 165; *Zero K* 100
"Demon" 95
Derrida, Jacques 100, 103, 105; and différance 101; and hauntology 106
Descartes, René 121
desire 43–47
Dick, Philip K.: *Ubik* 156
Digital Humanities (DH) 4, 102, 106–107
Donne, John 49, 176*n*5
Don't Tread on Me 20, 23, 26
Dreams in the Witch-House (film) 177*ch5n*3

Eagleton, Terry 114, 129, 132, 133, 139, 141, 177*ch5n*5
Edwards, Jonathan 63, 130
egotism 35, 56, 70, 82, 113, 135, 139–140, 143, 176*n*11
Eliot, T.S.: *The Cocktail Party* 81–83, 84, 87, 161; "The Four Quartets" 88, 134; "The Wasteland" 109
Elliott, Emory: *The Legacy of Puritanism* 179*n*16
Ellison, Harlan: "I Have No Mouth and I Must Scream" 176*n*4
Emerson, Ralph Waldo 164, 166
The Entity 165
"The Events at Poroth Farm" 5, 34–64,108, 165
evil 7, 41, 69, 139, 168, 170, 176*n*4
The Evil Dead 177*ch5n*3
The Exorcist 39

The Fog (film, 1980) 172
Foucault, Michel 79
"The Four Quartets" 88, 134
Frankenstein 120
Franny and Zooey 130, 178*n*7
Freud, Sigmund 11, 12, 72, 92, 107, 175*ch1n*3; *Civilization and Its Discontents* 11–16, 24, 32
"The Frolic" 177*ch3n*3
Fulci, Lucio: *The House by the Cemetery* 167
fundamentalist Christianity 4, 9, 58, 75, 77–78, 95, 117–135, 139, 144, 151, 152, 176*n*11
Furie, Sidney J.: *The Entity* 165

Gailly, Christian 5
Goffman, Erving 79
Gogol, Nikolai 60
"A Good Man Is Hard to Find" 78–79
Guattari, Felix 2, 32, 39; and becoming-woman 65; and BWO 178*ch6n5*; and deterritorialization 39, 62, 63, 78, 96, 143; and Kafka 74; and minor literature 142–143; *A Thousand Plateaus* 176*n*1
guilt 14
Gurdjieff, G.I. 29; *Beelzebub's Tales to His Grandson* 177*ch4n*1; and intentional suffering 95

happiness 31, 142
Haskins, David J.: *Who Killed Mr. Moonlight* 177*ch5n*5
The Haunting of Hill House 41, 50, 79, 98, 153, 176*n*8, 176–177*ch3n*2, 177*ch5n*4, 178*n*8
Hawthorne, Nathaniel: "Young Goodman Brown" 48, 169
"Heart of Darkness" 85–86, 89
Hegel, Georg Wilhelm Friedrich 100
Hell 126, 128–129, 132–134, 137, 139, 144, 150–151
Hell House 128–135, 178*ch6n*6, 178*n*8
hipster culture 18–19
Hough, John: *The Legend of Hell House* 129
The House by the Cemetery 167
"A Hunger Artist" 144–145, 149

"I Have No Mouth and I Must Scream" 176*n*4
In the Dust of This Planet 110–111, 113, 140, 175*Intro.n*1
Invasion of the Body Snatchers (film, 1978) 171
It Follows 25–26, 103, 177*n*2

Jackson, Shirley 49; *The Haunting of Hill House* 41, 50, 79, 98, 153, 176*n*8, 176–177*ch3n*2, 177*ch5n*4, 178*n*8
James, Henry 1, 2: "The Beast in the Jungle" 112; "The Turn of the Screw" 54
James, M.R. 1; "A Warning to the Curious" 20–25, 175*n*6
Jameson, Fredric 10, 16–17, 19, 28, 53, 175*ch1n*2
Joshi, S.T. 2, 6, 31–32, 33, 98
jouissance 30–31

Kafka, Franz 30; "A Hunger Artist" 144–145, 149
Kermode, Frank 117
King, Stephen 27; *The Shining* (film) 28, 39;

Index

"Why We Crave Horror Movies" 29, 156, 175n4
Klein, Melanie 175ch1n1
Klein, T.E.D. 1, 2; "Black Man with a Horn" 73–78, 79–80, 177ch3n5; *The Ceremonies* 1, 5, 34–64, 95–96, 120–121, 126, 153, 156–157, 165–173, 175–176n3, 176n6, 176n9, 176n12, 177ch5n4, 178n8; "Children of the Kingdom" 65–73, 135, 151–152; "The Events at Poroth Farm" 5, 34–64,108, 165; "Magic Carpet" 110; "Nadelman's God" 91–96, 108, 152, 163; "Petey" 83- 90, 152, 160, 168; "Raising Goosebumps for Fun and Profit" 97- 99, 107–108, 114, 159; "Well-Connected" 108–109, 162
Koedt, Anne 175ch1n3

Lacan, Jacques 11, 20, 22–25, 27, 30, 127, 142, 170, 172, 175ch1n2, 175n7, 178n11
Ladouceur, Liisa 148
Lakoff, George 151
The Last Exorcism 123–128
"The Last Question" 30
LaVey, Anton 90–91, 178n4
The Legacy of Puritanism 179n16
The Legend of Hell House 129
Le Guin, Ursala: "The Ones Who Walk Away from Omelas" 6
Ligotti, Thomas 135, 136, 178ch5n6; "The Frolic" 177ch3n3; "Professor Nobody's Liminal Fictions in Postmodern Culture 175n5
Little Lectures on Supernatural Horror" 28
literalism 4, 58, 88, 119–120, 141–143
Lords of Chaos: The Bloody Rise of the Satanic Metal Underground 175ch2n1
Lovecraft, H.P. 6, 10, 30, 58, 73, 74, 75, 76–77, 80, 86, 92, 95, 103, 107, 177ch5n5; "The Outsider" 90, 176n4; *Supernatural Horror in Literature* 9, 157
Lynch, David: *Blue Velvet* 36

Machen, Arthur 2; "The White People" 34, 60, 61–62, 67, 70, 176n13
"Magic Carpet" 110
Manhattan 116–117
Marxism 104
Maturin, Charles 108
Maugham, W. Somerset: *The Razor's Edge* 3, 176n11
Mayhem: *De Mysteriis Dom Sathanas* 175ch2n2
Meinhold, Wilhelm 108
Melville, Herman 31, 52

Men, Women, and Chainsaws: Gender in the Modern Horror Film 122
Mitchell, David Robert: *It Follows* 25–26, 103, 177n2
"More Dark" 135–139, 143, 163, 178–179n12
Moynihan, Michael: *Lords of Chaos: The Bloody Rise of the Satanic Metal Underground* 175ch2n1

"Nadelman's God" 91–96, 108, 152, 163
The New School 2, 52, 53, 54, 176n10
Nicoll, Maurice: *Psychological Commentaries on the Teaching of Gurdjieff and* "The Nine Billion Names of God" 145

Oates, Joyce Carol: "Demon" 95
O'Connor, Flannery: "A Good Man Is Hard to Find" 78–79
occult 62
"The Ones Who Walk Away from Omelas" 6
Oppenheimer, Judy: *Private Demons: The Life of Shirley Jackson* 176n7
Ouspensky 169
"The Outsider" 90, 176n4

patriarchy 49, 51
"Petey" 83- 90, 152, 160, 168
phenomenology 99
Phillips, Thomas: *Liminal Fictions in Postmodern Culture* 175n5
Plath, Sylvia 49
Play It Again, Sam 111
PMRC (Parents Music Resource Center) 146–147, 148
Point Omega 29–30
Pollock, Della 104
post-structuralism 121
Powell, Jason 100, 101, 103
The Power of Myth 178n1
Private Demons: The Life of Shirley Jackson 176n7
"Professor Nobody's Little Lectures on Supernatural Horror" 28
Psychological Commentaries on the Teaching of Gurdjieff and "The Nine Billion Names of God" 145

racism 10, 58–60, 76–77, 78
"Raising Goosebumps for Fun and Profit" 97- 99, 107–108, 114, 159
rape 50–51, 69
The Razor's Edge 3, 176n11
Reich, Wilhelm 169
Religion of Fear: The Politics of Horror in

Index

Conservative Evangelicalism 129–132, 135, 138
right wing politics 19
Roberts, Keenan 178*ch6n*6
Rosemary's Baby (film) 50, 122
Rotting Christ 148
Rusnak, Stacy 147–148

Salinger, J.D.: *Franny and Zooey* 130, 178*n*7
Sartre, Jean-Paul 27, 128
Satan 35, 50, 58, 59, 60, 87, 139, 149, 152; Satanism 127, 148, 150
satanic panic 147
The Satanic Temple 178*n*4
Satayana, George 107
Schopp, Andrew, safe-space fallacy 97
The Seventh Seal 77
sexuality 13
Shelley, Mary: *Frankenstein* 120
The Shining (film) 28, 39
Silverman, Kaja 18, 77, 121, 128, 179*n*14
Søderlind, Didrik: *Lords of Chaos: The Bloody Rise of the Satanic Metal Underground* 175*ch2n*1
Someone's Trying to Find You 55, 107
"Song of Myself" 178*n*3
Spinoza, Baruch 82, 83
Stamm, Daniel: *The Last Exorcism* 123–128
"Sticks" 71–72, 100
Strozier, Charles: *Apocalypse: On the Psychology of Fundamentalism in America* 117–121, 140
Supernatural Horror in Literature 9, 157
"Synagoga Satanae" 149–151

television 57

Tentacles Longer Than the Night 177*ch5n*5
Thacker, Eugene 178*ch5n*6; *In the Dust of This Planet* 110–111, 113, 140, 175*Intro.n*1; *Tentacles Longer Than the Night* 177*ch5n*5
A Thousand Plateaus 176*n*1
"To the Reader" 84, 137
Toussaint, Jean-Philippe 5
Trauma 103–104
Truth 65, 140
"The Turn of the Screw" 54

Ubik 156

Venom: *Black Metal* 35; *Welcome to Hell* 148
Virilio, Paul 33
Vonnegut, Kurt 153

Wagner, Karl Edward: "Sticks" 71–72, 100
Wallace, Allan 179*n*14
"A Warning to the Curious" 20–25, 175*n*6
"The Wasteland" 109
Welcome to Hell 148
"Well-Connected" 108–109, 162
West Memphis Three 147–148
"The White People" 34, 60, 61–62, 67, 70, 176*n*13
Whitman, Walt: "Song of Myself" 178*n*3
Who Killed Mr. Moonlight 177*ch5n*5
"Why We Crave Horror Movies" 29, 156, 175*n*4
Wilson, Edmund 97, 159

"Young Goodman Brown" 48, 169

Zero K 100

www.ingramcontent.com/pod-product-compliance
Ingram Content Group UK Ltd.
Pitfield, Milton Keynes, MK11 3LW, UK
UKHW042013140426
5217IPUK00015B/1142